Saint*Joseph*

Saint *Joseph*

His Life and His Role in the Church Today

Louise Bourassa Perrotta

Foreword by
Fr. Benedict J. Groeschel, C.F.R.

Our Sunday Visitor Publishing Division
Our Sunday Visitor, Inc.
Huntington, Indiana 46750

Our Sunday Visitor Publishing Division
Our Sunday Visitor, Inc.
200 Noll Plaza
Huntington, IN 46750

International Standard Book Number: 0-87973-573-2
Library of Congress Catalog Card Number: 99-75024

Cover design by Rebecca Heaston;
cover and text photo of the Flight into Egypt by George Martin,
from the collection of Guido Gockel, M.H.M.
PRINTED IN THE UNITED STATES OF AMERICA

For all the Josephs in my life,
including Joseph Anthony Perrotta,
Joseph Roger Locke,
Cardinal Leon Joseph Suenens,
and most especially for my father,
Roger Joseph Bourassa,
whose life has taught me much about St. Joseph.

Contents

Acknowledgments

I would be hard pressed to think of an author who needed more help and received it in greater measure than I did in the writing of this book. I owe special thanks to Father Benedict Joseph Groeschel, C.F.R., whose love for St. Joseph led him to write the foreword to this book. I am also indebted to:

Those who read. The following people gave freely of time and expertise in reviewing portions of the manuscript: John Boyle, of the University of St. Thomas theology department; Cindy Cavnar, author, editor, and faithful friend; Joseph F. Chorpenning, O.S.F.S., of Saint Joseph's University Press; Father John Echert, of the St. Paul Seminary School of Divinity; Roland Gauthier, C.S.C., founder of the Center for Research and Documentation at the Oratory of St. Joseph, Montreal, Canada; Michael C. Griffin, O.C.D., of Teresian Charism Press; Jeanne Kun, author, editor, and another faithful friend; Eugene LaVerdiere, S.S.S., of *Emmanuel* magazine; George Martin, founding editor of *God's Word Today* magazine, who also took the photograph of the cover and text illustration. I am grateful to Mike Dubruiel, whose comments and suggestions resulted in a more engaging and reader-friendly book, and to Henry O'Brien, who patiently and skillfully fine-tuned it.

Those who prayed. Among them: a Carmelite who prefers to remain anonymous; Maria Nyambu, a family friend; and especially my parents and my brother, Paul, who interceded nightly.

Those who helped. Mike Andaloro, for advice and information; editors Mike Aquilina, of *New Covenant,* and Greg Erlandson, of *Our Sunday Visitor*, for publishing my requests for St. Joseph stories; readers who responded; Father Guido Gockel, of the Pontifical Mission in Jerusalem, for providing artwork for the cover and text; Jim Manney, whose prodding got me going; Germano Pegoraro, S.C., of the Pious Union of St. Joseph, for information and inspiration; Susan Schaefer Pitman, for unexpected help in time of need; Pierre Robert, director of the Oratory of St. Joseph's Center for Research, and his assistant, Mariette Bédard, who guided me to the information I needed; my pastor, Father Edward Wojciechowski, for information and moral support.

Those who lived through it with me. Anna, Virginia, Maria, and Margherita, who took over the cooking, grocery shopping, and other tasks that I abandoned, and who also cheered my long working hours with gifts of flowers, treats, notes, and visits; Kevin, who was the first to say, "You should write a book about St. Joseph," and who followed up with ideas and comments, prayer, and loving encouragement.

Finally, heartfelt thanks to St. Joseph, whose presence, protection, and intercession became ever more real for me as I thought and wrote about him.

Foreword

As a lifelong devotee of St. Joseph I jumped immediately at the request to contribute the foreword to a book about this man whom I have always thought of as a personal spiritual father. But when Louise's manuscript arrived, I was initially puzzled by the length of the book. What had I gotten myself into? I had expected a slender volume with hard facts and a few theories and maybe a bit of devotion. Yet the pages of the still-unwrapped book looked like an encyclopedia of Josephiana. I feared a dreary volume of devotional fluff, despite what I know about the author.

Nothing of the kind! The author has done her homework very well and brings together a wide variety of sources to produce an outstanding example of popular religious writing, one that is both intelligent and engaging. This kind of writing is a task for which I have the deepest respect. Using the Fathers and Doctors of the Church, classical as well as contemporary theologians and scripture scholars, papal documents and spiritual writers, and drawing examples from everyday life, Louise Perrotta has woven together the most interesting tapestry of St. Joseph I have ever seen.

The subject of this book is one of the favorite saints of multitudes of older Catholics, the person closest to the Incarnate Word who, like the rest of us, had struggles with the effects of original sin. Imagine having your brunch (I learned in this book that that's what they had) every day with the Incarnate Word and the Immaculate Conception. No pope since Peter has had so daunting a responsibility as the contractor of Nazareth. (Most of you thought, as I did, all these years that he was a carpenter. Now check this out.) I've been reading Scripture and theology for nearly half a century and trying to present these powerful studies in a popular way, but I must admit that I have learned a good deal from this book.

Like many important people and things of Catholic life, St. Joseph got lost in the post-Vatican II shuffle. And, like many others, this faithful spiritual friend and marvelous guide is making a comeback. This book is a serious, well-thought-out, and, in many ways, delightful contribution to the literature on St. Joseph. Enjoy, and get to know this humble, holy, silent man who was closer to the divine mystery than any other human being and was chosen by God the Father Himself to be in that role of father for His Son on earth.

— Father Benedict Joseph Groeschel, C.F.R.

It Started with a Rosebush

To be more precise, it started with a *statue* buried under a rosebush. A three-inch plastic statue of the kind that I had seen advertised in "St. Joseph, Home Sale" kits. My husband, Kevin, unearthed it one overcast day as he planted a rosebush in the backyard of the house we had just bought.

"Look what I found," he said, handing me the grimy object.

I inspected it with mixed reactions. Should I take this as a sign of St. Joseph's presence and protection in our new home? Should I be disgusted at this run-in with what certainly appeared to be superstition? Not that I object to concrete, tangible expressions of faith. But burying St. Joseph, as I knew from articles in the real estate section of our local newspaper, was being touted as a hot technique for quick property sales. No faith in God, no relationship with St. Joseph required. Just bury the little statue and see it "work."

Without resolving the issue, I washed off the statue and set it on the kitchen windowsill. But the incident set me thinking.

As a lifelong Catholic raised by devout parents, I had always felt a basic appreciation of and devotion toward St. Joseph. At the same time, I had never really focused my full attention on him as a person in his own right. For me, he was simply the last and least member of history's most remarkable family — holy, yes, but hardly attention-grabbing.

But with the unearthing of that cheap statue, St. Joseph moved into my field of vision. *What do we really know about St. Joseph?*, I began to wonder. *How should we relate to him? Does he have any particular relevance for third-millennium Catholics?*

I looked more closely at the first chapters of Luke and Matthew, where Joseph appears. Other writings gave me food for thought: Pope John Paul II's 1989 apostolic exhortation on St. Joseph, *Guardian of the Redeemer*; anything and everything by Francis Filas, a Jesuit who shared his encyclopedic but nonpedantic knowledge of St. Joseph in works like *Joseph: The Man Closest to Jesus*; discoveries of St. Joseph's presence in the works of saints and spiritual writers.

My thinking was especially stimulated by a two-week visit (courtesy of a family friend) to Montreal's Oratory of St. Joseph. Besides being the world's largest shrine to St. Joseph, the Oratory is home to a research center that possesses what must be the world's most comprehensive collection of materials about him. As I read my way through many of them, Father Roland Gauthier, the center's founder, was putting the final touches on a definitive bibliography of "Josephological" writings. I have the finished product: a hefty tome almost three inches thick, containing over 19,700 entries.

There is, I discovered, no lack of words about "silent Joseph"!

At every stage of this journey to Joseph, Kevin and I discussed my findings. In fact, much of what appears in this work is the fruit of our conversations. As we talked and thought, it struck us that, far from being peripheral to the concerns of modern Catholics, Joseph is intimately involved in them.

It doesn't take a detective to see that big changes are afoot in many of the areas of patronage traditionally confided to him — marriage and family life, work, the interior life (or "spirituality"), death and dying. As patron of the universal Church, St. Joseph also plays a central role in key issues like evangelization and renewal. His very life, as described in Scripture, directs us to the heart of the Gospel message, to the incarnation. The more you look at St. Joseph, the clearer it becomes that he really does have "renewed significance for the Church in our day in light of the Third Christian Millennium" (*Guardian of the Redeemer,* No. 32).

This book is an attempt to share something of what I have learned about the significance of St. Joseph for today's Catholic. It opens with a look at the Gospel texts that provide the foundation for a healthy devotion, moves on to examine historical questions (for example, "What can we know about St. Joseph's daily life?"), and then focuses on a few areas of patronage.

Researching and writing this book has not only enriched my knowledge about St. Joseph, it has also led me to meet him in a deeper way. I hope that your reading will lead you to the same discovery.

St. Joseph, Real Estate Agent?

Who buried St. Joseph first? Who began the practice — now advertised on the Internet, recommended by some real estate agents, and apparently gaining in popularity — of trying to hasten property sales by planting his statue in the ground? No one seems to know.

Some people say it goes back to St. Teresa of Ávila (1515-1582), who prayed to St. Joseph when she needed more land for her convents and reportedly encouraged the nuns in her order to bury St. Joseph medals on likely sites. Another theory holds that German carpenters placed St. Joseph statues in the foundations of houses they built. Still another maintains that the practice comes from Sicily, where St. Joseph's intercession has traditionally been highly valued. Other people say the practice was popularized by Brother André Bessette (1845-1937), a saintly Holy Cross brother who was beatified in 1982. "I have concealed a medal of St. Joseph here," he told a companion one evening as they walked up a Montreal mountainside opposite the boarding school where he served as the hall porter. "Let us pray that we may be able to buy this piece of land. . . . St. Joseph needs it." Today an immense basilica dedicated to St. Joseph stands on the site.

As practiced by many today, burying St. Joseph statues to obtain a speedy closing is irreverent and superstitious. "We know you don't like to be upside down in the ground," runs one flippant "prayer" to St. Joseph that comes as part of a home sale kit, "but the sooner the escrow closes, the sooner we will dig you up and put you in a place of honor in our new home."

Abuses notwithstanding, it is not irreverent to express faith in God by making the right use of religious objects like medals and statues. After all, when properly blessed and used, these function as sacramentals — sacred signs that point us to God and open us to his action, often through the saints. For Teresa of Ávila, Brother André, and other friends of St. Joseph, burying statues and medals was a natural expression of trust in God's provision through a fatherly saint who spent much of his earthly life building houses and seeing to it that Jesus and Mary had a roof over their heads.

Part One

Discovering Scripture's Best Supporting Actor

I did not understand him well enough,
but that will change.

St. John of the Cross

Chapter 1

Joseph the Silent?

Scripture does not report a single word of his.
Silence is the father of the Word.
Paul Claudel

"Joseph's interesting. . . . But he's such a silent figure. What can you possibly find to say about him?"

Not infrequently as I was working on this book, this was the reaction I would encounter when people learned I was writing about St. Joseph. To be honest, there was a time when I would have reacted the same way.

Ours is a wordy culture of E-mails and chat rooms, talk shows and call-in programs, biographies and autobiographies the size of Manhattan phone directories. In our world, major news events are described and analyzed from every angle by choruses of commentators and correspondents who know how to make a short story long. Political fortunes are made or unmade by the ability to project "confidence" or "sincerity" by using just the right words in carefully crafted and executed speeches.

Without a single statement of his to go on, then, what are we word-hounds to make of St. Joseph? There are no flashy miracles to fill the gap of his silence, no indications that this workman's contemporaries saw him as anything but an "ordinary Joe." Perhaps we are left feeling like that anonymous Carmelite nun who wondered what the prioress would find to write in St. Thérèse of Lisieux's obituary notice. "She's very good," Thérèse overheard her say, "but she has never done anything worth talking about."

"The greatest things are accomplished in silence," Romano Guardini remarks in his meditative presentation of Christ's life, *The Lord.* "Not in the clamor and display of superficial eventfulness, but in the deep clarity of inner vision; in the almost imperceptible start of decision, in quiet overcoming and hidden sacrifice. . . . The silent forces are the strong forces."

We might think of Joseph's silence as a participation in what Father Guardini calls "the infinite stillness" that hovered over Christ's birth. This, he says, is "the stillest event of all — stillest because it

19

came from the remoteness beyond the noise of any possible intrusion — from God."

When the fullness of time had come, he who is the still turning point of the universe took flesh in a young woman entrusted to a man cloaked in silence. As portrayed in Scripture, Mary herself is a woman of few words: once she has dialogued with the angel Gabriel and sung her hymn of praise at Elizabeth's, her reported statements boil down to a question, an indirect request, and a directive to servants (Luke 2:48; John 2:3, 5). But Joseph says nothing at all.

Many people conclude from this that Joseph was "the strong, silent type." Pushing this portrayal to its limits, some have imagined him living as in a Carthusian monastery, where silence is the norm and an elaborate sign language serves for everyday needs. Although Scripture never once quotes Joseph, however, it nowhere says he never (or rarely) spoke. It is the *Gospel writers* who are silent — their muted presentation of Joseph most probably explained by their central focus, which is to present Jesus.

Keeping Joseph in silence does more than keep our attention on Jesus: it fits the overall part that Jesus' earthly father played in the drama of salvation history. In a 1657 sermon about this role, the eloquent French bishop Bossuet contrasted St. Joseph's mission with that of the apostles. In both cases Jesus is revealed, he pointed out, but for contrasting reasons. "He is revealed to the apostles to be proclaimed throughout the universe; he is revealed to Joseph to be kept quiet and hidden. The apostles are lights to make Jesus visible to the world; Joseph is a veil to cover him. . . ."

Joseph was charged with providing the safe setting for Jesus' quiet season of growth "in wisdom and in years, and in divine and human favor" (Luke 2:52). Is it surprising that the silence of those hidden years in Nazareth would also come to characterize their guardian?

All of this is not to say that we can know nothing about St. Joseph. The Gospels may not *seem* to give us much to go on, but like the five loaves and two fish that turned into a meal for more than five thousand (Mark 6:34-44), what they offer can become an abundant banquet for the soul. Scripture "grows through reading," said St. Gregory the Great. If we invite the Holy Spirit to guide that growth as we read and reflect on St. Joseph, we will find much to nourish our own relationship with the man who took Jesus into his fatherly care.

In fact, what the Bible says about St. Joseph is the indispensable foundation and starting point for understanding his role in the Church and in our own lives. For this reason, the next two chapters will offer a close look at these scriptural sources.

There are not many. The Gospel of John makes only passing mention of Joseph — and only as a way of identifying Jesus (see John 1:45; 6:42); Mark mentions him not at all. Matthew and Luke are the only evangelists to record anything about Jesus' birth and childhood, that part of his life in which Joseph plays an important role; they provide what New Testament information we have. We find all but three verses of that information in the first two chapters of each Gospel (as in John, the other references to Joseph serve to identify Jesus: Matthew 13:55; Luke 3:23; 4:22).

Matthew and Luke each offer us a different portrait of Joseph. Though clearly portraits of the same person, they are quite unlike. Matthew paints Joseph with bold, bright strokes and puts him in the foreground; Luke uses a restrained palette and an off-to-the-side placement. Each portrait faithfully conveys something important about who Joseph is, but each in its own way.

Why Matthew and Luke differ in their portrayals of persons and events connected with Jesus' infancy is a matter of ongoing discussion for Scripture scholars. One explanation is that the two evangelists had access to different sources: both made use of the Gospel of Mark, but each added material from some source unique to himself. Additionally, each Gospel was originally aimed at a different audience — Matthew's to Jewish Christians, Luke's to Gentile Christians; each was skillfully constructed to realize differing pastoral goals that we can infer only imperfectly.

But it doesn't take a Scripture scholar to understand the basic reason why we have two distinct portraits of Joseph: Matthew and Luke were two different people. Each had his own unique, Holy Spirit-inspired perceptions and skills.

In many ordinary ways you and I can see this dynamic at work every day. A high-school senior shows you her graduation photo, which reveals her as thoughtful and meditative; the candid photo next to it captures her equally characteristic "daredevil" side. Two people attend the same event — a family celebration, a business meeting, a retreat. They return with reports that agree factually (we can hope) but include different details and emphases.

My parents' first meeting, a blind date arranged by the family dentist, is a good example. My mother's account provided us chil-

21

dren with a treasured list of details: the look and feel of the hotel lobby where she sat waiting for Mr. Unknown, the identifying white carnation on her coat, her pleasant surprise when a handsome, red-haired Navy lieutenant materialized. My father's rendition centered on his sense of God at work: Dad had just finished a thirty-day novena for guidance about his vocation and realized right there in the Biltmore lobby how his prayer had been answered.

I always marveled at how my parents' accounts complemented one another, the differences resulting in a deeper, truer picture of how their relationship began than either one could have provided solo. This is the advantage of binocular vision.

People who study sight have found that, to a great degree, depth perception is made possible by the fact that each of our eyes looks at a scene from a slightly differing angle and point of view. Just as this disparity of images helps us toward a 3-D picture of the world, having Matthew's and Luke's differing portraits rounds out our picture of St. Joseph. Each of these inspired glimpses makes a valuable contribution to our understanding and leaves us spiritually richer.

We best appreciate the whole, however, by first appreciating its individual parts. In other words, before considering the composite picture of St. Joseph that results from combining Luke's and Matthew's portraits, it is worth studying each Gospel portrayal for itself. This is why, in chapter two of this book, you will find no references to Luke's Gospel and, in chapter three, just the briefest allusion to Matthew's.

Each evangelist has approached the same scene from different perspectives, producing different results. As we pay individual attention to the two portraits of St. Joseph, we will be enriched — and immeasurably so, for these are not simply works of art: they are first and foremost the inspired word of God.

Here, then, are a few practical remarks and suggestions to bear in mind as you read the next two chapters.

1. *Don't skip.* The Gospel passages that have to do with St. Joseph are so familiar that it might be tempting to flip past the pages where they are discussed. Consider, though, that what Scripture says about Joseph is the foundation for the Church's devotion to him. Consider, too, that looking at these familiar passages from a new angle — that is, to see what they reveal about St. Joseph — may yield insights you haven't had before.

In many cases, I have included the relevant Scripture verses in the sections where they are discussed. Still, you will benefit most by reading with a Bible at hand.

2. *Read carefully.* The approach to Scripture used here calls for careful, attentive reading. It does not require scholarly skills. Mindful of the Hasidic saying that every translation is "like kissing your beloved through a veil," I have included occasional discussions of the meanings of Greek or Hebrew words used in the original text. This is about as academic as this book gets. I myself am not a scholar, though I have drawn gratefully from the writings of scholars ancient and modern.

3. *Read separately.* Make an effort to forget what you know from the Gospel of Luke as you read what Matthew has written, and vice versa. This may take some doing, but the point is to cultivate a more focused approach to the particular Gospel at hand that will heighten your alertness to its unique qualities.

4. *Put questions on hold.* If, as you read Matthew and Luke, you find yourself wondering about some aspect of St. Joseph's life or about the events recounted, hold that thought! Perhaps your question will be answered in part two, which deals with discrepancies between Luke and Matthew and presents a bit of background. However, if your questions concern other types of issues — for example, how these Gospels originated and evolved — you will want to consult additional materials (the source notes offer some suggestions).

The aim of the next two chapters is simply to look at the Gospel texts as we have them. To paraphrase slightly what Luke Timothy Johnson explains in his commentary on the Gospel of Luke, "My only concern is with what [the evangelist] is saying and how he goes about saying it."

5. *Pray.* Whenever we read Scripture, we should begin with a simple act of turning mind and heart to God. George Martin, author of *Reading Scripture as the Word of God,* suggests that our pre-reading prayer should ask God two things:

> First, we should pray that the same Holy Spirit who guided the writing of Scripture will be present in us, inspiring us to correctly understand what we read, and to understand it in ever-increasing depth. . . .
>
> Secondly, our prayer should ask that we will be empowered to make what we read a part of our lives. . . .
>
> Such prayer should precede our every reading of the Bible.

For we do not approach the Bible as we approach any other book. We approach it as an opportunity to listen to him who speaks to us through the words of Scripture. Through the Bible, we approach God himself, and our attitude must be one of prayer.

Given the subject of this book, it would be appropriate to add another invocation as we turn to Matthew and Luke: "St. Joseph, pray for us!"

Pay a Visit

Visiting a shrine is good way to initiate or deepen your relationship with St. Joseph! A few possibilities for North Americans:

✓ *St. Joseph's Oratory* began in 1904 as a chapel built by Brother André (born Alfred Bessette), a brother in the Congregation of Holy Cross. Today it is the world's largest shrine to St. Joseph. Of special interest: the original chapel and reconstructions of rooms where Brother André lived, died, and received the multitudes who sought his counsel and prayers; the crypt church, where a round of daily Masses is celebrated in French and English; several adjacent rooms that house Brother André's tomb, a statue of St. Joseph where many visitors leave written prayer requests, and a votive chapel that displays crutches and other objects discarded by people who were healed through Brother André's prayers. A good place for private retreats, the Oratory offers walk-in spiritual counseling by a team of Holy Cross priests and affordable housing for pilgrims.

3800 Queen Mary Road, Montreal, Quebec, Canada H3V 1H6

(514) 733-8211 / www.saint-joseph.org

✓ *The Shrine of St. Joseph, Guardian of the Redeemer* was begun in 1952 but took on the second part of its name in 1993, in response to John Paul II's 1989 apostolic exhortation, *Guardian of the Redeemer.* Staffed by the Oblates of St. Joseph and overlooking the Pacific, the shrine offers many opportunities to participate in devotions to St. Joseph: prayers after daily Mass, Wednesday commemorations of his seven joys and sorrows, a March novena that ends with a celebration of St. Joseph's feast on the nineteenth, a yearly pilgrimage in August. Another encouragement to devotion is the shrine's exhibit of St. Joseph art.

544 West Cliff Drive, Santa Cruz, California 95060

(831) 457-1868

✓ *St. Joseph the Worker Shrine* originated in an 1868 mission

24

preached by a French-speaking Oblates of Mary Immaculate priest, André Garin, and attended by hundreds of Canadian immigrants employed in the area's booming cotton and woolen mills. Their donations, enough for a down payment on a church building, launched the downtown parish, which in 1956 was dedicated as a shrine to serve the spiritual needs of shoppers and workers. Daily Mass and confessions, devotions centering on prayer to St. Joseph as the model for working people, and information on Catholic social teaching are a few features of this shrine.

37 Lee Street, Lowell, Massachusetts 01852-1103

(978) 458-6346 / www.stjosephshrine.org

✓ *St. Joseph's Shrine* was founded in 1924 by Father Thomas Augustine Judge, a Missionary Servant of the Most Holy Trinity, whose particular desire was to empower laypeople to reach out to those in physical and spiritual distress. This commitment is reflected today in the shrine's various outreaches to the homeless, the hungry, and those who live in the inner city. Services to pilgrims include daily Mass, days of reflection, counseling from the priests on staff, and serene mountainside grounds conducive to meditation.

St. Joseph's Shrine, 1050 Long Hill Road, Stirling, New Jersey 07980

(908) 647-0208

✓ *Old St. Joseph's Church and National Shrine* is tucked away in an alley, a vivid reminder that when the church was founded — by Joseph Greaton, S.J., in 1733 — it was illegal for property dedicated to Catholic worship to be located on a public thoroughfare. Jesuits still staff St. Joseph's, which functions as a parish in Philadelphia's historic district and offers a regular schedule of daily Masses and other services.

321 Willings Alley, Philadelphia, Pennsylvania 19106

(215) 923-1733 / www.oldstjoseph.org

✓ *The Shrine of St. Joseph*, built by German immigrants in the 1840s, was the site of an authenticated miracle in 1864, when Ignatius Strecker was healed of a festering chest wound after venerating the church's relic of St. Peter Claver. That relic can still be venerated after Mass on Sundays. Beautifully restored, thanks to many donations of time and money, the shrine features an "altar of answered prayers" dedicated to St. Joseph, whose protection was invoked during an 1866 cholera epidemic.

1220 N. 11th Street, St. Louis, Missouri 63106

(314) 231-9407

Chapter 2

Matthew's Portrait: Joseph the Hero

Joseph conquered the devil; he conquered
a tyrannical king; he conquered himself. . . .

Jerónimo Gracián

We meet him in verse 16 of Matthew's Gospel — a discreet presence at the end of the long list of names that comprise "the genealogy of Jesus the Messiah, the son of David, the son of Abraham" (1:1). It is not the debut that most of us would have chosen for the first-century B.C. Jew we revere today as St. Joseph.

Roots: Matthew 1:1-17

Not that Americans have no interest in ancestries. Right now, an estimated nineteen million of us are engaged in tracing our family trees — and with the help of more than a million genealogical and local history websites and home pages on the Internet. Soon, trend-watchers predict, lineage-tracing will displace two perennials, stamp and coin collecting, as the most popular hobby in the U.S.

Yet even the most genealogically minded among us tend to find Matthew's opener alien, even daunting. We are not like the evangelist's first readers — first-century Jewish Christians, mostly — who were well-acquainted with the stories behind the "begats." Tossed into a heavy sea of names like Abiud and Jehoshaphat and Zerubbabel, we flounder and flail and finally skim.

Church Fathers like Augustine and John Chrysostom plunged into the genealogy with zest, diving deep to emerge with thoughtful, often ingenious insights into God's interaction with human beings. Similar enthusiasm characterizes modern Scripture scholars like Raymond Brown, a Sulpician priest who was twice appointed a member of the Pontifical Biblical Commission — by Pope Paul VI in 1972 and by Pope John Paul II in 1996. Until his death in 1998, Father Brown was waging a "somewhat solitary campaign" to make Matthew's genealogy a major topic of Advent preaching. Because these names contain "the essential theology of the Old and New Testaments," he felt, they should resound from the pulpit at least once a year.

Good news in Matthew's genealogy? Where is it? And what light can it shed on low-profile St. Joseph?

Matthew answers the last question indirectly by zeroing in right away on the identity of Jesus: he is "the Messiah, the son of David, the son of Abraham" (verse 1). In the largely Jewish Christian community for which Matthew wrote his Gospel, these titles proclaimed long-awaited good news. The One foretold by the prophets had come: Jesus, "who is called the Messiah" (verse 16)! God's pledge to David had been fulfilled! Jesus was the promised heir to the divinely established kingdom that, God had said, would "be made sure forever" (see 2 Samuel 7:8-16).

For Matthew's Gentile Christian readers, too, there was reason to rejoice. As "the son of Abraham," Jesus was also the heir to God's universal promises. "You shall be the ancestor of a multitude of nations," God had told Abraham at the very beginning of Israel's history; "by your offspring shall all the nations of the earth gain blessing" (Genesis 17:4; 22:18). Won by Jesus' death and resurrection, that blessing opened the way for non-Jews to join Abraham, Isaac, and Jacob at table in the kingdom of heaven (see Matthew 8:11).

Christ and Messiah, son of David, son of Abraham — by evoking these titles, Matthew situates Jesus within Israel's history and begins to present him and his message as the fulfillment of Israel's hope and tradition. This insistence on the continuity of God's action characterizes Matthew's whole Gospel and explains the presence of so many ancestors.

You might think of these ancestors as forming a sort of living extension ladder leading to Jesus. It is a long ladder in three sections, each one containing fourteen rungs, or names, that span Israel's history. Abraham leads off the first section, which extends through the time of the Old Testament patriarchs and up to the monarchy. Level two starts with David, takes us through the rise and fall of the kings of Judah, and extends to the period of the exile in Babylon. Stage three of the ascent to Jesus opens with two relatively obscure names, then moves on past some *real* unknowns (people who are not mentioned anywhere else) before finally leading up to history's most famous family.

Matthew's ladder — so neatly divided into fourteen-generation periods, its rungs so evenly spaced by the refrain "was the father of" — is a picture of symmetry. God is in control, this suggests; he has worked things out so that the whole history of Israel leads inevitably to the Savior, who appears at precisely the right moment.

But there is more to this ladder than its orderly appearance.

On closer inspection, it also reveals quite a different set of realities: that human history is *not* tidy, nor God's interventions predictable.

The inclusion of five women, an unusual departure from the pattern of biblical genealogies, is our first clue that there is something different about Jesus' birth record. For one thing, the four Old Testament women were seen as foreigners. Even more to the point: these are women whose marital histories carry a whiff of scandal, or at least irregularity.

• *Tamar*, a Canaanite, was left childless by the deaths of her first and second husbands, two brothers. In a last-ditch effort to continue their family line, she posed as a prostitute and seduced her father-in-law, Judah (see Genesis 38).

• *Rahab*, another Canaanite, was a real prostitute whose protection of Israelite spies made possible the fall of Jericho (see Joshua 2). Despite her shady past, she married into Jesus' family tree and gave birth to the great-grandfather of King David.

• *Ruth*, a widow, modeled faithfulness in caring for her family, yet she was a Moabite, a member of a people the Israelites held in special contempt. Her second marriage came about in an unusual way (see the Book of Ruth).

• *Bathsheba*, an Israelite whose connection with foreigners derived from her marriage to Uriah the Hittite, was either a victim of David's lust or a consenting partner to adultery (see 2 Samuel 11).

Another tip-off that Matthew's genealogy contains something unexpected is the disappearance of the phrase "the father of," as the genealogical ladder reaches Joseph. "Eleazar the father of Matthan, and Matthan the father of Jacob, and Jacob the father of Joseph the husband of Mary, of whom Jesus was born, who is called the Messiah" (1:15-16).

What Matthew intends by this disruption will soon become startlingly clear, but already it announces a halt to "business as usual." It suggests something peculiar about the marital situation of Joseph and Mary and raises questions about Joseph's position as father. "The fact that Joseph, the last descendant of David, is not a begetter is . . . disconcerting," observes French scholar René Laurentin. "It would appear to break the messianic chain."

From his first appearance in Matthew's Gospel, Joseph walks the edge between tradition and newness. He is a key player in a divine plan that is a surprising departure from the ordinary. Yet like Jesus, he is firmly rooted in the tradition of Israel.

His very name, "Joseph," is the name of the famous patriarch of the Book of Genesis. It means "may God add" — that is, "may God give us more children just like this one." Like Scripture scholar Joseph Fitzmyer, we might imagine St. Joseph's father, Jacob, and his unnamed wife exulting over their newborn son and deciding to name him Joseph as an expression of their delight.

We would not be off the mark if we also called Joseph a "son of David" and "son of Abraham." Only Jesus is *the* son of David, the Messiah. Still, "son of David" fits Joseph too, since it is in his lineage that Jesus' earthly identity is rooted. Joseph is a bona fide, if nonflashy, descendant of Israel's premier royal family: "son of David," the angel in his dream will call Joseph (verse 20). Matthew insists on this family tie because it fulfills the ancient prophecies that the Messiah must come from David's line.

Joseph is also a true "son of Abraham." Like the patriarch, who was called to set out in faith for an unknown land (see Genesis 12:1-9), he will exhibit obedient readiness to pick up and go at God's command (see 2:14, 21). He will see the promise to Abraham fulfilled when the Gentile magi travel from abroad to pay homage to the newborn "king of the Jews" (see 2:1-12).

Annunciation to Joseph: Matthew 1:18-25

A storyteller with a mission, Matthew presents Jesus' birth and infancy in five episodes that reveal the Child as the fulfillment of the messianic prophecies. Each episode either ends or climaxes in an Old Testament quotation that, like a thought-provoking punch line, brings out its deeper meaning.

After Jesus it is Joseph who stands out in this ensemble. The first story, which completes the genealogy in establishing Jesus' true identity, is especially important for understanding Joseph's. It begins:

> Now the birth of Jesus the Messiah took place in this way. When his mother Mary had been engaged to Joseph, but before they lived together, she was found to be with child from the Holy Spirit. Her husband Joseph, being a righteous man and unwilling to expose her to public disgrace, planned to dismiss her quietly.

The story of the most uncommon birth in history opens with a most common human event: a man has asked a woman to be his wife, and she has apparently said yes.

If all this took place according to the customs of the day, this was not a private proposal, with Joseph choosing a secluded, romantic setting in which to get down on one knee and pledge his undying love. Most marriages were arranged by the couple's families — not surprising in a society where women were commonly betrothed at twelve and men just a few years later. Nor, as with the engaged couples we know, did their engagement leave Mary or Joseph free to back out of the wedding ceremony if assailed by doubts and jitters.

For first-century B.C. Palestinian Jews, marriage was a family affair that took place in two acts separated by an intermission. Act one, an engagement usually ratified before witnesses at the bride's house, was a formal declaration of intent to marry; afterward, the couple were legally considered "husband" and "wife" (which is how Matthew refers to Joseph and Mary in verses 19, 20, and 24) and were bound to matrimonial fidelity, though they would not yet live together.

Act two, which took place with much fanfare about a year later, was the wedding ceremony in which the bride was escorted from her family home to the groom's. Perhaps Joseph and his family and friends arranged a festive torchlight procession for the occasion (as in Matthew 25). Perhaps they all feasted afterward, as a Cana couple would do some thirty years later (see John 2). Matthew offers no details. About this wedding, just one thing is known for sure: the bride came to it pregnant.

Mary conceived during the intermission separating acts one and two of the marriage process. Though considered married, a couple was not to have sexual relations during this interval. Mary's too-early pregnancy would thus have raised eyebrows and given neighborhood busybodies a juicy bit of gossip.

Joseph undoubtedly knew that people were jumping to false conclusions about his supposed lack of self-control. But what did *he* think about Mary's condition? Again, Matthew does not spell it out. We learn only that Joseph is "righteous," or "just" — a virtue that has made him decide to divorce Mary in the least humiliating way possible.

While agreeing on these basics, Christians reflecting on Matthew's text over the centuries have come to different conclusions about the nature of Joseph's justice and his motives. They theorize that he reacted to Mary's pregnancy in one of three different ways: awe, bewilderment, or suspicion.

• *Awe* is a credible theory only if Joseph discovered the pregnancy and its divine origin more or less simultaneously. Those who hold this view often interpret verse 18 — "she was found to be with child from the Holy Spirit" — to mean that the pregnancy itself somehow conveyed the knowledge that it was miraculous. Or they surmise that Joseph was enlightened by an earlier angelic appearance or by Mary. Like Moses before the burning bush or the centurion protesting his unworthiness to receive Jesus, they reason, Joseph would then have drawn back out of reverence, seeing himself as sinful and miscast in this divine drama.

"Joseph feared to be called the husband of such a wife," St. Basil wrote in the fourth century. And an ancient sermon incorrectly attributed to Origen explained why: "He recognized in her the power of a miracle and a vast mystery which he held himself unworthy to approach." In this scenario, Joseph's justice demonstrates itself mainly as an awed respect for God's plan of salvation.

Although the "awe" theory has appeal, it has problems too. For example, verse 18's news that the conception is miraculous is best read as Matthew's aside to the reader, not as information to Joseph. It is the evangelist's way of underlining Jesus' divine origin. Nowhere does Matthew indicate that Joseph already has this knowledge or suggest how he might have attained it. And why, if Joseph was already informed, would the angel in his dream give him directives followed by the explanation "The child conceived in her is from the Holy Spirit" (verse 20)? How often do angels announce what is already known?

• *Bewilderment* is another way Joseph might have reacted to Mary's pregnancy. Advocates of this idea focus on his perplexity before two seemingly irreconcilable realities: Mary could not have sinned, yet she was expecting a child that was not his. "He plainly saw the conception, and he was incapable of suspecting fornication," exclaimed an early commentator. Unable to make sense of the matter, runs this theory, Joseph did the gentlemanly thing; he suspended judgment and sought to end the relationship quietly. In other words, he was more concerned to let Mary off the hook than to guard against a possible transgression of the Mosaic law. "Knowing Mary's chastity and wondering at what had occurred," wrote St. Jerome, Joseph "concealed in silence the mystery he did not fathom." Here, then, his justice consists in mercy.

A major difficulty with both the "bewildered" and the "awe-struck" portrayals, however, is that they do not adequately explain why Joseph would choose to divorce Mary. No divorce could be completely hushed up, especially not in a small village. If Joseph believed Mary to be innocent, or at least could not bring himself to believe her guilty, how could he abandon her? Would a man described as "just" take such a step? Surely, he could not have expected people to draw enlightened, charitable conclusions about Mary's swelling figure — especially not when his retreat seemed to be a disclaimer of paternity.

• *Suspicion* is the traditional label for the theory that Joseph assumed Mary to have conceived in the normal way, either through adultery or rape. This was the majority view among the Church Fathers, including St. Augustine and St. John Chrysostom. It is also the one that best fits the story as Matthew presents it:

✓ It furthers the "scandal" motif evoked by the Old Testament women in the genealogy: Mary's pregnancy appears disgraceful to outsiders.
✓ It makes the best sense of the angelic message: Joseph is given the inside information he needs in order to proceed with the wedding.
✓ It does real justice to this Gospel's understanding of justice as sensitive obedience to the Mosaic law, and to its depiction of Joseph as "just."

For Matthew to call Joseph just, or upright, was to express the highest praise of his piety. It spoke of his desire to conform to God's will as revealed in the Torah, the teaching transmitted through Moses that covered every area of Jewish life. Normally, obedience to the Mosaic law would have been a privilege, not a burden, for someone like Joseph. In the face of Mary's disconcerting pregnancy, however, it presented this just man with a dilemma.

The Book of Deuteronomy spelled out what the law required when a bride came to her husband having lost her virginity: "The men of the town shall stone her to death, because she committed a disgraceful act in Israel by prostituting herself in her father's house" (22:21). Just how strictly this law was implemented in Joseph's day is unknown. However that may be, *something* unpleasant was clearly the norm for a woman in Mary's position — an unpleasantness Joseph was unwilling to inflict. A trial, perhaps (a procedure for a "trial by ordeal" of an adulterous wife is described in Numbers 5:11-31), or a public accusation of adultery through which a wronged

33

husband might establish his own innocence and his right to keep the dowry.

Joseph's decision to divorce Mary "quietly" proves him just, but also merciful. Deeply obedient to God and mindful of the sanctity of marriage, Joseph could not simply ignore the law "just this once" — not when he thought that Mary's pregnancy was of human origin. At the same time, he would not push for his rights at Mary's expense. Most likely, he decided to keep to the basic formalities — a writ of divorce and two witnesses — but without shaming Mary by demanding a trial or giving adultery as the reason for his action.

Does Joseph's "suspicion" — or better, his mistaken assumption about Mary — detract from his holiness? Not unless he can be faulted for not grasping a mystery that flesh and blood could not possibly have guessed!

Stacks of Christmas cards have arrived at our home over the years, but rarely have I found one that depicts the annunciation to Joseph. Perhaps the scene of a man asleep does not greatly excite the artistic imagination. Nonetheless, this is a dramatic moment in Matthew's Gospel, for it makes Joseph the first recipient, after Mary, of the good news of salvation through Jesus. (Matthew never reports the annunciation to Mary, but it is reasonable to suppose that he assumed something of the sort, since the incarnation required her informed consent.)

> But just when he had resolved to do this [divorce Mary quietly], an angel of the Lord appeared to him in a dream and said, "Joseph, son of David, do not be afraid to take Mary as your wife, for the child conceived in her is from the Holy Spirit. She will bear a son, and you are to name him Jesus, for he will save his people from their sins." All this took place to fulfill what had been spoken by the Lord through the prophet:
> "Look, the virgin shall conceive / and bear a son, / and they shall name him / Emmanuel," / which means "God is with us."
> When Joseph awoke from sleep, he did as the angel of the Lord commanded him; he took her as his wife, but he had no marital relations with her until she had borne a son; and he named him Jesus.

Matthew's annunciation centers on the identity and mission of Jesus, but it also reveals the identity Joseph is to have in God's plan. If ever Joseph had wondered, "Who am I?" or "Why am I here?" — this was God's mind-boggling answer.

Like the three other divine messages that Joseph will receive, this one comes in a dream, but not the sort that leaves a person woolly-headed or puzzling over subconscious meanings. This is a clear communication from an "angel of the Lord" — either Gabriel or another heavenly messenger, or God (see Exodus 3:2 and 14:19, for example, where "angel of the Lord" refers to God's presence). The message overturns Joseph's decision and gives him an active part in Jesus' coming. He is charged with two tasks, each accompanied by a supporting reason.

1. *Take Mary as your wife.* This is God's go-ahead to Joseph and Mary's original wedding plans. No need to withdraw banquet invitations or cancel that order to the wine merchant! Act two can, indeed must, proceed as scheduled, for Joseph is to take public responsibility for Mary and the child she is carrying.

The reason for this breakthrough is stunning news that sweeps away all impediments: "The child conceived in her is from the Holy Spirit." Completing the marriage process will not violate God's law, Joseph is assured. On the contrary, God has placed a particular seal of approval on Joseph and Mary's relationship by entering into it in a uniquely marvelous way.

2. *Name the child Jesus.* In a day when there was no such thing as DNA testing, Jewish law based paternity on a man's willingness to acknowledge a child as his own. "If a man says, 'This is my son,' he is to be believed," said a third-century Jewish law code. (A woman's testimony was considered unreliable: in order to avoid being accused of adultery, went the reasoning, she might well claim that her husband fathered a child he did not.)

Joseph's second task, to name the son that Mary has conceived, will signal that he accepts the role of father. While this is not the physical paternity that outsiders will assume it to be, it is no fiction either. *Legal* paternity was what integrated a newborn into an Israelite family. Joseph's cooperative obedience secured this and more for Jesus. The "more," as we have seen, involved his incorporation into Joseph's lineage, thereby ensuring the Davidic ancestry foretold of the Messiah.

None of the Gospels quotes Joseph directly. Matthew, however, reveals one word that he is sure to have said: "Jesus."

Religious-goods stores today often sell decorative plaques on which a person's name appears with a few words explaining its meaning. If Jesus had such a wall ornament hanging over his crib (and it's a sure bet he didn't!), there would have been two entries under his name. "Jesus" represents a shortened form of the Hebrew "Joshua," whose original meaning was "Yahweh helps." But since the name "Jesus" sounds like the Hebrew word for salvation, it eventually came to be interpreted, "Yahweh saves." The angel in Joseph's dream draws on this second meaning to explain why the child in Mary's womb must be called Jesus: "for he will save his people from their sins." In learning what name he is to confer, Joseph begins his initiation into the secret of Jesus' life and mission.

Joseph's naming will ensure Jesus' identity as Son of David and Savior. But as Raymond Brown points out, "There is a greater identity which Joseph must accept, but to which he cannot contribute: the child will be Emmanuel, 'God with us,' because Mary has conceived him through the Holy Spirit." Jesus is first and foremost the Son of God.

Only once before had the name "Emmanuel" been applied to anyone — and only symbolically, at that. Over seven hundred years before Jesus, the prophet Isaiah had given a frightened king a sign that his dynasty would survive the threat of an enemy invasion. This is the prophecy that Matthew now cites to underline Jesus' divine origin: "Look, the virgin shall conceive and bear a son, and they shall name him 'Emmanuel,' which means 'God is with us'" (Matthew 1:23; compare with Isaiah 7:14).

As a pious Jew who took God's word seriously, Joseph would have been familiar with this text. Those of us who have heard it proclaimed in many an Advent and Christmas liturgy may therefore wonder why he does not seem to have connected it with Mary's mysterious pregnancy — at least not in a way that removed his doubts.

But there is no clear evidence that anyone before Matthew had ever interpreted Isaiah's words to refer to a virginal conception. The Hebrew text of Isaiah spoke of a "young girl" conceiving. The Greek translation used by Matthew had used the Greek word for "virgin," but this word, too, could sometimes refer more generally to a young girl of marriageable age. The verse's most obvious meaning, then, was simply: a young girl has become pregnant; or (since the Greek translation of Isaiah indicated that the conception was a future event): a young girl now a virgin will become pregnant. Either way, no miraculous intervention was implied.

The original mother-to-be of Isaiah's prophecy was probably a new wife of Ahaz, the king to whom the word was addressed. His promised heir, as an ancient Jewish tradition attests, may have been Hezekiah, one of the few truly devout monarchs of David's line. (Not that Ahaz deserved any of this! He was a wicked ruler who made idols, worshiped pagan gods, and burned some of his sons as human sacrifices: see 2 Kings 16:1-4; 2 Chronicles 28:1-4.)

Guided by the same Holy Spirit who had inspired Isaiah's word to Ahaz, Matthew declared that word perfectly fulfilled in Jesus. God's own Son conceived by the Spirit's creative power, Jesus is the ultimate expression of "God with us," far beyond anything that Isaiah — or Joseph, for that matter — could have imagined.

"You are not your own" (1 Corinthians 6:19). "You have died, and your life is hidden with Christ in God" (Colossians 3:3). These words have not yet been written as Joseph wipes the sleep from his eyes, but their meaning will be illustrated by the way he now responds to God's message.

Awaking from sleep, Joseph awakens to a new life. He might have protested, "I was so looking forward to a normal married life," or, "Lord, you've put me in a very uncomfortable situation. I don't feel up to it." If any such regrets arose in Joseph's mind, they were quickly dismissed. We will not see him passive or pensive any more. He has become a man with a mission.

Having set out for one destination, Joseph promptly changes course as directed to head for uncharted terrain. He generously surrenders his own legitimate plans so as to accept a role for which there is no precedent. As John Paul II says, Joseph took Mary "in all the mystery of her motherhood," and with her, "the Son who had come into the world by the power of the Holy Spirit." What Joseph did showed his "readiness of will" toward God; it is "the clearest 'obedience of faith' " (Guardian of the Redeemer, Nos. 3, 4).

Matthew underlines the energy of Joseph's response with a quick succession of verbs: he awoke, did, took, named. One thing this man of action did not do, however: he had no conjugal relations with Mary "until she had borne a son." Matthew is making it perfectly clear that Jesus was not conceived by a human father.

About that little word "until." Doesn't it indicate that Joseph and Mary had sexual relations after Jesus was born? Not necessarily, linguists say. In Greek and Hebrew, an "until" clause is not a sure signal that a change will occur after the event it mentions. It might: "Flee to Egypt and stay there until I tell you [to do other-

37

wise]" (Matthew 2:13). Or it might not: "A bruised reed he will not break . . . until he brings justice to victory" (Matthew 12:20, quoting Isaiah 42:3). Commenting on this statement about Jesus, Father John Meier says: "Matthew certainly does not think that Jesus the gentle servant will turn harsh and cruel toward the weak and crushed after he makes God's saving justice victorious"!

In short, "until" says nothing one way or the other about the nature of Joseph and Mary's relationship following Jesus' birth. Matthew is not addressing the issue of Mary's perpetual virginity; he is affirming once again that Jesus was conceived supernaturally and was born of a virgin.

Surprise Visit: Matthew 2:1-12

If chapter one of Matthew's Gospel reads a bit like a *Who's Who*, chapter two is something of a travelogue. Place names appear, settings change, people journey. Jesus' birth (which Matthew mentions almost in passing) sets things in motion and provokes a two-fold reaction to a question that Joseph must already have been pondering: "Who do you say that I am?" (Matthew 16:15).

The first response comes from Gentile foreigners. "In the time of King Herod, after Jesus was born in Bethlehem of Judea, wise men from the East came to Jerusalem, asking, 'Where is the child who has been born king of the Jews?'" (verse 1).

Matthew might be surprised at our picturing the scene as a royal procession crossing hill and dale to hearty rounds of "We three kings of Orient are. . . ." He never specified how many travelers there were (Christians considered two, four, and twelve before finally settling on three, based on the number of gifts they presented), nor did he say they were kings. "Magi" seems to have been a generic term that could refer to sorcerers and charlatans, but also to men of genuine learning. Matthew's magi are true seekers after wisdom whose study of the stars draws them closer to God.

The second response to Jesus comes from a Jewish king who has a natural advantage over the magi: Herod has access to the Scriptures, which reveal what the wise men can perceive only dimly about the Messiah. Perversely, he chooses to ignore the truth and focuses exclusively on the possible threat to his own position. (After all, Herod's title was "King of the Jews." Who was this upstart?) With great guile he discreetly summons the magi to his Jerusalem palace and tries to recruit them as scouts, "so that I may also go and pay him homage" (verse 8). Father René Laurentin observes that Herod's "malevolent secretiveness" contrasts with the "compassionate secrecy of Joseph the just man," whose plan to divorce "quietly" was devised for Mary's good.

The story of the magi continues the "son of Abraham" and the "son of David" themes introduced in chapter one. The first theme is evident in Matthew's positive portrayal of the wise men as pioneers and models for Gentile believers in Christ. The second theme is sounded in the four references to Bethlehem. Located five miles south of Jerusalem, Bethlehem was David's ancestral town, where he was born and anointed king. Old Testament prophecies like the one quoted to King Herod in verse 6 specified that it would be the Messiah's birthplace as well (see Micah 5:2).

Matthew confirms that Jesus was born in Bethlehem, which he seems to view as Joseph and Mary's place of residence. Bethlehem is the first place name the evangelist mentions. It appears at the beginning of chapter two, with no sign that the setting has changed from chapter one. With only Matthew's account to go by, one would naturally assume that Bethlehem is where the events surrounding Joseph's "annunciation" have taken place. Also, the magi find Mary and Jesus in "the house" (2:11) — which sounds like the family's permanent dwelling.

Is Joseph present during the magi's house call? The story mentions him not at all, which is surprising, given his prominence elsewhere in these two chapters. Some commentators take his absence as a possible subtle reminder that Jesus had no human father. (But if so, why didn't Matthew absent Joseph more consistently?)

It seems more likely that Joseph goes unmentioned because his presence would have been taken for granted by Matthew's readers. Theirs was a patriarchal society, where women lived lives centered on the home, under the authority and protection of husband, father, or other male relative. There were strict limits on the mingling of the sexes. Social historian Léonie Archer points out that "the most important rule of conduct for women when moving in public was that they should never, under any circumstances, speak to a man." Even within the home, she says, wives attended but did not generally sit with their husband and male visitors. If, in an exceptional case, a married woman had cause to meet with a man in her husband's absence, "then a chaperone was required to be present. This rule applied even to male relatives (excepting sons)." In such a social climate, it would have been quite improper for Mary to receive the magi on her own.

Besides, this would not have been a fifteen-minute stop to drop off gifts! The wise men, who had been "overwhelmed with joy" upon seeing the star (verse 10), would doubtless have wanted to linger in the presence of the One who caused it. We can imagine animated conversation, the visitors telling of their discovery, the couple confirming it. Then, too, the Jewish approach to hospitality demanded more than American-style entertaining — especially when the visitors had come from afar. Being a host meant receiving strangers into one's care and looking to their needs, a responsibility that would have fallen to Joseph.

Maybe Matthew made a point of referring to Mary because his first readers would not have assumed *her* presence! Another possibility, based on Father Roland de Vaux's study of ancient Israel, derives from the exalted position accorded to the queen mothers of newborn or newly installed Davidic kings. Some scholars think Matthew may have been evoking this idea through his mention of "the child with Mary his mother" (verse 11) — a young king of David's line receiving homage in David's city in the presence of the queen mother.

However the wise men's visit took place, it gave Joseph much to ponder about the child he had taken to his heart. Signs in the heavens, learned foreigners paying homage and bringing tribute — like the just man described in Psalm 1 who meditates day and night on God's word and deeds, Joseph surely marveled over the mystery unfolding before him.

Flight and Murder: Matthew 2:13-18

A joyful scene turns somber in the next two stories, as the magi leave and Herod's jealousy explodes into murderous rage. From Jerusalem come deadly orders to exterminate all Bethlehem boys two and under. Based on estimates of that town's population and of birth and infant mortality rates of the day, the number of victims might have been twenty or so.

If this bloody incident is all a person knows of Herod, it will come as news that history calls him Herod the Great and that, in many ways, he was a ruler of outstanding administrative and political ability. During his thirty-three-year reign, the country was mostly at peace, trade flourished, and building projects abounded — most notably, the magnificent Temple in Jerusalem.

But Herod kept a ruthless grip on power. He did not slaughter on the scale of a Stalin or a Pol Pot, but he was merciless in eliminating both real and imagined rivals to his throne. The Jewish historian Josephus, born about thirty years after Herod's death, reported that by the time of Jesus' birth, the king's long list of victims included a favorite wife and two sons. Another son, whom Herod had once named as his successor, was executed only days before Herod's own death, on Herod's orders.

While Josephus said nothing of the Bethlehem massacre, a modern biographer points out that the incident is consistent with Josephus' description of Herod's character — "his restlessness, his rage, his guile, and his cruelty," especially toward the end of his reign. Always paranoid, Herod became even more so with age and illness. The Herod encountered by the magi was, according to a modern physician's interpretation of the symptoms described by Josephus, "an aged arterio-sclerotic . . . becoming increasingly prone to mood changes, delusions of persecution, uncontrolled outbursts of hypertensive cerebral attacks."

The magi's unannounced departure precipitates the outburst of fury that costs the "holy innocents" their lives but fails to accomplish Herod's purpose. His soldiers do their bloody work in vain. The child they seek is safely out of reach, thanks to Joseph's swift obedience.

> An angel of the Lord appeared to Joseph in a dream and said, "Get up, take the child and his mother, and flee to Egypt, and remain there until I tell you; for Herod is about to search for the child, to destroy him." Then Joseph got up, took the child and his mother by night, and went to Egypt, and remained there until the death of Herod. This was to fulfill what had been spoken by the Lord through the prophet, "Out of Egypt I have called my son."

Again Joseph has received a divine command through a dream, and again he has obeyed promptly and to the letter. "Get up, take, flee, remain." He "got up, took, fled, remained." "Have you ever beheld such obedience?" asked John Chrysostom, the fourth-century bishop of Constantinople, in his commentary on the Gospel of Matthew:

> When Joseph heard this message, he was not offended nor did he say, "Here indeed is something very puzzling! You told me but recently, 'He shall save his people,' and now he is un-

able to save himself, and we must flee on a long journey and a change of place? This is contrary to your promise." No, he uttered nothing of this sort, for he was a man of faith. Nor did he inquire the time of the return even though the angel spoke vaguely, saying, 'Remain there until I tell you.' Thus, Joseph did not become slothful, but he obeyed and bent his will, and he bore all his trials with joy.

The journey to be undertaken in such haste was not a Sunday outing, under any circumstances. From Bethlehem to the Nile delta was a two-hundred-mile trek, with no fast-food restaurants or motels to sustain the weary. Travelers planned ahead; they gathered supplies, chose beasts of burden, decided whether to go it alone or join up with a caravan for protection. But Joseph was given no time for planning. Warned by night, he acted by night — immediately, secretly, and no doubt resourcefully.

We would like some information about how he did it, but Matthew offers no explanation of Joseph's actions or thoughts. Told only that he "departed" with Jesus and Mary, we are left to wonder: What route did he choose? The Way of the Sea, the major trade thoroughfare that ran along the Mediterranean, was the shortest and most convenient; the alternative desert route was arduous, but perhaps safer for someone who was being hunted down as a political subversive. Did Joseph consider disguising the family's identity? Did he anxiously look back over his shoulder for signs of pursuit? The angel had not told him just how Herod would carry out his "search and destroy" mission for Jesus, and Joseph knew that Herod had a long arm.

Fortunately, that arm did not reach into Egypt, which had become a Roman province in 31 B.C. In 40 B.C. Rome had appointed Herod "King of the Jews" — but not of those Jews who lived outside his geographical domain. Egypt had long been a place of refuge for those fleeing trouble in Palestine, and although it was a pagan land, Jews had begun settling there after the Babylonian exile (586 B.C.). By Jesus' day they were quite numerous. In the city of Alexandria, to mention only one possibility, the refugees from Bethlehem would have found a sizable and thriving Jewish community.

Where did Joseph settle his family? Apocryphal writers and popular traditions were not shy about filling in the blanks. They supplied an itinerary that took the Holy Family south on the Nile (a trip they could afford, thanks to the magi's costly gifts), far past the pyramids of Gizah and the bank where Moses had been hidden in the bulrushes. None of this can be read into Matthew's account, of course. The evangelist hints only at the significance of Egypt as the family's destination.

It seems odd that Matthew cites the Old Testament prophet Hosea — "Out of Egypt I called my son" (2:15; Hosea 11:1) — as Joseph is leading Jesus and Mary *into* Egypt. Hosea was referring to the exodus from Egypt, and perhaps Matthew wanted to allude to this defining event in Israel's history at the first possible opportunity.

By evoking the exodus, Matthew draws attention to the parallel between Moses, who led his people out of Egypt and bondage to Pharaoh, and Jesus, who will lead his people out of bondage to sin. Like Herod, Pharaoh issued orders to kill Jewish boys, but one was marvelously saved (Exodus 1:16, 22; 2:1-10). Like Jesus, Moses fled into exile because of death threats but returned once the wicked king had died (Exodus 2:15, 23; 4:20). "Go back to Egypt," the Lord told Moses; "for all those who were seeking your life are dead" (Exodus 4:19). "Go to the land of Israel," the angel will tell Joseph, "for those who were seeking the child's life are dead" (Matthew 2:20).

Matthew points back to Moses in order to further his portrait of Jesus as the Savior who fulfills God's promises to Israel. But the sufferings of Moses and the Israelites under Pharaoh also point forward to the passion and death of the new Moses. Right from the beginning of his earthly life, Jesus, along with his family, is acquainted with hardship and sacrifice.

Going Home: Matthew 2:19-23

> When Herod died, an angel of the Lord suddenly appeared in a dream to Joseph in Egypt and said, "Get up, take the child and his mother, and go to the land of Israel, for those who were seeking the child's life are dead." Then Joseph got up, took the child and his mother, and went to the land of Israel. But when he heard that Archelaus was ruling over Judea in place of his father Herod, he was afraid to go there. And after being warned in a dream, he went away to the district of Galilee. There he made his home in a town called Nazareth, so that what had been spoken through the prophets might be fulfilled, "He will be called a Nazorean" (Nazarene in other translations*).

---

*Note: "Nazorean" instead of "Nazarene" is used throughout this work.

Matthew's mention of Herod's death provides information about the year of Jesus' birth and perhaps also a clue as to the length of the Egyptian interlude.

Most historians agree that Herod died in 4 B.C. Seen along with other data — including Herod's instructions to kill boys two years old and under, based on the magi's information (2:16) — this fact suggests that Jesus was born somewhere around 6 B.C., up to two years before the king's death. (It also opens the possibility that Jesus was older than a newborn at the time of the magi's visit.) As many have remarked, it is one of the curiosities of history that Jesus' birth took place in the time "before Christ." Blame it on the miscalculation of a sixth-century monk and calendar-maker!

While hard facts about dates are elusive, Matthew gives the general impression that Jesus was born not too long before the end of Herod's reign and that his stay in Egypt was relatively short. In support of the second point, John Meier observes that Matthew uses "the same diminutive word *paidion* ('little child') to describe Jesus during the visit of the magi (2:11), the flight into Egypt (2:13), and the return from Egypt after Herod's death (2:20)." Additionally, he says, the fact that Jesus was known as "the Nazorean" (2:23) might be taken to imply that his residence in both Bethlehem and Egypt was short and his residence in Nazareth long.

It takes two dreams to get Joseph and his family back to Israel and settled in Nazareth. The first one follows a familiar pattern: told to "get up, take, and go" back, Joseph promptly "got up, took, and went."

His first thought, it seems, was to return to Bethlehem. That idea lost its appeal once he learned that the region was now governed by Archelaus, the least competent and most brutal of the three sons among whom Herod's domain had been divided. Joseph had good reason for his fears. "Archelaus had all his father's defects of character with but little of his administrative and diplomatic ability," says professor of New Testament history F. F. Bruce. So tyrannical was his rule that the Roman emperor found it necessary to depose and banish him after nine oppressive years.

Redirected through another dream, Joseph heads north to Galilee, where Archelaus's brother Herod Antipas had come to power. This Herod was more able and more restrained than his brother — except in his personal life. His marriage to the ambitious and infamous Herodias, his niece and another brother's wife, was to involve him in a disastrous war with a neighboring king and bring about his own banishment in A.D. 39. The marriage also produced an equally infamous daughter, Salome, who is remembered for her role in the beheading of John the Baptist, a relative of Jesus.

Joseph's travel assignments come to an end in Nazareth, which Matthew introduces in verse 23, as if the family has not been there before. An insignificant backwater village not mentioned anywhere in the Old Testament or in historical literature up to this time (and not even in later rabbinic writings), Nazareth was not the kind of place to attract a ruler's attention. This makes it an ideal home for returning exiles who want to raise their child in peace.

According to Matthew, settling in Nazareth also fulfills the prophets' word that the Messiah "will be called a Nazorean" (verse 23). It is not clear which Old Testament text this refers to, or whether it has messianic as well as geographical overtones. Whatever the case, Matthew's use of the prophecy reemphasizes that God's plan of salvation is being fulfilled, often despite appearances to the contrary. It is no accident that Joseph has brought Jesus and Mary from David's royal city of Bethlehem to Egypt to the "nowheresville" of Nazareth. God has orchestrated the whole thing! And just as he prepared the Savior's birth through the saints, sinners, and scandalizers in Jesus' family tree, so God the Father has used human events and agents — some of them unwitting and even wicked — to get Joseph and his family to Nazareth.

Had Joseph spoken to the Herods after his last move, he might have quoted an Old Testament Joseph: "It was not you who sent me here, but God" (Genesis 45:8). One of the patriarch Jacob's twelve sons, this earlier Joseph had aroused his brothers' jealousy by his prophetic dreams and favored-son status. Sold into slavery by them, he ended up in Egypt as Pharaoh's right-hand man in charge of food supplies. This was where his astounded brothers found him once famine struck the land of Canaan and drove them to the granaries of Egypt. *Don't be afraid!* was the substance of Joseph's reassurance when they discovered his identity. *I'm not out for revenge. God worked everything out to achieve the good result he intended all along.*

In this and other ways, Matthew's portrayal of Joseph of Nazareth deliberately recalls Joseph of Egypt. Both receive revelation in dreams, journey to Egypt, and cooperate in a divine plan to save their people. St. Bernard of Clairvaux elaborated on these points and others in a masterly sermon:

Remember this great patriarch who was once sold into Egypt (Genesis 37:28) and know that he [Joseph of Nazareth] inherited not only his name, but also his chastity, his innocence, and his graces. . . .

The first Joseph, out of faithfulness, resisted the enticements of his master's wife. [Genesis 39 tells how the wife of Pharaoh's chief steward attempted to seduce Joseph.] The second Joseph, out of respect for the virginity of his Lady, the mother of his Lord, faithfully kept himself chaste.

The first Joseph was given the gift of interpreting dreams; the second, the gift of knowing and cooperating in heaven's plans (Matthew 1:20).

The first gathered reserves of wheat for himself and for all the people (Genesis 41:47-57). The second received into his care, for both himself and the whole world, the living Bread come down from heaven (John 6:51).

Audiences do not generally react well when favorite characters are retired early. When Charles Dickens was writing his magazine installments of *Little Dorritt*, all England pleaded with him to spare his saintly heroine's life and was distressed when he didn't. Sir Arthur Conan Doyle killed off his famous detective, Sherlock Holmes, then had to resurrect him in response to public demand.

Some of us, perhaps, wish we could have persuaded Matthew to keep Joseph in his story a bit longer. But somewhere in between chapter two and chapter three, which recounts Jesus' baptism, Joseph has vanished. Without a word of explanation, Matthew has retired the hero, the second most important character in his account of Jesus' birth and childhood. Except for one indirect comment related to Jesus — "Is not this the carpenter's son?" (13:55) — he will not mention Joseph again.

Modern biographers would have given Joseph's story a different ending, just as they would have opened it with something other than a genealogy. But Matthew has not been writing biography as we know it, much less a biography of Joseph. His concern is to present the life of Jesus in a way that will inspire faith in him as the risen Savior and the perfect fulfillment of God's plan. Other characters are drawn into this presentation only insofar as they contribute to its focus.

Joseph advances Matthew's faith-eliciting portrayal of Jesus in several important ways:

- Joseph provides the right family tree in which to root Israel's promised Messiah, who must come from the House of David.

- He resembles the Old Testament Joseph and thereby points to the continuity between Jewish tradition and scripture and Jesus' message.

- He is a "son of Abraham" who sees the ancient promise of salvation for the Gentiles begin to be realized through the magi's visit.

- He is a "just," or "righteous," man who by his respect and love for the Jewish law prefigures Jesus' fulfillment of it. As Raymond Brown explains: Matthew's Joseph "fulfilled every jot and tittle of the Law and the Prophets, worthily serving as a father to a son who would insist on the fulfillment of the Law and the Prophets" (see 5:17; notice also that Jesus' first words in Matthew have to do with fulfilling "all righteousness": 3:15).

- He reveals the understanding of justice that Jesus articulates and exemplifies and which, says one commentary, is the hallmark of Matthew's Gospel: a sensitive interpretation of the Mosaic law that emphasizes compassion (see 7:12; 9:13; 12:7-8).

- He demonstrates faithful obedience, the virtuous action that Matthew holds up throughout his Gospel as the essential quality of discipleship. Joseph is the type of *doer* commended by Jesus, who hears God's word and acts on it (7:21; 21:28-32).

Joseph plays a critical practical role in salvation history by becoming Mary's husband and Jesus' legal father. But he is not just a figurehead. He is a real husband and a real, though not biological, father; he exercises real authority and responsibility in a real, though unusual, family situation.

Because of his obedience, Joseph also qualifies for membership in Jesus' real family, those who hear God's word and do it. Later, Jesus will stress the priority of this kinship over all other relationships when he tells the crowds, "Whoever does the will of my Father in heaven is my brother and sister and mother" (12:50).

And, he might have added, "my father" (with a small "f").

'Incarnational' Prayer to St. Joseph

"The Virgin shall conceive and bear a son, and they shall name him 'Emmanuel,' which means 'God is with us'" (Matthew 1:23) — which also means that God is with us in a new way in the physical universe he created. Just as the Son of God humbled himself and took on a human body to bring us salvation, he draws near with his saving grace as we turn to him using humble, everyday things to express our faith.

A good model of this "incarnational" prayer is Blessed Brother André Bessette, who has been called the twentieth-century apostle of St. Joseph. "We are not walking brains," he used to say. "We need to see, to touch, and to feel." As concrete aids, he especially recommended medals and oil taken from a lamp that he kept burning in front of a statue of St. Joseph. "Take a medal of St. Joseph with you and hold it in your hand while you're talking," he used to tell people who faced some difficult encounter. "St. Joseph will help you." Says one of his biographers, Bernard LaFreniere, C.S.C., "holding a medal was for him almost like holding St. Joseph's hand." Brother André also routinely recommended that prayer for physical healing be accompanied by the use of oil and medal. Many of the one hundred twenty-five healing stories recounted during his beatification process were from people who had followed his advice.

In 1912, a little girl came who was about to lose one eye after an accident. Brother André gave her some St. Joseph's oil, and she recovered, just as he had promised.

"I have eczema, and the doctor says he can do nothing" [a young man told Brother André one day in 1916]. "Rub yourself with this medal," said Brother André, "and use some of this oil. There is nothing like St. Joseph to help you!" The young brother said afterwards, "I went to bed and did exactly what Brother André had said. And on the following day, the eczema had totally disappeared. I have been well ever since."

In 1931, a two-year-old crippled child was brought to Brother André. Both his legs were so twisted and his feet so deformed he could not walk. He too was healed after his parents rubbed his legs with St. Joseph's oil.

(Bernard LaFreniere, C.S.C., *Brother André According to Witnesses*, Oratory of St. Joseph, 1997, pp. 86-87)

Chapter 3

Luke's Portrait: Joseph the Hidden

Silent and humble, he always stands
on the side, letting the mother and child
go ahead of him. . . .

Catherine Doherty

For reasons we cannot penetrate, the third Gospel centers its account of Jesus' conception and early years around Mary. The man who played one of the leads in Matthew's account is recast by Luke as a retiring supporting actor, "a man whose name was Joseph, of the house of David" (Luke 1:27).

Some scholars see this as Luke's way of emphasizing that Jesus did not have a human father. Theories abound, but fundamentally "it is impossible to say what dictated Luke's choice," observes biblical scholar Luke Timothy Johnson. "Was it a historical reminiscence, a special tradition, his predilection for presenting positive women?" Whatever the case, it is Mary who stands out here.

By focusing on Mary as the privileged mother of the Redeemer, however, Luke is not belittling the man who was her spouse or implying that she and Joseph were mismatched. On the contrary, Luke's presentation provokes reflection about Joseph.

"What must have been the level of a man who deserved such a woman?" wrote Sor Juana Inés de la Cruz, a seventeenth-century Mexican nun and poet, in a carol to St. Joseph. As the illegitimate child of a macho gadabout, Sor Juana was in a position to love and appreciate St. Joseph for having quietly assumed his family responsibilities and background role without touchiness about male honor and prerogatives.

Using Scripture as a springboard for meditation, many Christians like Sor Juana have come to their own deep appreciation of the "man whose name was Joseph." By carefully reading Luke's Gospel, so can we. Much of it does not deal directly with Joseph; we may find it beside the point at first. But Luke is describing the world in which Joseph lived and the events in which he participated. If we keep him in mind as we go, we can count on becoming better acquainted.

Annunciation to Mary, Part 1: Luke 1:26-33

Sometimes the day's take of bills and bulletins and junk mail in my letterbox reads like a study in negative one-upmanship: there is distressing news followed by even more distressing news! Chapter one of Luke's Gospel operates on the opposite dynamic: there is good news followed by *incredibly* good news. It is like finding two delightful and unexpected birth announcements in the mailbox — one from friends who had given up hope of ever being able to conceive, the other from . . .

Well, every comparison limps.

Truth is, nothing can compare with the good news announced to Mary. To underscore the point, Luke uses a splendid split-screen effect for his first two chapters, which depict parallel scenes from the lives of John the Baptist and Jesus. Similar events appear on both screens: an angel announces an extraordinary conception; a son is born, named, circumcised, and revealed as a divinely sent agent of salvation. But the scenes are hardly a matching set, for each pair clearly presents the superiority of the Savior over the herald.

As my husband, Kevin, has suggested, John the Baptist serves partly for comparison. To give an idea of the scale of something huge, like the pyramids, photographers often get a human figure in view. Likewise, Luke portrays the magnitude of Jesus by bringing his precursor into view. "How great was Jesus? Well, consider John the Baptist. He was filled with God's Spirit from before birth and led a life of total dedication to God's word. Yet, compared to Jesus, John is like the 'little' figure in the photograph, gazing up at the pyramid."

Luke says that John will be "great in the sight of the Lord." But Jesus will be "great" because he is "the Son of the Most High" (1:15, 32). John will be filled with the Spirit "even before his birth," from his mother's womb, but Jesus from conception (1:15, 35). "Many" will rejoice over John's birth, but Jesus' coming will be "good news of great joy for all the people" (1:14; 2:10). John will "make ready a people prepared for the Lord"; Jesus will rule them as the Son of David whose kingdom will have no end (1:17, 33).

Given the patriarchal nature of the societies in which Jesus was born and Luke wrote, you would expect the evangelist's point-counterpoint treatment to feature the fathers who are to receive and raise these unique sons. At first glance, this seems to be the case. Chapter one opens with the parents-to-be who hold the best credentials: the aged Zechariah and Elizabeth are both from priestly families and described as "righteous" in God's eyes and "blameless" in following his commands (1:6). The privileged status of Zechariah, in particular, is highlighted by Gabriel's appearing as he offers the evening incense in the sanctuary of the Jerusalem Temple, Israel's holiest setting.

Contrasting with Zechariah "in all his glory," as Father René Laurentin puts it, are "the humble villagers Mary and Joseph." Luke's presentation of the young couple is spare, with no praise of their righteous conduct. Even so, Joseph's distinguished family background warrants a mention.

> In the sixth month the angel Gabriel was sent by God to a town in Galilee called Nazareth, to a virgin engaged to a man whose name was Joseph, of the house of David. The virgin's name was Mary.

Luke seems to envision both Joseph and Mary as residents of Nazareth, today a bustling, plain-Jane town of about seventy thousand, but then an inconsequential village with a population of perhaps only a few hundred. They are most likely teenagers (if they are within the normal age range for betrothal), probably counting the days till they can begin their married life, and certainly not brimming over with worldly advantages. True, Joseph is from the royal house of David. But like those European blue bloods who have to convert the family castle into a bed-and-breakfast to make ends meet, he has the lineage without the wealth.

> And he came to her and said, "Greetings, favored one! The Lord is with you." But she was much perplexed by his words and pondered what sort of greeting this might be. The angel said to her, "Do not be afraid, Mary, for you have found favor with God."

"Greetings, favored one!" With Gabriel's deceptively simple, deeply significant greeting to Mary in verse 28, Luke's parallel takes an unexpected turn. Centuries ago, Origen, the Church's first great biblical scholar, pointed out that Mary was the first person to be so addressed on God's behalf; she was also the last. Of all persons past, present, or future, Mary is *the* most favored.

Luke accentuates God's choice of Mary by deliberately contrasting her not with Joseph but with the most prominent member of this foursome, Zechariah. Unlike the priest, notes Luke Timothy Johnson, Mary has no official position or prestige. "She is among the most powerless people in her society: she is young in a world that values age; female in a world ruled by men; poor in a stratified economy. Furthermore, she has neither husband nor child to validate her existence." Mary herself exemplifies what she will celebrate in her beautiful song of praise: God's ways are surprising, overturning human expectations and exalting the lowly (1:46-55).

In Mary, singular grace goes hand in hand with a singular mission. "The Lord is with you," Gabriel tells her. As Mary would have known, God or his angels had sometimes spoken these words in the past to reassure a chosen person of divine help for a tough assignment (see Gideon's story: Judges 6). Is this why Mary is "much perplexed" (or, as some translations render it, "greatly troubled")? And as she hears about her own stupendous calling, does she hope against hope that Joseph, too, will help her and play a part in it?

> "And now, you will conceive in your womb and bear a son, and you will name him Jesus. He will be great and will be called the Son of the Most High, and the Lord God will give to him the throne of his ancestor David. He will reign over the house of Jacob forever, and of his kingdom there will be no end."

"The Madonna is not pleased when she is put above her Son," said Pope John XXIII. Quite displeasing indeed must be certain interpretations of the annunciation that displace the Son for his mother. One corrective is to recognize the above verses as the heart of Gabriel's message: the primary emphasis is not on Mary but on the coming of Jesus. The same will be true of Gabriel's explanation of the "how" of Jesus' conception (verse 35): Mary's virginal conception is affirmed, but it appears primarily to explain Jesus' identity rather than Mary's privileged status.

And what about Joseph? While Mary's calling is a secondary but crucial theme of Luke's annunciation story, Joseph's calling does not figure in at all. Interestingly, though, Luke presents his key character as linked and even defined by this marginal figure: his one allusion to Mary's identity is that she is Joseph's fiancée. Presumably, this reveals something about the need for Joseph's assent to the divine plan!

In his masterful commentary on the Gospel of Luke, Joseph Fitzmyer calls the angel's message "a dramatic, two-stage declaration" about the child Mary is to bear. Stage one (verses 32-33) identifies him as "the Son of David," the promised Messiah. In this description of Jesus' greatness, Mary would have caught echoes of the messianic prophecy to King David (compare with 2 Samuel 7:9, 13-14, 16).

We can only wonder what Mary made of stage two, which identifies her child as "Son of God" (verse 35). Did she immediately grasp that the Creator of the universe was about to take flesh within her womb? Or did her understanding of the mystery unfold as she pondered it over time? Overall, the second view seems to best fit the portrayal of Mary as pondering "in her heart" (2:19, 51) and of both her and Joseph as sometimes "amazed," "astonished," and even puzzled by Jesus (2:33, 48, 50).

In any case, while Gabriel's message directly affirms that Mary's child will be the Messiah, it only leaves open the possibility that he will be divine. As Father Fitzmyer remarks, the title "Son of God" (along with its variant, "Son of the Most High") had a long history in the ancient Near East in general and in the Old Testament in particular and "could imply many things."

Even the name "Jesus" — to us so sacred, so obviously reserved for God-made-man — would not have given away the divine identity. Those of us who are not from Spanish-speaking backgrounds would never dream of giving it to our sons. But the Spanish and Latino practice is closer to that of first-century Palestine, where the name was common. Perhaps, when told to "name him Jesus," Mary wondered more at Joseph's role than at the name itself: by not assigning Joseph a role in Jesus' naming, was God excluding her fiancé from the picture?

Annunciation to Mary, Part 2: Luke 1:34-38

> Mary said to the angel, "How can this be, since I am a virgin?"
> The angel said to her, "The Holy Spirit will come upon you, and the power of the Most High will overshadow you; therefore the child to be born will be holy; he will be called Son of God."

Mary's question seems puzzling. The problem she advances — literally, it reads, "since I do not know a man" — is not a denial of her relationship with Joseph. It is an expression meaning that she

53

has not had sexual relations with him or anyone else. Why does Mary see this as an obstacle to the conception the angel has announced? Since Gabriel has said nothing so far about a virginal conception, why doesn't Mary assume that the announced conception will take place in the usual way, after her upcoming move to Joseph's house?

Starting with the Church Fathers and continuing till the present day, various explanations have been proposed — some ingenious, some absurd. Most represent attempts to penetrate Mary's inner motives and reactions. Among Catholics, an especially popular theory — and the one that most directly concerns Joseph — involves a possible vow of virginity. In other words, Mary's words are taken to mean, "How can I conceive, since I have pledged never to have a sexual relationship?"

This view, it seems, was first articulated by the fourth-century theologian Gregory of Nyssa, in an age when ascetic ideals ran high and women were taking monastic vows for the first time. Other Church writers adopted and popularized it. Medieval theologians brought Joseph into the picture, deducing that both Mary and Joseph had been inspired by God *before* their marriage to commit themselves to celibacy.

While firmly asserting Mary's virginity, however, Church Fathers held various opinions about a pre-annunciation vow, as do Scripture scholars today. In fact, there are some serious objections to the theory.

• *It makes little sense within Luke's story.* If Mary has vowed to remain a virgin, why has she accepted Joseph's marriage proposal? If Joseph, too, has pledged virginity *before* the annunciation — that is, before realizing that God's unique plan for him and Mary might call for a unique response — why is he planning to marry? Is he simply supporting Mary in *her* decision to remain a virgin? How will this be a real marriage?

Almost invariably, this approach gives a strange impression of Joseph and Mary's relationship. At best, it emerges as a marriage of convenience — not devoid of love, but not marked by spousal love. At worst, it takes on a caretaker-ward flavor, with the caretaker made "safe" by being stripped of his virility and portrayed by pious legends as a doddering old man of 80, 120, and even 200 years!

All of this assumes something other than what Luke has written. "Mary's words in themselves merely express a simple denial of sexual intercourse and have nothing to do with an antecedent vow or resolve of perpetual virginity," says Joseph Fitzmyer. "The context in which they occur scarcely implies anything of the sort."

• *It is historically improbable.* What we know of Palestinian Judaism also casts doubt on the theory that Mary and perhaps Joseph committed themselves to virginity before Gabriel's announcement. Such vows were unknown in the Old Testament and also among first-century Jews (with the possible exception of some members of the ascetic community associated with the Dead Sea Scrolls). So was "family planning." For everyone the ideal was to have many children, and the more the merrier. "May you . . . become thousands of myriads," ran the somewhat daunting blessing prayed over one Old Testament woman (Genesis 24:60).

It is reasonable to suppose that Mary and Joseph at first shared this common aspiration for a large family. Having children was seen as the obedient response to God's command ("Be fruitful and multiply" — Genesis 1:28), and also as a sign of his favor. Infertility was considered a trial, a humiliation, or God's punishment for wrongdoing. As Raymond Brown points out, Luke "uses the words 'disgrace' and 'low estate' to express what the Jewish mentality toward . . . childlessness would be" (see 1:25, 48).

Like a gun in a movie about King Arthur, a vow of virginity before the annunciation is an anachronism. For Mary and Joseph it would make sense only *after* Gabriel's announcement; for everyone else, only after the example of celibacy modeled by Jesus and, later, St. Paul. "Christian virginity is a response to the eschatological kingdom of God when it has already arrived," specifies theologian Karl Rahner; "it is not to be thought of as a preserving of oneself from the power of sexuality considered as dangerous or even as sinful."

"How can this be?" Perhaps we simply do not have enough information to understand what lies behind Mary's question. Luke, after all, is not reporting on her inmost thoughts! Without understanding it fully, though, we can at least note that the question draws attention to the obstacle that God must overcome. Luke tells us — twice in one verse (27) — that Mary is a virgin. Gabriel announces that she is to be a mother. The "problem," Luke hints, is Mary's unprecedented calling: she is to be a living contradiction in terms, simultaneously virgin and mother. Gabriel addresses the issue by asserting the virginal conception.

Some people contend that Gabriel's explanation of the Spirit's overshadowing Mary (1:35) is not an airtight affirmation of Jesus' divine origins. They take it to mean simply that Jesus is to be uniquely equipped and sanctified.

But the structure of chapters one and two gives clear evidence that Luke *is* speaking of a virginal conception. As already mentioned, two birth stories are shown in parallel, with Jesus' side always coming out ahead. Since John the Baptist's conception has required a miracle, Raymond Brown argues persuasively, the "one-upmanship" dynamic calls for an even greater miracle in Jesus' case. Luke's presentation of Jesus' superiority "would fail completely," he says, if Jesus was conceived in a less amazing manner than John the Baptist. On the other hand, "it would be continued perfectly" if Jesus was virginally conceived.

After all, God had overcome the obstacles of age and barrenness before. But to become pregnant without a loss of virginity — the difficulty posed in Mary's question — here, says Father Brown, is "an extraordinary action of God's creative power, as unique as the original creation itself."

> And now, your relative Elizabeth in her old age has also conceived a son; and this is the sixth month for her who was said to be barren. For nothing will be impossible with God." Then Mary said, "Here am I, the servant of the Lord; let it be with me according to your word." Then the angel departed from her.

In Old Testament birth announcements, the angel never hangs around for a response. Now, however, with life-and-death issues at stake, Mary's cooperation is sought and awaited. "On your response depends the salvation of all the children of Adam, of all your race," exclaimed St. Bernard in a sermon that catches the drama of the moment. "Answer quickly, O Virgin! Lady, say the word for which heaven and earth are waiting!"

Mary does not delay. History's pivotal conversation ends with her obedient yes.

Visiting Elizabeth: Luke 1:39-56

Mary embraces God's plan with eager enthusiasm, not the grim resignation of a martyr personality. The next scene pictures her traveling "with haste" to a town roughly ninety miles south of Nazareth to visit the relative whose surprise pregnancy, still hidden to outsiders, has been revealed to Mary as a sign of God's power and faithfulness.

Elizabeth, too, has been touched by mystery. At this point, she may be the only person who can begin to appreciate what has happened to Mary. Joy breaks out at their meeting — two women and their unborn babies swept up in a mighty outpouring of the Spirit.

No husbands are on the scene for this glad encounter. Zechariah is mentioned but absent; he has been sidelined for the duration of Elizabeth's pregnancy as a penalty for disbelief. His imposed muteness stands in sharp contrast to the women's delighted greetings and loud cries, Elizabeth's words of blessing, and especially Mary's *Magnificat*. Joseph is unmentioned, but not because of anything about his character: most likely it is to confirm that he has played no part in Jesus' conception.

Unlike Zechariah, Mary has heard and believed. "Blessed is she who believed that there would be a fulfillment of what was spoken to her by the Lord," Elizabeth says in praise of her (1:45).

Where is Joseph during his fiancée's three-month absence from Nazareth? Many spiritual writers find it unthinkable that he would not have accompanied Mary on her journey to Elizabeth's. The sixteenth-century Dominican Isidore of Isolano goes so far as to say that no rational person or person possessed of Catholic feeling could deny it! St. Francis de Sales, who saw "a thousand lights" in the episode of the visitation and gave its name to the religious order he founded with St. Jeanne de Chantal, pictures Joseph and Mary en route and speculates about their thoughts and conversation, as well as about their stay with the elderly couple.

Though Luke gives no such particulars, his presentation does raise practical questions and leaves room for conjecture. No first-century Jewish girl was free to undertake a four-day journey on her own. If unmarried, she lived under her father's authority and was generally restricted to the home; if married, she had greater freedom of movement, but only insofar as her husband permitted it. Since Luke's allusions to time are often vague, it is impossible to tell where Mary was living just before setting out for Elizabeth's. Verse 56 of chapter one says she returned to "her home" afterward — but was this her family's house or Joseph's? Either way, she needed permission to make her visit.

She also needed protection. Galilee and the hill country of Judea were generally safe. Still, prudent travelers everywhere banded together to discourage roving outlaws. The question is not whether Mary had some sort of protective escort, but whether it was Joseph.

More timing questions: When did Joseph learn that Mary was expecting? And was Mary present when John was born?

Luke is silent on the first question and ambiguous on the second, saying only that Mary stayed three months with Elizabeth. Some commentators hold that she rushed back to Galilee before John's birth to begin life with Joseph and stave off scandalous rumors about her own pregnancy. Others maintain that Mary stayed with Elizabeth in her hour of need and that she paid for her charitable delay by being found obviously — and shockingly — pregnant upon her return to Nazareth.

It is worth noting that Luke never raises the issue of scandal in connection with Mary's unique pregnancy. No one, including Joseph, is portrayed as troubled or perplexed by it; no one presumes illegitimacy. Theories that connect the length of Mary's visit with concerns about her pregnancy's giving scandal are attempts to harmonize Luke's account with information that does not appear within his Gospel.

A Son Is Born: Luke 2:1-7

Just a name in chapter one, Joseph takes center stage in the first verses of chapter two. He is shown as a law-abiding citizen who is following a government order, at some inconvenience to himself and Mary. Though Jesus will be sentenced to death on charges of civil disobedience and rabble-rousing (see 23:2, 5, 14), he will not grow up in a household where political revolutions and ambitions are nurtured!

> In those days a decree went out from Emperor Augustus that all the world should be registered. This was the first registration and was taken while Quirinius was governor of Syria. All went to their own towns to be registered. Joseph also went from the town of Nazareth in Galilee to Judea, to the city of David called Bethlehem, because he was descended from the house and family of David. He went to be registered with Mary, to whom he was engaged and who was expecting a child.

The command that Joseph is obeying requires him and everyone in "all the world" to stand up and be counted in "their own towns." Nazareth is Joseph and Mary's "own town" (2:39), but Joseph must register eighty-five miles away in Bethlehem, where his ancestor David lived forty-two generations before him.

As Luke presents it (and his scenario is contested), the census sounds like a bureaucratic nightmare. How could Augustus — "that most rational of Caesars," historian E. P. Sanders calls him — have expected people to comply? How would anyone know where to go?

True, this was a world in which lineage was important. There were no blood types and Social Security card numbers to memorize, but each Israelite was to keep track of immediate ancestors and tribal origin, at the very least. Some people could go back many generations (see Tobit 1:1 and Judith 8:1). Nonetheless, Sanders points out, "No one could trace his genealogy for forty-two generations." Even with today's research tools and access to archives and public records, most of us would find this a challenge. But there may be more to this than tribal memory, some scholars suggest; perhaps Joseph's family still owns land in Bethlehem.

On another level, we wonder why Mary is traveling so close to her due date, so far from the midwives and female relatives who might have assisted her in Nazareth. How could Joseph have agreed to this risky trip? Or does Mary have to register too?

A modern biographer might have explained all this in a historical study of Roman census procedures and explored Joseph and Mary's psychological reactions and motivations. Luke's main concerns lie elsewhere, and he does not provide us with information by which to answer modern questions. For him the census functions primarily as a fitting background for Jesus' birth and an instrument for the fulfillment of prophecy.

A FITTING BACKGROUND • Like computer software that gives you a look at a continent and then lets you zoom in to country, region, city, and even street, Luke's census evokes a wide-angle view of "all the world" on the move, before narrowing in to one region, one town, one couple on a journey. Jesus' birth is significant not just for the Jews, Luke is hinting, but for all the peoples of the earth. (We can imagine his first readers — most of them non-Jewish Christians — as especially sensitive to this message of salvation offered to all.)

The census also gives Luke an opportunity to contrast Jesus' greatness with worldly greatness, represented by Caesar Augustus. Grand-nephew and adopted heir of Julius Caesar, Augustus brought an end to years of civic strife and ushered in a long golden age of peace (27 B.C. to A.D. 14). For this his subjects acclaimed him "god" and "savior." By situating Jesus within his reign, Luke points to "the real bearer of peace and salvation to the whole world," says Joseph Fitzmyer. "The child thus born under the *Pax Augusta* will eventually be hailed as 'the king, the One Who is to come in the name of the Lord' — and the result will be, 'Peace in heaven and glory in the highest heaven' (Luke 19:38)."

Might and majesty surround Augustus, while Jesus is born in lowly circumstances, to politically powerless parents of humble means. But things are not what they appear. "Ironically, the Roman emperor, the mightiest figure in the world, is serving God's plan by issuing an edict for the census of the whole world," observes Raymond Brown. "He is providing the appropriate setting for the birth of Jesus, the Savior of all those people who are being enrolled." Augustus can move the world's peoples around like figures on a chessboard, but he himself is an unwitting agent in the hands of the Prime Mover.

AN INSTRUMENT FOR PROPHECY'S FULFILLMENT • The census brings Joseph and Mary to Bethlehem and ensures that Jesus will be born there. Bethlehem is the appropriate setting because of its connection with King David, to whom the Messiah was promised. In this small town about five miles south of Jerusalem, David was born and later anointed king. Now, in fulfillment of prophecy, the Messiah will be born there too.

Jesus' link with David has already been established by the fact that his legal father is "from the house and family of David" (2:4). His birth in Bethlehem draws attention to that link, as well as to God's faithfulness: God fulfills the words of his prophets.

Even while emphasizing this Davidic lineage, though, Luke keeps Jesus' divine origins clearly in view. Perhaps this explains his rather surprising reference in verse 5 to Mary as Joseph's betrothed, "to whom he was engaged," not his wife. "The function of this unusual usage," surmises René Laurentin, "is to remind us that Mary 'did not know man' [a Semitic euphemism for sexual intercourse: see, for example, Genesis 4:1, 17] and that Jesus is not the son of Joseph."

> While they were there, the time came for her to deliver her child. And she gave birth to her firstborn son and wrapped him in bands of cloth, and laid him in a manger, because there was no place for them in the inn.

"Give me the details," I tell my husband whenever he returns from a solo visit to far-off children and grandchildren. "Give me the details," I might tell Luke if time-travel were possible. But obviously, the story of Jesus' birth was not written at the prodding of the inquisitive!

Exactly when and how Mary delivered, whether or not she endured labor pains, what role Joseph played and whether he experienced the nervousness of a waiting-room father — such items are not on Luke's agenda. Still, the two above verses do furnish some significant details:

FIRSTBORN SON • Putting this together with later references to Jesus' family — for example, Luke 8:19, which speaks of "his mother and his brothers" — some people conclude that Joseph and Mary had other children after Jesus was born. Scholars both Catholic and Protestant are agreed, however, that "firstborn" does not have to mean "first of many." As supporting evidence, Joseph Fitzmyer and others cite the grave inscription of a Jewish woman who died in Egypt in the fifth century B.C. "In the pangs of giving birth to a firstborn child," it reads, "Fate brought me to the end of my life." Obviously, this woman's firstborn was her lastborn.

Luke mentions Jesus' birth order not to imply that siblings will follow, but to indicate that none have preceded. To Jesus belong the rights and responsibilities that the Mosaic law gave firstborn sons. But Jesus' privileged status points to a hidden reality. It is not just a question of his inheriting a double portion of Joseph's estate: in this family, the "favored son" is God's only-begotten Son.

As such, Eugene LaVerdiere points out, Jesus *will* eventually have siblings — namely, all who come to be associated with him after his passion and resurrection. In a theological sense, says Father LaVerdiere, "firstborn son" is "a statement about Jesus' relationship to his future followers."

If so, what might this suggest about his followers' relationship to Mary and Joseph?

BANDS OF CLOTH • Perhaps Joseph helped Mary to make their newborn as comfortable as possible. They would have washed him first, then rubbed him with salt. ("Palestinian peasants still say 'it makes them strong,'" reports Father Roland de Vaux, who mentions this custom in his book *Ancient Israel*.) However that may be,

Mary alone carries out the next step, wrapping Jesus in strips of cloth, or "swaddling clothes."

Although this detail has often been interpreted as a sign of poverty and hardship ("all meanly wrapt in the rude manger" is how John Milton describes Jesus), Luke probably intended it to signify quite the opposite. From the first moment of Jesus' coming, Luke shows him enfolded by — literally, wrapped up in — the love of the most loving of mothers. Mary's maternal care ensures that Jesus is received like the king he is. Solomon's words in the book of Wisdom indicate that even this richest of Israel's kings was not welcomed more royally: "I was nursed with care in swaddling cloths" (7:4).

MANGER • The path to the manger starts at the inn door. We picture a tired couple gazing wistfully at a quaint, cozy cottage with a "no vacancy" sign in the window. What Luke pictured is not so clear. The Greek word translated "inn" was a general term for any place of hospitality — anything from a guestroom in a private home to a caravansary, where groups of travelers slept in lodgings surrounding a courtyard parking lot for camels and donkeys.

Luke tells us three times that Jesus' crib is an animal feeding trough (2:7, 12, 16). Justin, the second-century Church Father, spoke of its being in a cave — possibly the back area of a house built into the side of a hill and usually set aside to shelter animals in bad weather. Other writers pictured the manger in a barn or even an open-air feeding area.

We are free to speculate on what Joseph and Mary thought of their primitive nursery, but Luke at least shows none of the pathos that *we* may feel as we sing Christmas carols about the "poor baby" lying "asleep in the hay." While not denying Jesus' poverty, Luke seems once again to have a different point in mind.

Expressing the views of many early and modern commentators, Joseph Fitzmyer thinks the manger is probably meant to evoke God's reproach in Isaiah 1:3: "The ox knows its owner, and the donkey its master's crib; but Israel does not know [me], my people do not understand [me]." At long last, Luke is saying, Israel's king is being recognized and received — first, by Mary and Joseph, then by the rustic group that now makes its entrance.

Shepherds Hear and Visit: Luke 2:8-20
"In that region there were shepherds living in the fields, keeping watch over their flock by night." All unsuspecting, probably groggy

with sleep, a band of simple guys on the job see the sky light up with angels who proclaim astounding news. Manger, swaddling clothes, Savior, Messiah, and Lord — the shepherds must have found it an unlikely, if exhilarating, mix of elements. But then, they themselves were not the likeliest of recipients. Like the unprepossessing young couple chosen to care for God's Son, the lowly shepherds witness to God's "preferential option" for those with little worldly status.

The shepherds' presence also reinforces the theme of the Davidic lineage that has come to Jesus through Joseph. David, too, was a Bethlehem shepherd. He was tending his sheep (perhaps in the very fields where angel voices sang?) when summoned into town for a kingly anointing and sudden career change (1 Samuel 16:1-13). Now, in his city, one of David's descendants has become the adoptive father of Jesus, the Good Shepherd and King of kings. How fitting that fellow shepherds — David's successors in the fields — will be the first to greet this child, rushing off to him like Mary to Elizabeth.

> So they went with haste and found Mary and Joseph, and the child lying in the manger. When they saw this, they made known what had been told them about this child; and all who heard it were amazed at what the shepherds had told them. But Mary treasured all these words and pondered them in her heart. The shepherds returned, glorifying and praising God for all they had heard and seen, as it had been told them.

Awestruck parents watching over their newborn: here is the familiar scene so beautifully commemorated in song, poetry, and painting — and, unfortunately, so often trivialized today. What *would* Joseph and Mary think of a "kneeling Santa" at the crib? Of nativity sets where all the characters are portrayed as cute bears?

What would they think of another misguided, though less objectionable, tendency of Westerners at the manger: our overly sentimental insistence on its piteousness? The poverty of the Holy Family is "a simple fact" of Luke's Gospel and gives "abundant food for meditation," explains Cistercian writer Michael Baily. But sentimentalizing adds abject details that never entered Luke's head. "It sets the birth of Jesus at a time and in a place that makes the Babe truly pitiable." Poets and other writers depict him rejected by a hardhearted innkeeper, forced to turn to animals for warmth and hospitality. He is born "in the frost" (Chesterton); "in freezing winter night" and is "alas, a piteous sight" (Southwell); "in the bleak midwinter," while "frosty wind made moan" (Christina Rossetti); and even as "the thatched eaves bend beneath the snow" (Gautier). Never mind that it rarely snows in Bethlehem and that winter temperatures do not usually dip below the mid-forties!

"By any standard, the birth of Jesus was surrounded by poverty," Father Baily agrees. But, he says, we go astray if we judge the manger according to current Western ideals of comfort. Life was harsher and people more used to roughing it in first-century Palestine, as in today's Third World. "Contemporaries of Jesus would not have been particularly surprised at the circumstances of his birth, nor would they see any reason to pity him," says Father Baily. Luke himself gives no hint that Jesus, Mary, and Joseph are to be pitied. "The only sentiment recorded is one of great joy."

Great joy, great awe. It is natural for new parents to marvel at the mystery of life and to think their child a wonder. But who can imagine the depths of Joseph and Mary's wonderment? To paraphrase St. Augustine, God had become man so that man might become God. The proof of it now lies in the manger before them: an infant who cries, nurses, drools, and fills his diapers like any other helpless newborn — and who is Emmanuel, God with us.

The many practical tasks involved in caring for a newborn make it something other than a contemplative experience. And yet, as Mary and Joseph tended to Jesus, they must have felt caught up in heavenly mysteries. Knowing, as only they could know, that their child had been virginally conceived, they must have reflected more and more deeply on what they knew of his identity.

It seems only normal to us, who have heard the story so often, that shepherds would come calling. But Joseph and Mary are not expecting the early morning visit of a breathless bunch of unkempt strangers (and their flocks of silly sheep?). Are they taken aback at this eagerness to see their baby? Luke reports only that they are "amazed," like everyone else, by the shepherds' story.

"To you is born this day in the city of David a Savior, who is the Messiah, the Lord," the angel told the shepherds (2:11). For Mary and for Joseph too, here are more depths to ponder.

Fulfilling the Law: Luke 2:21-40

> After eight days had passed, it was time to circumcise the child; and he was called Jesus, the name given by the angel before he was conceived in the womb.

Isaac, Jacob, Joseph, Samuel, and other Old Testament figures were named immediately after birth, but by Jesus' day a son's naming had been combined with his circumcision. Mosaic law set the time: "On the eighth day, the flesh of his foreskin shall be circumcised" (Leviticus 12:3). The procedure took place in the home, not the Temple; it was normally done by the father, sometimes by a physician or specialist, never by a priest.

Circumcision was the mark of a man's incorporation into the community of Israel, a physical sign of God's covenant with Abraham and his descendants (Genesis 17:9-14). It was an event that called for celebration with neighbors and relatives, as Luke shows in his parallel scene about John the Baptist (1:58-66).

What's in a name? Judging from the perennially brisk sales of books with titles like *The Right Name for Your Baby*, new parents generally approach this subject with some intensity. Names are important. They shape and reveal, which is one reason why Catholic parents are urged to give their children saints' names or names that express Christian mysteries or virtues.

Joseph and Mary don't have to agonize over what to call their little one. "You will name him Jesus," Gabriel had said to Mary (1:31). Curiously, Luke does not specify which parent carries out this commission. Whatever his reasons for this, his wording calls attention to both Joseph and Mary's obedience to God's command, as well as to Jesus' divine origins.

"Yahweh saves." We can imagine that this meaning of "Jesus" is remarked and discussed by his parents. Like everyone in the ancient Near East, Mary and Joseph would need no reminders about the revealing aspect of names. In their culture, explains Roland de Vaux, "the name defines the essence of a thing: to name it is to know it." A person's name "reveals the character and destiny of the bearer. The name becomes the expression of a hope." In Jesus, name and mission converge perfectly to address the human heart's deepest hopes and longings.

On a lesser plane, some scholars find it significant that Jesus and all his relatives bear the names of men and women who figured at key points in Israel's history. This is "probably not by accident," observes Father John Meier.

"Jesus" comes from a shortened form of Joshua, the name of the hero who succeeded Moses and led Israel into the promised land. "Joseph" commemorates the ancestor who went to Egypt as a slave but was raised up to save his people from famine. "Mary"

— Miriam in Hebrew — recalls the sister of Moses and the exodus from Egypt. James, one of Jesus' four "brothers" (relatives), is a form of "Jacob," the patriarch whose sons began the twelve tribes of Israel. The names of Jesus' other "brothers" — Joses, Simon, and Judas — are variations on those of three of Jacob's sons. (Mark 6:3 and Matthew 13:55 list the names; Luke 8:19 omits them.)

Jewish parents who selected names from the glorious past may well have been expressing hope for Israel's restoration and renewal, says Father Meier. Nothing strange about that. For similar reasons, Americans have named their sons after George Washington and Robert E. Lee. Puritan parents often reached back for obscure Old Testament names like Jedidiah to emphasize their belief in renewal through a return to *every* part of the Bible. And somewhere, there must be Catholic parents whose passion for monastic ideals and renewal has led them to name their children after St. Thérèse of Lisieux and her sisters, or after the holy brothers-and-sister trio of Basil, Gregory, and Macrina!

It strikes us as perfectly natural that the names in Jesus' family should come from the glory days described in Genesis and Exodus. But as John Meier points out, in the first century this was a relatively recent trend: "For most of the Old Testament period Israelites were not named for the great patriarchs."

Paradoxically, the popularity of these names had been spurred by Antiochus Epiphanes (175-164 B.C.), a ruler who made an aggressive attempt to force Greek customs on the Jews. (For example, he made circumcision punishable by death.) But, as with Polish Catholics under Communist rule, persecution sparked a resurgence of national and religious identity.

Most probably, says Father Meier, "the fact that all of Jesus' immediate family bear 'patriarchal' and 'matriarchal' names betokens the family's participation in this reawakening." As he sees it, Joseph's claiming descent from King David makes this conclusion "all the more likely."

What we glimpse of Jesus' family through the "names" peephole is confirmed by Luke's portrayal of Joseph and Mary as devout and pious Jews who observe the basic practices of the Mosaic law. Obedient to the law of the land, they are *zealously* obedient to the law of the Lord. The two have already complied with the requirement of circumcision. Now, they bring Jesus from Bethlehem to the Temple in Jerusalem. Luke showcases their fidelity in his account of the purification and presentation, where he mentions the law five times (2:22, 23, 24, 27, 39).

> When the time came for their purification according to the law of Moses, they brought him up to Jerusalem to present him to the Lord (as it is written in the law of the Lord, "Every first-born male shall be designated as holy to the Lord"), and they offered a sacrifice according to what is stated in the law of the Lord, "a pair of turtledoves or two young pigeons."

The parents of the One who will one day insist that his message must continue and fulfill the law of Moses (see 16:16; 24:44) would have known that law well — and observed it more precisely than this passage indicates! Luke, it seems, was a non-Jewish Christian who was generally well-informed about Jewish rituals, but a bit fuzzy on the details. Here he has confused two customs: the mother's purification and the consecration of the firstborn son (commanded in Leviticus 12:1-8 and Exodus 13:1-2; 11-16, respectively).

But in no way do Luke's inaccuracies undermine the scene's purpose, which is to reveal Jesus as the fulfillment of Israel's heritage. Like a composer blending old melodies to form a new song, Luke uses a mix of Old Testament motifs to sound the theme of Jesus' future greatness and its continuity with God's past action.

We catch echoes of a much earlier presentation at the sanctuary: that of Samuel, the priest who traveled to Bethlehem and called David away from his sheep to anoint him king (1 Samuel 1:24-28; 16:1-13). We meet Simeon and Anna, figures who mirror Zechariah and Elizabeth in both their age and their piety. The two might have stepped out of an Old Testament story. Simeon, "righteous and devout," symbolizes the Mosaic law; "the prophetess Anna" represents the Prophets ("the law and the prophets" is Lucan shorthand for Israel's heritage: see 16:16). Simeon especially is a spokesman for the past as he takes Jesus in his arms and proclaims the dawning of a new age.

Something about the encounter takes Joseph and Mary by surprise. "And the child's father and mother were amazed at what was being said about him" (2:33). Is it the discovery that their baby is known and awaited? Is it the passion with which an elderly stranger has greeted Jesus and declared himself now able to die happy? Is it his emphatic identification of him as "salvation" for

Jews and Gentiles alike (2:30-32)? As for Simeon's next words, what forebodings must they have stirred in the couple's hearts?

> Then Simeon blessed them and said to his mother Mary, "This child is destined for the falling and the rising of many in Israel, and to be a sign that will be opposed so that the inner thoughts of many will be revealed — and a sword will pierce your own soul too."

Simeon peers into the future and prophesies both glory and rejection. Jesus' coming will bring "peace on earth," but also a painful testing — a sword that will pass through even families to separate out the true disciples (see 12:51-53). Mary herself will not be spared the trial, though she will emerge triumphant as her Son's first and model follower.

And what about Joseph? Why doesn't Simeon address him too? One possible answer is that Luke, wanting to turn up the volume of the Old Testament leitmotifs in his story, is sticking close to the Old Testament model of Samuel's presentation, in which the mother, Hannah, plays the dominant role. Another possibility is that Simeon's words are not applicable to Joseph because this particular test will pass him by. Jesus will not be viewed as a sign of contradiction until he is about thirty and begins his public ministry. But will Joseph live to see this day?

Temple duties fulfilled, the little family heads home to "their own town of Nazareth." Here begin those tantalizing hidden years whose events Luke compresses into one verse: "The child grew and became strong, filled with wisdom; and the favor of God was upon him" (2:40).

Losing and Finding: Luke 2:41-52

Alone among the evangelists, Luke does recount one telling episode from the hidden years. It is instructive for what it reveals about Jesus' relationship with his father on earth and his Father in heaven.

> Now every year his parents went to Jerusalem for the festival of the Passover. And when he was twelve years old, they went up as usual for the festival. When the festival was ended and they started to return, the boy Jesus stayed behind in Jerusalem, but his parents did not know it. Assuming that he was in the group of

travelers, they went a day's journey. Then they started to look for him among their relatives and friends. When they did not find him, they returned to Jerusalem to search for him.

Passover-Unleavened Bread was one of the three pilgrimage festivals of the Jewish year. It commemorated two episodes of the exodus: God's sparing the Israelites during the tenth plague, after they marked their doorposts with the blood of a lamb, and their ensuing departure from Egypt, so hasty that there was no time for bread to rise (see Exodus 12).

How was Passover celebrated in New Testament times? Scholars are unsure of the details. Later Jewish tradition specified that all adult male Jews were expected to celebrate Passover in Jerusalem with observances that included the sacrifice of a lamb, a commemorative meal, and a seven-day celebration. Women were dispensed from attending, as were boys under thirteen. These customs may well have obtained in the first century. If so, the Holy Family's piety stands out in the fact that both Jesus and Mary accompany Joseph to Jerusalem, though under no obligation to do so.

Later Jewish tradition also saw Passover as a golden teaching moment that trained a boy in his future responsibilities by assigning him an active role in the ritual. At the Seder meal where the Passover lamb was eaten, the youngest son was to ask the question that triggers an explanation of what is being celebrated: "Why is this night different from other nights?" (see Deuteronomy 6:20). Did Jesus learn this ritual? For us who foresee the Passover at the end of Luke's Gospel (chapter twenty-two) and who hear "this is the night" proclaimed in the Easter vigil's *Exsultet,* it is poignant to imagine Joseph teaching this question to the Lamb who will be led unprotestingly to slaughter (Acts 8:32).

Passover was a religious celebration, but also the year's big holiday. "Whole towns emptied as people streamed to Jerusalem," says E. P. Sanders. The crowds ran between three hundred thousand and four hundred thousand, he thinks; another historian guesstimates a more conservative hundred thousand. Archaeological finds and water systems suggest that perhaps fifty thousand people lived in Jerusalem at the time; so, by any reckoning, the Passover influx was a major break in business as usual. Anyone in Paris or Denver or Manila for Pope John Paul's World Youth Day visits will get the idea.

The Nazareth caravan of family and friends would have covered the eighty miles to Jerusalem in perhaps four days. Did Joseph and his family stay with friends who lived there? in nearby villages? in a tent pitched outside the city walls?

Curiosity turns from mild to wild if we start psychologizing about Jesus' disappearance: How could Joseph and Mary not have noticed his absence? How could Joseph in particular, as head of the family, have been so remiss? How could Jesus have been so indifferent to the distress he caused?

"To ask such questions is to miss the whole point of the episode," Joseph Fitzmyer warns. "It was not meant to bear such weight." Attention should be focused instead on Luke's main point — expressed in Jesus' own words — about his identity and priorities.

> After three days they found him in the temple, sitting among the teachers, listening to them and asking them questions. And all who heard him were amazed at his understanding and his answers.

Clearly, Jesus is unique. His understanding astounds. His actions astonish and perplex even his parents, who know him best. But Luke does not strain credulity by making him into an unreal, untouchable, divine walking encyclopedia. As Father René Laurentin observes: "Jesus performs no miracle. Nor does he proclaim new revelations. He does not refute the teachers. He does not dispute. He is not even presented as a 'one-way' teacher. On the contrary, he listens and questions."

Jesus is fully human, as well as fully divine. Even at twelve, he demonstrates a talent for relating to people very different from himself. He engages them in discussion, listens, asks questions — something Mary and Joseph must have experienced often as the family sat around the dinner table in Nazareth!

> When his parents saw him they were astonished; and his mother said to him, "Child, why have you treated us like this? Look, your father and I have been searching for you in great anxiety." He said to them, "Why were you searching for me? Did you not know that I must be in my Father's house?" But they did not understand what he said to them.

Why is it Mary who speaks up as the anxious parents finally come upon Jesus in the Temple? A social historian would find her initiative-taking entirely in keeping with the particularly close, protective way in which Jewish mothers of her day related to young sons. But Mary's action also seems to signal the beginning of what has been called "the eclipse of Joseph." He will be mentioned only twice after this episode, in passing references that have to do with Jesus' origins (3:23; 4:22).

"I must be in my Father's house" — or, as the Greek can also mean: "I must be in the temple, . . . involved in my Father's affairs, . . . with those who belong to my Father's household." Any way you look at it, these first words ascribed to Jesus in Luke's Gospel certainly dim the lights on Joseph!

To a mother who comes speaking of "your father and I," Jesus declares another Father's prior claims. It must have been an unsettling moment for Joseph and Mary. There was the element of surprise: apparently the child Jesus was normally docile — not given to running away or to self-asserting statements. Then, too, there was the fact that the exchange took place in public, with Temple teachers looking on. However sweetly Jesus may have answered his mother, it still came off as a mild reproach. How was that perceived in this culture so sensitive to issues of honor and shame, where a son's duty toward his parents — especially his father — was prompt, silent obedience?

Jesus is no adolescent cutting the apron strings in order to discover his identity. He knows who he is. And by distancing himself from Mary and Joseph, he helps them toward the same understanding.

The Father must increase, Joseph must decrease.

What do Mary and Joseph fail to grasp about Jesus' reply? Venerable Bede, the English Doctor of the Church, expresses an opinion also held by St. Bonaventure, St. Bernard, and other writers: "His parents do not understand the word that he speaks to them concerning his divinity."

Though many believers will not allow that Mary in particular could have lacked complete knowledge about the incarnation, Luke does seem to portray it as incomplete. His references to the couple's bewilderment (2:18, 33, 47-48, 50) and to Mary's pondering (2:19, 51) suggest that Joseph and Mary's understanding of Jesus evolved. They no doubt knew they were touching mysteries. But penetrating those mysteries would come over time and at a price.

Expanding on this view, a number of commentators connect

71

Mary and Joseph's incomprehension of Jesus' words with Simeon's prophecy, uttered to Mary twelve years before and experienced by the two of them now. Losing Jesus was hard, but finding him has a sting too. The sword becomes a painful reality: as Jesus will warn would-be followers one day, even the closest family ties must yield before God's plans. "Whoever comes to me and does not hate father and mother, wife and children, brothers and sisters, yes, and even life itself, cannot be my disciple" (14:26).

Besides making the best sense of Luke's text, the "evolving understanding" approach counters our tendency to misrepresent life in the Holy Family as too ethereal and exalted for ordinary people to relate to. Scripture tells us that Jesus came on earth to share our lot and live a truly human life, to be like us in every way excepting sin (Hebrews 2:17; 4:15). English writer Edmund Sutcliffe suggests that this purpose would be "more perfectly achieved" if full knowledge of Jesus' divinity were still hidden from Joseph and Mary during his childhood years. Then, he says, it is easy to imagine Jesus living "a normal human life" and being treated by his parents "as other children are treated."

To think that Joseph and Mary may not have understood Jesus fully is not to depreciate their holiness. On the contrary, their virtue would seem all the more admirable for having developed through situations in which they did *not* enjoy a sort of infused knowledge of the big picture. Mary and Joseph were told what they needed to know at each stage — but no more. Each of us can relate to that!

Paradoxically, the "eclipse of Joseph" coexists with what seems to be an emphasis on his real fatherhood. As Luke's story ends, Joseph is repeatedly referred to as Jesus' father (2:33, 48) and parent (2:27, 41, 43, 48). St. Augustine commented that "Luke did not call Mary [Christ's] sole parent; he had no hesitation in calling both his parents." And notice, says Origen, that "Mary herself says in the Gospel, 'Behold, your father and I were seeking you with anxiety.' "

Augustine stresses that Jesus' explanation of his disappearance "does not mean that God is his Father in such a way that he denies Joseph to be his father." He goes on to prove his point from one of Luke's ending remarks about Jesus' childhood years: "Then he went down with them and came to Nazareth, and was obedient to them" (2:51). Noting that Luke did not say Jesus was subject only to his mother but rather to *them*, to both parents, Augustine affirms Joseph's real fatherhood: "Both were parents to whom he

72

was subject with that condescension by which he was the Son of Man."

The subject of many meditations about the divine humility, this verse stressing Jesus' obedience really is "quite dramatic," says Raymond Brown — especially when it is set alongside Jesus' amazing understanding and claim of a unique vocation. Just think of it, marveled Pierre d'Ailly, the author of a fifteenth-century treatise in praise of Joseph. "Who was subject to whom?" God's very Son was subject to his parents — "and principally to St. Joseph himself, to whom Mary as a humble wife was subject also. . . . O wonderful event! Joseph supports and cherishes by his aid him who supports and cherishes all things and governs the whole world!"

Indeed, Pope Leo XIII affirmed in an 1889 encyclical, "the Word of God was obedient to Joseph, was attentive to his commands, and held him in all honor, as children must necessarily tender honor to a parent." Joseph governed his family "as with paternal authority."

In a patriarchal society, this authority is no figure of speech. The world in which Jesus grew up assigned the father an all-important position within the family unit. "Authority was vested in the father," says historian Léonie Archer, "and obedience to his dictates was enjoined on minor children and their mother alike."

What humility on God's part. What responsibility on Joseph's!

Supposed Son of Joseph: Luke 3:23-38

It could be read as a sneering put-down of Jesus — a remark worthy of some upper-class snob in an Austen or a Dickens novel: "Is not this Joseph's son?" (Luke 4:22). Or could it be a backhanded compliment of Jesus, at Joseph's expense? Have the people of Nazareth noticed a discrepancy between the ordinary-looking father and the son who has just spoken so amazingly in the synagogue? The episode does not end well (admiration turns to murderous rage), but the townspeople's comment does serve to suggest that up till he was thirty, Jesus had normal-looking family relationships.

The citizens of Nazareth had not grasped that Jesus was the reflection of a Father who did not live in the village. Joseph was a real father to him, but not in the biological sense. "Joseph played no part in the generation of Jesus, other than through his service and his affection," Origen specified. "It is because of this faithful ministry that Scripture gives him the name father."

Luke, too, both affirms and denies Joseph's parentage: his ref-

73

erences to Joseph as the father of Jesus are offset by his allusions to Jesus' real roots. There is Gabriel's announcement to Mary that she will conceive the Son of God through the power of the Holy Spirit and the Most High (1:35). There is Luke's "one-up" construction of parallel scenes from the lives of Jesus and John the Baptist and his unstated but unmistakable conclusion about their conceptions: it is more miraculous to be conceived of a virgin than of an aged mother. There is the fact that Luke does not mention Joseph in connection with Mary's visit to Elizabeth (though it makes sense to picture him as her traveling companion).

Finally, there is the short, significant tip-off with which Luke introduces Jesus' genealogy: Jesus "was the son (as was thought) of Joseph son of Heli. . ." (3:23). Luke's off-the-cuff "as was thought" can only be interpreted as meaning that he did not view Jesus as Joseph's natural son. And despite far-fetched attempts old and new to find here a hint that Jesus had a human father other than Joseph, it is obvious that the evangelist is clarifying Jesus' *divine* origins. Placed as it is after the account of Jesus' baptism, the genealogy demonstrates what the Father has just spoken: "You are my Son, the Beloved" (3:22). As Joseph asserted his apparent fatherhood by naming Jesus, the Father now claims and names him "my Son."

Jesus' family tree is important for what it shows about Jesus' legitimacy (legally, he is Joseph's son) and his mission (as David's descendant, he has the lineage expected of the Messiah). But Luke's interest in human ancestors takes a backseat to his interest in Jesus' divinity. Accordingly, he uses a simple "son of" construction, makes no comments about any of the seventy-seven men on his list (thirty-six are never-heard-ofs, but even famous ancestors like David and Abraham go unremarked), and presses on toward a singular climax: Jesus is "son of Seth, son of Adam, son of God."

As far as scholars can determine, God had never before figured in a person's genealogy. But Jesus transcends human history and breaks all the molds. The "supposed" son of Joseph is first and foremost the Son of God.

Luke's genealogy includes an Old Testament patriarch named Enoch (3:37), who mysteriously disappeared after a virtuous life: "Enoch walked with God; then he was no more, because God took him" (Genesis 5:24). Continuing on in Luke's Gospel, we become aware that, like Enoch, Joseph is "no longer here." He has been onstage only briefly. Now he moves completely out of range.

Before asking why Joseph has disappeared, it might be helpful to review what Luke has told us about him. It adds up to more than we might have thought.

There are vital statistics: lineage, village of residence, names of relatives, time and place and circumstances of birth of his legal son. There are character references: good citizen, supportive husband, concerned father, devoted servant of God. There is the outward indication of normal family life, but also the hidden inner reality of unique family relationships. Joseph is called father by a son whose conception he had nothing to do with; he is called husband by a wife whose miraculous pregnancy gives an unprecedented direction to their marriage.

If twentieth-century reporters were to cover Joseph's life, they would emerge at key moments, microphone in hand, to take his emotional pulse by asking repeatedly, "How do you feel right now?" Luke records one, and only one, reaction to the mystery of Jesus' identity: like Mary, Joseph is amazed, astounded, astonished, and finally uncomprehending (2:18, 33, 47-48, 50).

So why has Joseph vanished? More to the point, why has Luke not told us more about him?

Some commentators have theorized that Joseph is "hidden" because Luke drew on some account (unknown to us) of Mary's reminiscences. One of the many questions left unanswered by this theory is why Luke would give a confused description of the Jewish rituals surrounding the birth of a firstborn son (see page 67). Mary would hardly have made such mistakes! And is it likely that she would have made Joseph a minor player in the story? This does justice neither to his role nor their relationship. (What happily married woman would downplay her husband in the memoirs of her early years as wife and mother?)

More plausibly, Luke's lack of attention to Joseph is a consequence of his highlighting Mary's growth into her Son's most faithful follower. Joseph cannot play this role, for he does not seem to have survived long enough. (He never figures in the accounts of Jesus' ministry years, though three Gospels mention his name there.)

For Luke, Mary is the bridge figure linking Jesus' hidden life with his public life. "She is the only adult in his infancy narrative who will last into the public ministry and even into the Church," notes Raymond Brown. And in that later portrayal, there is no negative note of misunderstanding.

Like those who heard the shepherds' report and Jesus' conversation with the teachers, Mary has been astonished. But unlike them, she retains, ponders, and finally penetrates what had at first eluded her. Later, in an episode that two other Gospels present rather negatively, Jesus will commend his mother's faith; their family tie is both biological and spiritual, for Mary is one of "those who hear the word of God and do it" (Luke 8:21).

Mary's active faith marks her out as the first and model disciple. Through it she is led on to new frontiers, cooperating in the birth of the Church, as she did in the birth of the Messiah (see Acts 1:14, where Luke mentions Mary among the believers at Pentecost). Mary is like the good soil that receives the seed, in Jesus' parable of the sower. She exemplifies "the ones who, when they hear the word, hold it fast in an honest and good heart, and bear fruit with patient endurance" (Luke 8:15).

Surely, Joseph, too, is "good soil." All evidence points to his generous welcome and pondering of God's word along with Mary. His growing season on earth was shorter than hers. But we can justifiably imagine Joseph living on as a just man "planted in the house of the Lord" (Psalm 92:13-14), yielding a rich harvest in an unseen field.

Those Hidden Years

Among the Church's rich tradition of meditations and devotional writings centered on the Holy Family's hidden life in Nazareth are many contributions by saintly men and women who had a special appreciation for St. Joseph. Here are just two examples.

St. Francis de Sales (1567-1622) expressed his devotion to Joseph in a number of ways: he composed a litany in his honor, named him patron of the religious order he founded with St. Jeanne de Chantal, carried only his image in his breviary, and always made it a point to preach on the saint's feast day, March 19. Francis' meditations on the hidden life centered especially on the Holy Family's loving union of hearts, a theme that stands out in his influential *Treatise on the Love of God* (1616). Its dedicatory prayer to St. Joseph sets the tone, evoking an ideal of deeply affectionate human relationships centered in God.

Great St. Joseph, most beloved spouse of the Mother of the Beloved, ah, how many times have you borne in your arms the love of heaven and earth! All the while, inflamed by the sweet embrace and kiss of that divine child, your soul was dissolved in joy. All the while — O God, how sweet it was! — he spoke tenderly into your ears and told you that you were his great friend and his beloved father.

(*Treatise on the Love of God* 1, trans. John K. Ryan, Doubleday/ Image, 1972, p. 34)

Charles de Foucauld (1858-1916), a French playboy whose conversion eventually led him to become a hermit in the Sahara, was so drawn by the example of the Holy Family's hidden life that he actually moved to Nazareth, where he pursued his own hidden life of prayer and humble work for three years. Later, he recalled his arrival with thanksgiving: "The first Wednesday [the weekday traditionally dedicated to St. Joseph] I spent there you led me, O God, through the intercession of St. Joseph, to enter the convent of St. Clare as a servant. O the peace, happiness, consolation, blessings, and wonderful happiness I knew there! . . ." De Foucauld was murdered by Muslim nationalists in Morocco, but his ideals live on today in the Little Brothers and the Little Sisters of Jesus and other religious congregations and associations inspired by his example. For Charles de Foucauld, the hidden life at Nazareth was above all a witness and a call to humility.

"And he went down with them and came to Nazareth and was subject to them" [Luke 2:51]. He went down, he humbled himself — his life was one of humility. Being God, you took the appearance of a man; as a man, you made yourself the least of men. Your life was one of *lowliness:* the place you took was the lowest of all. You went down *with* them to live their life with them, the life of the poor laborer, living by working. Your life, like theirs, was one of *work and poverty.* They were obscure, and you lived in the shade of their *obscurity.* . . .

I must believe no work beneath me, for Jesus was a carpenter for thirty years, and Joseph all his life. . . . I must welcome with love and readiness any occasion for humility. . . .

(*Charles de Foucauld,* ed. Robert Ellsberg, Orbis Books, 1999, pp. 37, 48-49, 56)

Part Two

In Search of the Historical Joseph

Joseph, Son of David, who are you?
Bernard Martelet

Chapter 4

Inquiring Minds Want to Know

If the quest for the "historical Jesus"
is difficult, the quest for the "historical relatives
of Jesus" is nigh impossible.

John Meier

My sister, Jeanne, and I tell two different versions of the mousetrap story, each as we honestly remember it from our childhood. Mine is a cautionary tale about resisting a sibling's dares to do something adventurous — like sticking your finger in a strange round thing that turns out to be a mousetrap. Jeanne's account is a melodrama that centers on a miscarriage of justice: she was an innocent by-stander ("I even warned you not to do it!") who received a parental rebuke when she cried in empathy.

Jeanne and I agree on a nucleus of historical material: there was a round mousetrap in the shed under an old sofa; Louise poked her finger in and got it caught; she ran crying to mother. But our versions are contradictory in every other respect.

Experiencing this sort of discrepancy — about an incident that involved me and happened not *that* long ago — only increases my respect for Matthew and Luke's fundamental agreement about the Gospel events in which St. Joseph played a part. Neither evangelist witnessed these events, though Luke does mention eyewitnesses (1:2). Both wrote some years after the actual happenings. And yet they are remarkably united on the key elements of Jesus' early life and their significance.

This is an important indicator that these key events actually occurred. If two independent accounts agree (and no one has ever been able to prove that Luke and Matthew depended on one an-other as they wrote), they are all the more credible.

Guided by the Holy Spirit, Matthew and Luke addressed the same basic issues, observes Father René Laurentin: "The two evan-gelists were clearly answering the same question: Who was Jesus at the beginning of his life. . . ? Both confront two major difficulties: How is it that the Messiah was not born from Joseph, son of David? How is it that he came from Nazareth in Galilee, a place tradition-ally held in contempt?"

Specifically, Luke and Matthew agree on the following points that touch on the life of St. Joseph:

✓ Jesus is conceived by Mary, a virgin. She is engaged to Joseph, but they are not living together.
✓ Joseph is not involved in Jesus' conception: it takes place through the Holy Spirit.
✓ Jesus' birth is announced by an angel — to Mary in Luke, to Joseph in Matthew. He identifies Jesus as Savior and specifies what name he is to be given.
✓ Joseph and Mary have come to live together by the time Jesus is born in Bethlehem, in the reign of Herod the Great.
✓ Joseph is of the house of David. Through him, Jesus is recognized as a son of David.
✓ Joseph and Mary raise Jesus in Nazareth, where Joseph is thought to be the boy's natural father. Joseph disappears from the scene before Jesus begins his public ministry.

Luke and Matthew concur so cordially on these fundamentals that we scarcely ever think about the differences in their accounts of Jesus' early life. Or we unconsciously form composite pictures that smooth them over. The Christmas crèche is a good example, combining Matthew's star and magi with Luke's manger, angels, and shepherds (and, of course, Isaiah's ox and donkey).

But Matthew and Luke *are* different, and their portrayal of Joseph is only one example of it. Think about the structure and mood of the Gospel texts we examined in the last two chapters. Think about their side characters and episodes. In addition to the nativity-scene contributions mentioned above, only Matthew tells us about the annunciation to Joseph, the massacre of the innocents, the flight to Egypt. Only Luke reports the annunciation to Mary, the visitation, the census, the presentation and finding in the Temple. Zechariah and Elizabeth, Simeon and Anna, and the canticles (1:46-55, 68-79; 2:29-32) also come to us courtesy of Luke.

As exemplified by the Christmas crib, some of the unique features from Matthew and Luke fit together quite nicely. Others can be harmonized only by devising ingenious (critics would say far-fetched) solutions. But sometimes the two accounts seem to stand in tension. Here are two discrepancies, as they involve St. Joseph.

Is Joseph living in Nazareth or in Bethlehem just before Jesus' birth? Luke specifies that Nazareth is Joseph and Mary's "own town" (2:39; see also 1:26) and presents the census as the reason why Jesus was born in Bethlehem. In Matthew there is no hint of a census or a journey to Bethlehem: Joseph and Mary already live there in "the house" (2:11) where, presumably, Jesus is born.

Which evangelist has the facts right? Or is one providing us with details that the other has chosen to omit? There seems to be no way of finding out. While historical certainty eludes us, though, we *can* appreciate what each evangelist is trying to highlight. Matthew's emphasis on Bethlehem, King David's ancestral town, stresses Jesus' role as the promised messiah, "the son of David" (1:1). Luke points to Bethlehem and beyond by adding mention of a census for "all the world" (2:2): Jesus will be the Savior of all peoples.

The census presents historians with another puzzle, as there is no evidence for its happening at the time and in the way Luke describes it. But again, to fixate on historical details is probably to miss the point. Whether or not he has gotten the details right, Luke makes use of Joseph's civic obligation to make a statement about Jesus' role and identity. This is how the third-century Church Father Origen explained it:

> I can imagine someone saying: Evangelist, what use to me is the story that the *first registration* of the entire world took place under Caesar Augustus, that along with everyone else *Joseph too with Mary his betrothed (she being with child)* put his name on the census-book. . . ? But if you look more closely, you will see that a great mystic sign is set before us: for in the registration of the entire world, Jesus Christ had to be included. His name was written down with all the others in the world so that he might sanctify the world, and transform this roll of registration into the book of life, so that the names of those who were registered with him and who believed in him might be written down in heaven.

Who was Joseph's father? I grew up in a family where discussion of local events often ground to a halt as my father, aunts, and uncles tried to situate the people involved within the larger context of their family relationships.

"Don't you remember? She's a Bernier. Her brother married a

LaVerdiere who was second cousin to Mrs. Roy who lived on Monument Street."

"No, no, she's a Carey! Her mother was from the Fairfield branch of the Taylor family — you know, the ones who are related to Dr. Fortin on his father's side."

More often than not, Dad and his siblings reached agreement. Luke and Matthew, whose genealogies reach back to include seventy-seven and forty-one names respectively, did not.

Who *was* Joseph's father? Was it Jacob (Matthew 1:16)? Or was it Heli (Luke 3:23)? Was his grandfather Matthan (Matthew 1:15) or Matthat (Luke 3:24)? What about his great-grandfather — and almost every other ancestor all the way back to King David?

Beginning early in the second century, Church writers struggled to penetrate the reasons for the differences between the two ancestral lists. One theory suggests that Matthew gives us Joseph's family tree, while Luke gives us Mary's. The obvious objection is that Luke proposes the genealogy as Joseph's, not Mary's (3:23). Also, he presents Mary as related to Elizabeth, from the tribe of Levi (1:5, 36), whereas both lists are lineages from within the tribe of Judah.

St. Augustine tried to resolve the two-list problem by suggesting that Joseph was adopted. Later he opted for an earlier theory based on the ancient Jewish custom of "levirate marriage" (see Deuteronomy 25:5-10), where the brother of a man who died childless was expected to marry his widowed sister-in-law and continue the deceased husband's lineage. In this scenario, Jacob and Heli would have been brothers who successively married the same woman. Her firstborn son would have been Joseph, legal son of the first (deceased) husband, and natural son of the second. Two fathers, two genealogies, goes this theory.

But if Jacob and Heli were brothers, why do *they* have different fathers, grandfathers, and so on? And as Raymond Brown asks, if the whole point of a levirate marriage was to produce a legal heir for the deceased father, why preserve a record of ancestry through the natural father?

Attempts to explain Joseph's two family trees continue, but like so much about the man, his biological ancestry will probably remain mostly mystery. But whether it is Matthew or Luke who is closer to the historical reality, Father Brown points out, both genealogies "can be scriptural and truly inspired by God [even] if only one or neither was a historically accurate family record. . . . Genealogies serve different purposes. . . ."

The purposes underlying the structure of Luke's and Matthew's genealogies would have been immediately obvious to their first readers, who would have understood that the evangelists were using them to reinforce truths about Jesus' identity. They are largely lost to us, who are products of a later and a vastly different culture.

But whatever other purposes Luke's and Matthew's lists may serve, each one provides what my father and his siblings were trying to get at in their debates over local lineages: an answer to the question "Who *is* this person?" When the person is Jesus, "son" of Joseph, the truest answer does not center on facts like whether his grandfather was Heli or Jacob. The truest answer is theological. Jesus is "son of David, son of Abraham" (Matthew 1:1) and "son of Adam, son of God" (Luke 3:38).

Who are the "brothers and sisters" of Jesus? Over the centuries, one of the most tantalizing questions for inquiring minds that want to know about "the historical Joseph" has involved a subject on which Luke and Matthew do *not* disagree. In fact, they are in accord not only with one another but also with Mark, John, and other New Testament writers. You might phrase the question as "How large a family did Joseph preside over in Nazareth?"

The mysterious "brothers and sisters" of Jesus make brief appearances here and there in the Gospels:

> "Is not this the carpenter's son? Is not his mother called Mary? And are not his brothers James and Joseph and Simon and Judas? And are not all his sisters with us?"
>
> Matthew 13:55-56 (see also Mark 6:3)

> Then his mother and his brothers came to him, but they could not reach him because of the crowd. And he was told, "Your mother and your brothers are standing outside, wanting to see you." But he said to them, "My mother and my brothers are those who hear the word of God and do it."
>
> Luke 8:19-21 (see also Matthew 12:46-50; Mark 3:31-35)

> After this he [Jesus] went down to Capernaum with his mother, his brothers, and his disciples. . . .
>
> So his brothers said to him. . . . (For not even his brothers believed in him.) . . . But after his brothers had gone to the festival. . . .
>
> John 2:12; 7:3, 5, 10

The brothers of Jesus also surface in the Acts of the Apostles among Mary and the other disciples who are gathered for prayer and then filled with the Holy Spirit at Pentecost (1:14). They reappear in St. Paul's first letter to the Corinthians (9:5). And finally, "James the Lord's brother" is spotted in Galatians 1:19.

Who are these siblings? Not Mary's children, for she was a virgin not only at the time of Jesus' birth, but all her life. This belief in Mary's "real and perpetual virginity" developed in the early Church as an outcome of deepened faith in Christ's virginal conception (see the *Catechism of the Catholic Church,* No. 499). It was not a fringe or a late-breaking view, as scholars on an ecumenical task force sponsored by the National Lutheran/Roman Catholic Dialogue agreed: "The title 'Ever Virgin' arose early in Christianity. . . . It was a stock phrase in the Middle Ages, and continued to be used in Protestant confessional writings."

With no family tree to provide direction about how to view these "brothers and sisters," Christians over the centuries have subscribed to different explanations of their parentage. In the second century, one approach was circulating in a popular apocryphal writing called the *Protoevangelium of James.* Here Joseph figures as an aged widower with sons by a previous marriage, including the James who is presented as author of the work. In this picture, then, the brothers of the Gospels are Jesus' stepbrothers, and Mary is their stepmother. (If this view of Mary had taken root in popular devotion as deeply as did "old Joseph," would the "wicked stepmother" stereotype be going strong today?)

The theme of "Joseph widowed, with children" recurs often in other apocryphal writings. The *History of Joseph the Carpenter,* an Egyptian work dating from about 400, adds the interesting, if dubious, details that Joseph was ninety-one and Mary thirteen at the time of their marriage and that James was still very young when Joseph's first wife died. It even supplies the names of Joseph's daughters: Lysias and Lydia! (Another tradition calls them Esther and Tamar.)

Influenced largely by the family portrait offered in the *Protoevangelium of James,* most Church Fathers in the East as well as some in the West adopted the idea of Joseph's earlier marriage. Among them were Clement of Alexandria, Epiphanius, Gregory of Nyssa, Ephrem of Syria, and Hilary of Poitiers. Ambrose, John Chrysostom, and, in some early writings, Augustine also seem to have viewed the "brothers" in this light.

In his commentary on Matthew's Gospel, Origen acknowledges very frankly why "some persons" (including himself, as is clear elsewhere in his writings) are so taken with the apocryphal depiction of Joseph as a widower with children: "Those who hold this view wish to preserve the honor of Mary's virginity throughout. . . ."

Thinking of Joseph as an *aged* widower was like an extra guarantee of Mary's marital virginity — an easily understood explanation for any heretic who would deem it impossible for a young married couple to live together without having sexual intercourse. As Father Francis Filas dryly observes, however, "We do not have to postulate senility as a necessary means to preserve virginity, especially in so unique a marriage as existed between two people so holy as Joseph and Mary. God's grace is more than sufficient to observe continence if such be God's will."

The explanation that Jesus' so-called brothers and sisters were really his cousins — and, by extension, that both Joseph and Mary were lifelong virgins — was introduced by St. Jerome in the late fourth century. A certain hapless Helvidius, in an excess of zeal to show Mary as a model of both perfect virginity and perfect married love, had revived a minority view held by several Church Fathers, notably Tertullian, who had affirmed the virgin birth but not Mary's continued virginity. Like them, Helvidius presented Joseph and Mary as the biological parents of Jesus' brothers and sisters. Jerome reacted to Helvidius's treatise with his usual acerbic vigor, resting his defense of Mary's perpetual virginity on two main points:

✓ Jesus' brothers were children of another Mary, sister of the Virgin, who was present at the cross and identified as both "Mary the mother of James and Joseph" (Matthew 27:56; Mark 15:40) and "Mary of Clopas" (John 19:25).

✓ "All Scripture indicates that cousins are called brothers." Neither biblical Hebrew nor Aramaic has a word for cousin, Jerome explained, so the word for brother was often used instead. When the Old Testament was rendered into Greek, these "brother/cousin" references were translated literally, emerging as the Greek word for brother.

Jerome presented his case with rather more conviction than was warranted by the Gospel texts. To date there is still no consensus on the complex question of the relationships and identities of Jesus' relatives and disciples. Nor, as Jerome maintained, does "all

Scripture" illustrate that the Greek word translated brother (*adelphos*) is regularly used to mean cousin.

In the Greek translation of the Old Testament, there is "perhaps only one" indisputable example of this usage, says Father John Meier. In the New Testament *adelphos* "means only full or half-brother," except when referring to relationships of another order (brothers in Christ, for example).

Additionally, Paul's description of James as "the Lord's brother" (Galatians 1:19; 1 Corinthians 9:5) weakens the "cousin" interpretation. Noting that the usual Greek word for cousin, *anepsios,* appears in Colossians 4:10, scholars ask themselves: If St. Paul meant to call James a cousin of Jesus, why didn't he use this perfectly good word for cousin rather than writing *adelphos*? After all, in composing his letters Paul wasn't dealing with issues of translation!

Even so, though much remains unclear, many scholars concur with Jerome's basic insight that "brother" describes a more elastic relationship than might have been supposed. Without nailing it down to cousin or trying to specify the family connections involved, they think the Greek word may indeed reflect an underlying Semitic meaning — a broader sense of kin or relative.

So who are the "brothers and sisters"? There are, it seems, only three possibilities. And only the first two are consistent with Catholic teaching based on the belief of the early Church.

They are near relatives. For Catholics, belief in Mary's lifelong virginity has been a key factor in the search to identify the brothers and sisters. Consequently, as the *Catechism* states, the Church has always seen them not as children of Mary but as "close relations" of Jesus (No. 500).

Of course, Catholics can and do speculate about the specifics. The "brothers and sisters" are . . . children of Mary's sister? . . . of two of Joseph's siblings? . . . adopted children of deceased relatives? . . . children of Mary's nearest relatives, with whom Mary lived after Joseph died but while Jesus was still young? . . . Within the range of doctrinally acceptable possibilities are some that are rather different from our usual picture of just three places at the Holy Family's dinner table!

They are children of Joseph and a deceased wife. For Eastern Christians, some Catholics, and other Christians who honor Mary

Ever-Virgin, this remains the most convincing scenario. "Psychologically, this rings true to me," explains Scripture commentator George Martin. "In my own family, I can remember a time when all five of our children were under age nine. I was in my thirties then, and if my wife, Mary, had died, I would certainly have been willing to consider remarrying!" And, he points out, given the early marrying ages in first-century Palestine, "Joseph the widower" need not have been decrepit.

Interestingly, an Anglican scholar who does *not* hold to Mary's perpetual virginity also makes a case for the widower/stepchildren portrait. Richard Bauckham argues that:

✓ It is the oldest explanation and should not be discounted simply because it appears in apocryphal writings. These "works of imagination" preserve an accurate historical memory and "are evidence of a well-established tradition in (probably early) second-century Syrian Christianity that Jesus' brothers and sisters were children of Joseph by a previous marriage."

✓ If Luke can call Joseph Jesus' parent or father without implying blood relationship, he can do the same with regard to Jesus' brothers and sisters.

✓ The evangelists seem to present Joseph, Mary, Jesus, and the brothers and sisters as a nuclear family; marital or legal ties would suffice to hold this unit together.

✓ The people of Nazareth call Jesus "son of Mary" (Mark 6:3): this would distinguish him from the children of Joseph by his first wife.

Objections can be raised to the family portrait of Joseph the widower and Mary the stepmother presiding over their unique blended family. Western Catholics, accustomed to honoring St. Joseph for his lifelong virginity, tend to find it jarring. "We believe that just as the mother of Jesus was a virgin, so was Joseph. . . ." God "placed the Virgin in the care of a virgin," wrote St. Thomas Aquinas, affirming and restating the theological opinion that the Church in the West has followed, by and large, since the fifteenth century. And so St. Joseph stands, lily in hand as a symbol of his virginity, in the statues and paintings that are still to be found at many a side altar.

At the same time, however, Joseph's perpetual virginity is not an article of faith for Catholics. It may be traditional — many would say preferable — to view St. Joseph as a lifelong celibate, but Catholics are not bound to accept this as official Church teaching. In principle, there is no reason why a holy widower who accepted God's invitation to a virginal marriage could not qualify as the Virgin's chaste guardian and spouse.

They are biological children of Joseph and Mary. This is the dominant view among most Protestants and is commonly assumed to be one of the issues over which Protestants and Catholics have always disagreed. It therefore comes as something of a shock — "a startling fact," says John Meier in reporting it — that this view developed only with the rise of the Enlightenment in the eighteenth century and was not the view of Protestant Reformers like Martin Luther and John Calvin. Like Jerome, says Father Meier, "they held to Mary's perpetual virginity and therefore did not consider the brothers and sisters of Jesus to be true siblings."

"I am inclined to agree with those who declare that 'brothers' really means 'cousins' here," wrote Luther in a sermon on the Gospel of John. To which one of Luther's editors adds the note: "It is significant that among the interpretations of the word 'brother' which Luther discusses, he does not even consider the possibility that Mary might have had other children than Jesus. This is consistent with his lifelong acceptance of the idea of the perpetual virginity of Mary."

Is the "quest for the historical relatives of Jesus" just about impossible, as John Meier states in this chapter's opening quote? "Could be," we may conclude after our exploration of these historical questions raised by Luke and Matthew. Inconclusive results, however, do not make the search pointless, unimportant, or unexciting.

On the contrary, we have much to gain by reflecting on the Gospel events and situations involving St. Joseph. Not absolute certainty, perhaps, but a better understanding of their historical underpinnings and a deeper appreciation of the spiritual truths they convey. Guided by the Church's inspired interpretation of Scripture, our "inquiring minds" can discover new facets of St. Joseph there, as well as in past writers and present findings.

Even better: as we ponder "the historical Joseph" behind the Gospel passages, we can expect to meet the "real Joseph" — alive and active in the Body of Christ, which he in a special way protects.

St. Joseph: How Artists Saw Him

Taking their cue from writings like the *Protoevangelium of James,* the artists of the Middle Ages almost always pictured St. Joseph as elderly, bearded, and bald. Furthermore, observed noted art historian Emile Mâle, they never dreamed of portraying Joseph alone, but only as a character in scenes from Jesus' birth and infancy: "The least saint of our provinces had his statue; St. Joseph did not have his."

Some of the Italian Renaissance artists were the first to challenge this view of "old Joseph." Following in the tradition of scholars like Jean Gerson (1362-1428), they reasoned that only a younger, vigorous man could have withstood the rigors of a trek to Egypt and years of heavy labor as a carpenter. An early example of this new view was Raphael's 1504 *Marriage of the Virgin,* which features a thirtyish Joseph.

The new look took root a bit later in Spain, once Teresa of Ávila's writings had begun making the country into "the chosen land of St. Joseph," as Emile Mâle put it. El Greco, Zurbaran, and especially Murillo, "the painter of St. Joseph," picture the saint as a strong man in the prime of life. Handsome, too! "Why must we think that Joseph was ugly?" St. Teresa's co-worker, Jerónimo Gracián, had asked in his *Summary of the Excellencies of St. Joseph.* On the contrary, he maintained, St. Joseph was the man who most resembled the adult Christ.

Identifying symbols of St. Joseph in religious art from the sixteenth century on fall into two categories. *St. Joseph the worker* appears with the tools of his trade — ax, saw, plane, hammer, and the like. *St. Joseph, guardian and protector,* is depicted carrying Jesus or leading him by the hand; or he holds a lily (courtesy of the apocryphal accounts of his miraculous selection as Mary's husband), a palm (symbol of fortitude and perseverance), or, in Nativity scenes, a candle or lantern.

Chapter 5

An Ordinary Nazorean

What does me a lot of good when I think of the Holy
Family is to imagine a life that was very ordinary.
St. Thérèse of Lisieux

No halo marked St. Joseph out from the other household heads of Nazareth. No trail of miracles led to his door. No angels materialized to do his planing and pounding. No ecstasies, no prophetic preaching, no inspired writings, no spiritual fireworks whatever are reported of him.

Certainly, the people of Nazareth were unaware that Joseph was anything special. After hearing Jesus speak in the synagogue, they protested in astonishment, "Where did this man get this wisdom and these deeds of power? Is not this the carpenter's son?" (Matthew 13:54-55). Apparently, nothing about Joseph had prepared them for Jesus' performance. Like the pearl of great price before it was pried from its oyster, Joseph's extraordinary virtue was hidden under the appearances of a very ordinary life.

As we have seen, the "search for the historical Joseph" can go only so far in exploring the particulars that make St. Joseph extraordinary. On the other hand, that search sheds valuable light on his "ordinary" side — that is, on the experience of life that he shared in common with other residents of Nazareth. Here, history, archaeology, anthropology, and linguistics come to our aid to help us picture Joseph in context, living an ordinary life "totally like ours," as Thérèse of Lisieux liked to imagine.

And yet, for all its ordinariness and approachability, his life was in many respects very different from ours. Never underestimate the culture gap between modern America and Palestine two thousand years ago!

"The past is a foreign country. They do things differently there," a British novelist observed. Just how differently they did things in St. Joseph's day has been discussed in enough books to fill a library. Still, it may be helpful to examine here, on a very modest scale, some of the specifics relating to daily life in the time of Joseph.

Think of this chapter, then, as a mini-guide that you are consulting to prepare for an extended stay in the home of a long-lost cousin in Nazareth sometime between the years 10 and 20. Like a regular guidebook, it contains assorted facts and figures, practical information, and some miscellaneous "things you should know."

YOUR GUIDE TO FIRST-CENTURY NAZARETH

Facts and Figures

Nazareth is located in the lower portion of Galilee, which is the northern region of Palestine. Lower Galilee covers about four hundred seventy square miles and now, in the first century, is mainly a rural area of fertile plains and low hills whose rocky slopes shelter numerous peasant villages and hamlets.

Unlike Judea in the south, which Rome governs directly through a prefect in Jerusalem, Galilee is a semi-autonomous kingdom that Rome governs through the local ruler, Herod Antipas. Since Herod faithfully pays the required tribute and maintains public order, you will not generally see Roman soldiers on the streets. Even so, Galileans bear no love for Herod, who is viewed as an apostatizing collaborator, and still less for the Romans.

Taxes are one sore point. Besides being burdensome, they are collected through a system that fosters graft and corruption. And though Rome keeps a discreet distance, every villager is aware that the Roman eagle hovers overhead, ready to swoop down at any sign of protest. Looking northwest from Nazareth, you can see the city of Sepphoris, which revolted in 4 B.C. The Romans burned it, sold its people into slavery, and crucified two thousand on charges of rebellion.

The Galilee you are planning to visit is being swept by winds of change. The region is moving from a barter economy to a market and money economy, and peasants and small landholders especially are feeling the pinch. Some are losing their lands. Some are becoming tenant farmers on large estates owned by absentee landlords, struggling to pay the rent in cash or crops. Biblical studies professor John Riches observes that with much of the land, "probably the markets, and certainly wages" in the control of a few wealthy landowners, many peasants are living on the edge, threatened with "debt, loss of tenancies and ultimately slavery." Some are giving up and moving to the cities in search of a better life. Others are taking to begging. Still others are choosing the way of crime or violence — becoming thieves, bandits, or resistance fighters.

Another major change is the breakdown of the family. This

94

sounds like a familiar theme to modern Americans, but in first-century Galilee it has a different twist: it is the *extended* family that is breaking down here, not the nuclear family.

For longer than anyone can remember, adult sons and their wives have normally settled in or near the parental household, with daughters married out to live with or near their in-laws. The oldest son inherited the family home and a double share of the land; the rest was divided among his brothers. But now, with the population booming and the family land divided and subdivided, individual plots are becoming too small to support even one person. Many younger brothers have no choice but to sell their land and consider their options. They can become farm laborers or construction workers, learn a craft or trade, sell, beg or steal, or move. In this area, where geographical mobility has been unknown and occupations are handed down from father to sons, this is a big change indeed.

A younger son's employment prospects are probably brightest in the cities. First-century Lower Galilee has four: Caesarea Maritima and Akko on the Mediterranean coast and Sepphoris and Tiberias, two pet projects of Herod Antipas. Sepphoris, 3.7 miles from Nazareth, is a large-scale urban renewal project; it will serve as Herod's capital until displaced by Tiberias, a new city on the southwestern shore of the Sea of Galilee.

But moving from village to city is more easily said than done. As in many societies, "city mouse" and "country mouse" live on opposite sides of a great divide in lifestyle and outlook. In Palestine the traditional tensions are heightened by different approaches to an infiltrating language, with its culture and institutions.

Greek came to the Near East through the military campaigns of Alexander the Great, some three hundred fifty years ago. Since then it has become the main language of the Roman empire, the cement that holds together a complex mosaic of many different peoples. If you want to get ahead in first-century Palestine, you'll need Greek. This is especially true for city-dwellers, but even country people who market their wares and skills outside the village have to learn the rudiments of business Greek.

The problem, as many Jews see it, is not with Greek as a language (by now the Hebrew Scriptures exist in Greek, translated by Jewish expatriates in Egypt), but with Greek as a culture. Greek architecture, literature, styles, schools, sports stadiums, theaters, temples — in Palestine's cities especially, Greek is "in." Some of the powerful urban Jewish families have embraced this trend as the road to success. But people in the countryside view Greek culture the way many modern Christians in the West view the media culture: as a threat to traditional religious beliefs and moral values.

This inbred suspicion of Greek culture colors the way the people of Nazareth relate to the nearby city of Sepphoris, which Herod is rebuilding in grand Greek style with sumptuous buildings, baths, and a theater. The Nazoreans take food and other goods to sell in the Sepphoris market, no doubt. Perhaps some Nazoreans also pack a lunch and walk there daily to work on Herod's construction projects. But you will surely not find them attending the Greek games and theater and acquiring a veneer of urban sophistication!

If your stay in Nazareth coincides with one of the year's three pilgrimage festivals, you might travel with the villagers to the one city that they hold dear. This is Jerusalem, traditional center of the Jewish nation and home of the Temple. Evidence of Greek culture is here, too, but Jerusalem is revered nonetheless as the holy city, the only place where sacrificial worship can be offered. Galileans loyally support the Temple, its rituals, and its priesthood (though often distrusting the high priests, who are chosen by Rome and Herod).

Peasant piety runs deep and sticks to the basics of Judaism, you will notice. In addition to pilgrimages, these basics include belief in one God, his covenant with the Jewish people, and the Scriptures; circumcision; observing the Sabbath and other special days; following dietary laws and other rules of purity and impurity; prayer, fasting, and tithing. There is probably a synagogue in Nazareth, where people gather regularly for prayer and teaching. Pious parents arrange for their sons to receive religious training there.

Strangely enough for people who are basically pious and resistant to foreign influences, Galileans are often scorned by other Jews, who see their geographical proximity to pagan nations as violating the purity laws. (Phoenicians live north and west of Galilee, Samaritans to the south, and a federation of ten Greek cities lies to the southeast.) Also, the Galileans' country bumpkin manners and speech can cause them to come across as people who do not think deeply about God and his word. The opposite is true, as you will discover during your Nazareth stay.

But prepare yourself: Nazareth really is a hick town! Located away from the Sea of Galilee and off any major road, the hillside village has somewhere between one hundred and five hundred residents. Many are related by blood or marriage. One author guesstimates that Nazareth covers just one acre; sixty acres, says another. Whichever, almost any modern American will find Nazareth small and backwater.

Practical Information

ACTIVITIES • Descriptions of village life in first-century Galilee abound with phrases like "dominated by work." The children of Nazareth play games — the boys especially (girls are introduced to child-care and household tasks very early). But the adults have few if any recreational activities. No one in Nazareth has the energy or the inclination for sports. No one would ever dream of hopping over to Sepphoris to catch the latest Greek play. Enjoyment, says one author, is "confined to the odd visit of a wandering minstrel or the religious festival."

CLIMATE • Forget about five-day forecasts and weather channels, although Nazoreans are sensitive to meteorological "signs of the times" in nature. Spring and autumn are foreign to their experience; "wet" and "dry" are the seasons they know.

Summer ("dry") is from about mid-April to September and is characterized by virtually cloudless days. Winter ("wet") lasts from about mid-September to March; it is not a nonstop downpour, but rather a series of two- or three-day rainstorms followed by several days of dry weather. No one here groans over the winter rains: both the "early rain" of September-October and the "later rain" of March-April are critical for good harvests and full cisterns for the dry months.

January is the coldest month in Nazareth. But anyone who has lived through winters in the northern United States and Canada will find the seasonal variations very moderate. Temperatures normally fluctuate between 45 and 80 degrees Fahrenheit over the course of the year.

DRESS • No designer showings or fashion fads here. A few basic articles of clothing serve everyone, year in, year out.

The tunic is a neck-to-ankle rectangle of linen or wool with head and arm openings. It comes in a variety of lengths and colors (often darker and more varied for women), and more than one can be worn. Over it is the mantle, or cloak, a short-sleeved or sleeveless coat that is loose-fitting, sturdy, and all-purpose. Men's cloaks have bluish-purple tassels at the corners, a visual reminder to obey

God's law (see Numbers 15:38-39). Everyone wears a belt: with it you can turn your cloak into a carry-all pouch, or you can "gird your loins," that is, tuck up your garments for greater freedom of movement. The wardrobe is completed by a pair of simple sandals and a cloth head-covering for protection against sun and wind: men secure it with a headband, women drape or wrap it around the head and sometimes also use a face veil.

Galilee is known for its linen and Judea for its wool industries, and ready-made clothing can be bought in the cities. In a tiny village like Nazareth, though, making the family's clothing is yet another task on a woman's long to-do list.

FOOD AND DRINK • By necessity, first-century villagers in Galilee eat the "Mediterranean diet" now being marketed to health-conscious Americans. Grains provide half the caloric intake; the rest is from fruits, vegetables, olive oil, and dairy products. You won't eat meat except at village wedding banquets and religious feasts; in Nazareth, which is not near any body of water, fresh fish is rare too.

Most likely, two daily meals are the norm. The late-morning meal/work break might be bread dipped in olive oil, accompanied by grains, fruit, and water or diluted wine. The early-evening meal is more substantial and includes a hot dish like a vegetable soup or stew.

Grains are eaten either parched (roasted on a hot griddle), as porridge, or as bread. Wheat is the grain of choice, but in a poor village like Nazareth, bread is usually made from a mixture of ground wheat and barley or millet. Vegetables include cucumbers, leeks, onions, beans, garlic, lentils, and squash, which most villagers grow in fields or garden plots. Most also have at least a few fruit and olive trees and grapevines. Local fruits — figs, grapes and raisins, pomegranates, and apples — are sometimes made into sauces, spreads, and syrups.

Most of the dairy products come from goats, which are more resilient than sheep or cows (they can graze on marginal land and go up to two weeks without water). Plentiful and easy to digest, goat's milk is made into buttermilk, yogurt, cheese, and curds, as well as drunk sour out of skins. Other than goat's milk, your beverage choices are table wine and water.

HEALTH • Don't get sick while in Nazareth. Treatment is limited to bandages, salves, poultices, and possibly bone-setting.

Dental care is unknown, so don't get a toothache either. Most older people here have gum diseases and dental problems — not tooth decay but attrition, where teeth are gradually ground down by eating coarsely milled grains. Flies and the challenges of hygiene contribute to common health problems like intestinal parasites, skin diseases, and trachoma, a contagious eye infection that can cause blindness.

"Older," by the way, is what modern Americans would call early middle age. Thirty to forty-five years is probably the average life expectancy of first-century Nazoreans: almost thirty percent of live births are dead by age six, seventy-five percent by their mid-twenties. Maybe only three percent make it to their sixtieth birthday.

HOUSING • During your stay in Nazareth, you will be living in a house containing a few rooms adjoining an open courtyard. Houses have stone walls (in some areas, a cave may serve as a room), floors of earth, clay, or small stones, and flat roofs made by laying slats or poles across wooden beams and then covering the whole thing with clay or plaster. Roofs, reached by outside stairs or an inside ladder, are flat and are centers of domestic activity: laundry, bathing, hot-weather sleep-outs, and drying food, fodder, and fuel. Courtyards are all-purpose areas for household tasks, sheltering animals, and even cooking; if the family has an oven, it may be situated here in a corner away from the wind.

How many rooms in a house? It depends on the family's size, income level, and occupation. Farmers need more indoor space for animals and feed, equipment, and the like; an artisan like the village carpenter needs a workroom. Whatever the house size, though, every family divides its space into what modern anthropologists call a "living domain," where they eat, sleep, prepare food, and entertain, and an "economic domain" that houses what is needed for survival (food, fuel, tools).

For many reasons, your lodging will take some getting used to. Doors and windows are kept to a minimum, so rooms are generally dark and close. Oil lamps provide some light, but nothing like the wattage you consider normal. Even if you are an animal-lover, you may not appreciate living so close to sheep, goats, and donkeys (no pampered cats or dogs here, but the family milk goat is often kept like a pet within the house complex). You will certainly not have your own room: in this culture, personal privacy as we think of it is not even an ideal.

LANGUAGES • Four languages are used in first-century Palestine, but for ordinary, everyday communication you will need only Aramaic. You probably know a few words already: *abba* and *golgotha;* perhaps you have also heard of *maranatha* and *talitha koum* — "little girl, get up" (Mark 5:41). Some of the villagers — the especially devout ones — have learned Hebrew in order to read the Scriptures. Merchants and craftsmen have also picked up at least enough Greek for business transactions in nearby cities. Latin is the language of the Roman officials; it is unlikely that anyone in Nazareth speaks it.

MONEY • For in-town purchases, use the small change coined locally by the Roman procurators and the Herods. Imperial coinage from Rome, Alexandria, and Antioch includes the large silver denarius, which is the usual salary for a day's work. Because of uncertain exchange rates and the many types of coins in circulation, changing money is a complex matter. Go out to the gate of one of the larger cities and find yourself a good money changer.

OCCUPATIONS • It will be made clear to you that work is strictly divided along gender lines, with women tending to things within the home and men to things outside it. Women help with harvesting but stay together in clusters separate from the men.

If you do "woman's work" in Nazareth, you will sweep and clean, do laundry, spin and sew, draw water from the local spring, and cook. You will learn to make bread: first you mix flour, water, salt, perhaps honey, and some old dough for leavening; then you knead and shape the dough into round loaves — some small, some large, some thin; after rising, the loaves are baked on a flat hot stone or in an oven (probably the communal village oven). Less appetizing but vital, since there is very little wood to burn, is the task of making fuel patties out of camel and donkey dung. Salted and sun-dried, these provide reliable cooking fuel especially during the rainy season.

Most people in Nazareth are what we would call farm families who support themselves by selling produce and livestock, as well as homemade goods, at the city markets. Local products — grains, vegetables, figs, olive oil, grapes, and wine — are exported, but with most of the profit going to well-to-do landlords and business owners who typically live outside the village.

Though the soil is fertile here, agriculture is difficult. Farming methods are laborious, involving terracing and water storage for the dry months. Family-owned plots are small and must be intensively cultivated for maximum yield. Tenant farmers are under particular pressure to produce.

Other Nazoreans support themselves through a craft or trade. Important among these is the village carpenter, Joseph, who works with his son, Jesus. "Carpenter," as we use the word, is too narrow a description of their work, however: the precise Aramaic word for it is unknown, but Greek speakers would call Joseph a *tekton*, meaning a woodworker or, broader still, a craftsman who works with any hard material such as wood, stone, or bricks. If this carpenter were to advertise in the yellow pages, he might list bricklaying and stonemasonry among his skills.

Typical projects for "Joseph and Son, Inc." would include house construction and repair, especially preparing and placing heavy roof beams, and making doors and doorframes, windows and window fittings, locks and bolts. Villagers probably turn to Joseph when they need agricultural implements (plows, yokes, winnowing forks); they most certainly do when they need furniture: beds, tables, stools, lampstands, and storage containers like chests, cabinets, and boxes.

You may be surprised at the relatively high quality of workmanship. Woodworking tools and techniques in first-century Galilee are not too different from those used in colonial America. Most of Joseph's tools — among them, the hammer, mallet, chisel, saw, drill, plane, lathe, square, and straightedge — will look familiar to you. Being the Nazareth *tekton* requires both muscle and a fair level of technical skill.

TRAVEL • Don't expect any sight-seeing excursions during your stay in first-century Nazareth. As one author says, travel in this world is "very difficult and never a pleasure . . . fraught with risk and danger." Sensible people stay at home as much as possible; wanting to "go out and see the world" — to leave the protective, predictable set of relationships that give you an identity — is considered deviant. The danger of travel comes from wild animals and bandits; the difficulty from poor roads, punishing heat, tolls, long distances on foot (seventeen to twenty-three miles is the daily average), and the lack of reliable food and lodging. No surprise that the people of Nazareth are mainly stay-at-homes.

But don't jump to the conclusion that Nazareth is a hamlet of couch potatoes. Everyday life here calls for more walking than you can imagine — much of it uphill, none of it in Reeboks. No Nazorean needs a treadmill or exercise bike in the family room.

Just getting around on foot keeps everyone fit.

Things You Should Know

Your stay in first-century Galilee will be smoother if you are alerted beforehand to a few crucial differences in manners and mentality. The following list highlights a few of these areas. It is by no means exhaustive, nor is it meant to be anything but suggestive of issues you may want to explore more thoroughly.

IT'S A MAN'S WORLD • At every level of this society, power and leadership are male prerogatives. Men make the decisions, relate to the outside world, and generally maintain the family honor in their social and business dealings. Except for childless widows, divorced women with no family ties, and prostitutes, every woman lives under male protection. Her part is to avoid dishonor, especially by shunning any potentially compromising contact with men. This means she is at home most of the time, especially in those parts of the house reserved for "women's work."

American women who visit first-century Galilee and get restless at this unaccustomed seclusion should know that the common Aramaic word for prostitute is an expression that means literally "she who goes outside"! American men who are inclined to relate directly to the local women should know that their friendliness will be interpreted as an affront to the family honor.

OLDER IS BETTER • Biblical scholars like Ben Witherington point out that "the wise old man" of ancient Palestine is often "the most revered person in a village or town." Cultural anthropologist Bruce Malina confirms this first-century view: "The older an individual is, the higher the status."

We are miles away from the youth culture of the modern West.

PERSONAL SPACE IS FOR SHARING • In America, males who hold hands or lock arms with one another are assumed to be advertising their sexual orientation. In first-century Palestine, this is simply a sign of friendship, with no sexual connotations. Friends value being included within one another's personal space, so they touch and jab more than we do and also feel free to handle possessions without asking permission. This is an expressive culture, where touching and show-

102

ing emotion are normal, even (and maybe especially) for men.

By the way, stand closer to the people you converse with here — about six to eight inches away, rather than the sixteen to eighteen inches you feel comfortable with. In the ancient Middle East, it is rude *not* to breathe into a person's face when conversing.

MIND YOUR TABLE MANNERS • For meals in the village you will sit cross-legged on the floor around a low table or a mat spread on the ground. If you dine with the urban elite, you will probably eat propped up on one elbow and lying on a couch or mat pulled up to a square table. Water will be provided for washing your hands before and after the meal. The reason for this will soon become obvious: all eat out of a common dish, with fingers or flat bread serving as utensils. Men and women do not normally eat together, though wedding banquets may be an exception.

THERE'S NO TIME BUT THE PRESENT • Nazoreans will laugh at you if you pull out your daily organizer or look at your watch. Time is not an abstract concept here, nor something to be measured and scheduled. People live in the present, their daily routines guided by things like the location of the sun and their own internal clocks ("Gee, I'm hungry; it must be dinner"). They remember the past in terms of specific events ("the year the locusts came") and consider it foolhardy beyond belief to try and plan an uncertain future that only God can know. You will do best to forget about schedules and punctuality and discover time Mediterranean-style.

NO INDIVIDUALISTS HERE • First-century Palestinians see themselves not as individuals but as members of groups — family first, then a variety of in-groups such as friends, neighbors, and fellow villagers. Being a nonconformist, marching to your own drummer, focusing on your unique potential — all of this they would consider extremely weird.

In-group members have first claim on one another's time and services; only with good reason can their requests be denied. Out-group members such as foreigners are viewed with suspicion, indifference, or hostility — unless, of course, they are distant American relatives doing time-travel to first-century Galilee!

Returning to the Twenty-first Century

In most respects the society Joseph lived in was one that few modern Westerners would want to endure for very long. As John

Meier observes, "A comfortable, middle-class urban American would find living conditions in ancient Nazareth appalling." It is worth noting, however, that we enjoy exceptionally high standards of living, even compared to most people in our own world. The average person now living in a developing country like China and India would have an easier time in first-century Nazareth.

Many features of first-century life would strike us as strange, however, and many others galling — gender issues, the value placed on conforming and meeting in-group expectations, the lack of opportunities for travel and for "moving up in the world" (no American-style success stories here: from one generation to the next, people generally stay at the same social and economic level). On the other hand, certain features of life in Nazareth — the struggle to keep land in the family, to keep the family together, to maintain traditional religious beliefs and values against a powerful pagan culture — might have a familiar feel.

A lengthy stay in ancient Nazareth would no doubt bring us new insights into ways of living and thinking that seem strange from a distance. But once our initial culture shock had worn off, the greatest surprise of all might be to realize that the life of Joseph the carpenter and his family was so terribly ordinary. They lived like everyone else in the village, like ordinary Nazoreans.

Feasting at St. Joseph's Table

We can't join the Holy Family at the Nazareth dinner table, but for many centuries Italians have celebrated the feast of St. Joseph by preparing a table of special foods in his honor. In some parts of Italy, a great banquet was set out in the town square after Mass on March 19: three people presided as stand-ins for the Holy Family, and the poor were especially well served. In Sicily, a feast table was set up in every home as a sort of altar of thanksgiving, with foods displayed, blessed, enjoyed, and distributed to the needy in memory of St. Joseph's intervention during a severe drought. As Ann Ball points out in her cookbook of traditional Catholic recipes, Italian Americans have continued the tradition, sometimes in their homes, sometimes in parish halls. Each St. Joseph's altar is unique, she says, but there are some common features.

The altars generally have three tiers to symbolize the Blessed Trinity. A statue of St. Joseph and a statue or picture of the Holy Family are placed on the top tier and decorated with flowers, greenery, and fruit. The altar is blessed by the priest, usually in a special ceremony, before anything is removed from it. If the altar is set up on the eve of the feast, people often visit to pray and to leave petitions and donations for the poor. . . .

The beautiful breads are baked in symbolic shapes. . . . Some of the symbols pictured on the St. Joseph's altar are the monstrance, chalice, cross, dove, lamb, Bible, hearts, wreath, palms, lilies, sandals, beard of St. Joseph, ladder, and tools. A braided loaf symbolizes the staff of St. Joseph. . . . Other traditional foods are also found on the altars. *Mudica* is a type of seasoned bread crumb for the pasta which represents the sawdust of Joseph the carpenter. *Pignolatti* are fried pastries in the shape of pine cones. Legend tells that the Child Jesus played with pine cones for toys as a child. . . . In addition to other fruits, there are generally grapes, olives and figs because these are grown abundantly in Sicily.

(Ann Ball, *Catholic Traditions in Cooking,* Our Sunday Visitor, 1993, pp. 96-97)

Chapter 6

Is That All There Is?

There is always a tendency among the devout to look for
something more because they have not looked deeply
enough into what they already have.

Benedict J. Groeschel, C.F.R.

Think of yourself as a biographer who wants to write a life of Joseph of Nazareth. Having gleaned all you can from Scripture and from the findings of archaeologists and other modern researchers, you look around for other possible sources of information.

First-century historians, perhaps? But as you soon discover, their references to Jesus himself are few and meager. The Jewish historian Flavius Josephus, who was born around A.D. 37, makes just two remarks about Jesus in his twenty-volume *Jewish Antiquities*. The Roman writer Tacitus (about 56-118) alludes in passing to Jesus and his followers when describing the great fire of Rome under Nero. And here ends the list of undisputed, independent, non-Christian sources of information about Jesus in the first century!

For Joseph the list is even shorter: there are no entries at all.

At this point, Joseph's biographer might want to explore the historical value of some writings called the *apocrypha* (Greek for "secret, or hidden, things"). These are various early Christian writings, mostly from the second and third centuries, that expand on the Gospel presentation of Jesus, his family, the apostles, and even lesser characters like Pilate. Though some of these writings call themselves "Gospels" and claim a link with the apostles, they were eventually excluded from the Church's official canon, or list, of New Testament books considered inspired Scripture.

Is there any historical value to the apocrypha? A number of Church Fathers said yes, accepting at least some of the writings at face value. Others took a contrary position. "Delirious nonsense!" thundered St. Jerome, who judged the apocrypha lacking in common sense, historical accuracy, and scriptural foundation. Today some scholars assess the apocrypha in terms reminiscent of Jerome: "a field of rubble, largely produced by the pious or wild imaginations of certain second-century Christians." Others are cautiously open, finding them "not completely worthless for historical reconstruction."

But the apocryphal writings cannot be overlooked by anyone wishing to know St. Joseph, for he figures in a number of them. Even if they are of dubious historical merit, says Italian scholar Tarcisio Stramare, O.S.J., they were widely circulated and thus exerted "a profound influence on popular devotion, sacred preaching, the interpretations of the holy Fathers and Church writers, works of art, and also the liturgy."

Despite being rejected and sometimes officially condemned by Church authorities, some apocryphal books — especially those dealing with Jesus' birth and childhood — increased in popularity for centuries. Even now, works like the *Infancy Gospel of Thomas* continue to fascinate. Like today's best-selling biographies and magazines about the lives and lifestyles of the rich and famous, they appealed to people's curiosity. Unlike the modern muckraking approach, though, these early writings sprang out of a simple, somewhat gullible faith that tended to fill information gaps by inventing pious details. This made for a lively, popular, sometimes sensational style very different from the more reserved spirit of the Gospels.

Curiosity was not the only factor driving the production of apocryphal writings. Defending Christian truths against heretical attacks was another important concern. As Mary's virginity and Jesus' divinity came under fire, apocryphal writers explored Joseph's relation to each in ways that provided ammunition for counterattack.

The resulting picture of Joseph was not always faithful to him or even to the Gospel. For example, when it began to be rumored that Jesus was the illegitimate son of Mary and a Roman soldier, the apocryphal *Gospel of Philip* and the *Acts of Pilate* stressed that Joseph was Jesus' biological father. As we saw in chapter four, more mainstream apocryphal writers upheld Mary's virginity by aging Joseph dramatically (impotence is the between-the-lines message).

Since the apocryphal accounts have added significant touches to the common picture of St. Joseph, it is worth taking a look at a few of them.

Protoevangelium of James *(second century)*

Having endured discrimination and derision for their childlessness, the devout and wealthy Joachim and Anna beseech God to make them fruitful. Mary is the answer to their prayers. Coddled and cared for at home by her parents and a bevy of carefully selected babysitters, she is taken to Jerusalem when she turns three and is presented to the high priest at the Temple. There she lives for the next nine years, receiving her food from the hand of an angel.

Joseph comes on the scene when the high priest, Zechariah, summons all the local widowers to determine which one is to take care of Mary. Miraculously designated by a dove flying out from his staff, Joseph protests: "I already have sons and am old, but she is a girl. I fear lest I should become a laughing-stock to the children of Israel." He yields to Zechariah's entreaties, takes Mary to his house, and leaves for a long-term construction project while Mary stays home spinning thread for the veil of the Temple.

In spite of receiving not one but two angelic annunciations of Jesus' birth, one at the well and one inside the house, Mary seems to forget the divine origin of her pregnancy. Six months later, when Joseph returns and discovers her condition, she counters his anger and bitter tears with a simple "I do not know whence it has come to me."

Joseph's agonizing has a scriptural ring: "If I conceal her sin, I shall be found opposing the law of the Lord. If I expose her to the children of Israel, I fear lest that which is in her may have sprung from the angels and I should be found delivering up innocent blood to the judgment of death." Also familiar are Joseph's decision to divorce Mary quietly and his angelic dream. But fantasy steps in again when the high priest orders both Joseph and Mary to drink "the water of the conviction of the Lord" as a test of their innocence.

Acquitted of guilt, the couple and Joseph's two sons set off to obey the census requirement. Before they reach Bethlehem, Mary senses that she is ready to deliver. Joseph settles her in a cave in the care of his sons and leaves in search of a midwife. Something strange happens as he goes: "Now I, Joseph, was walking, and yet I did not walk. . . . And I looked up at the vault of heaven, and saw it standing still and the birds of the heaven motionless. . . ." It is the moment of Jesus' birth, and all creation has paused in solemn, silent recognition.

Enter the midwife, who returns to the cave with Joseph and emerges praising God that "a virgin has brought forth." Less trusting is her friend Salome, who refuses to believe "unless I put forward my finger and test her condition." Salome has no trouble believing once her hand drops off (it is, of course, restored in answer to her repentant pleas).

The *Protoevangelium of James* ends with the death of Zechariah, martyred by Herod's soldiers in the Temple sanctuary for refusing to divulge the whereabouts of his son, John the Baptist. Simeon, the elderly prophet who figures in Luke's account of Jesus' presentation, is chosen to replace him as high priest.

Reading through this sometimes hilarious weave of biblical allusions, legends, and oddities, one is inclined to St. Jerome's general opinion of the apocrypha. The Jewish customs described are wildly inaccurate (girls never lived in the Temple, for example). Some conflict with the Gospel accounts (Zechariah was not the high priest; he was part of the "section" of priests that was "on duty" at the time Luke describes: see 1:8-9).

But despite its flaws, says Joseph Fitzmyer, the *Protoevangelium of James* is unique among writings of its type. It "may contain some genuine historical details. Whether legendary or not, it is an important piece of ancient Christian literature, which shows us how second-century Christians recalled the family of Jesus, Mary, and Joseph."

Infancy Gospel of Thomas *(late second century)*

This short collection of stories, written to highlight Jesus' divinity, describes his exploits at ages five, six, eight, and twelve. There is the episode of the clay birds: as Jesus plays by a brook with a group of other children, he fashions twelve sparrows out of clay and brings them to life. He thereby violates the Sabbath — an offense for which Joseph rebukes him.

Some of the stories anticipate the healings Jesus will perform later in life. He raises children from the dead, heals a young man who has gashed his foot with an axe, and cures Joseph's son James of a poisonous snakebite. In other stories Jesus uses his supernatural powers for everyday activities like sowing wheat and carrying water from the well. When Joseph's rustic carpentry skills (he usually makes "ploughs and yokes") cause him to botch a bed-making job, Jesus saves the day by stretching a too-short board to the right length. "Happy am I that God has give me this child," exclaims the inept carpenter.

But gratitude is not the predominant reaction to Jesus in the *Infancy Gospel of Thomas.* And for good reason. The scholar who describes its portrayal of Jesus as that of a "self-willed little brat" and "sinister superboy" who belongs "more in a horror movie than a gospel" is not overstating things! In an excess of desire to stress the supernatural powers of Jesus, notes another scholar, the author of *Thomas* has depicted him as "no better than a god of Greek mythology in a bad mood."

"Meek and humble of heart" this Jesus is not. In the class-room he is sassy and arrogant, calling his teachers hypocrites and showing them up with obscure sayings about the letters of the al-phabet. Some are driven to violence and hit Jesus. One calls him a "wicked boy" and wants to know when Joseph is going to take steps so that his son "may learn to be fond of children of his years and may honor old age."

Neither is Jesus' out-of-classroom behavior a report to make a parent proud. "You insolent, godless dunderhead!" he calls a boy who has broken up his pool and dam dirt-works. And the child withers up like the Gospel fig tree. Another boy is made to drop dead because Jesus is "exasperated" at having been bumped into accidentally. "Teach him to bless and not to curse," the villagers plead with Joseph. "For he is slaying our children."

One side effect of this emphasis on Jesus' super-powers is to make Joseph look ridiculous. Repeatedly confronted by adults who are incensed at little Jesus' abusive behavior, Joseph is upset but powerless. His feeble attempts to scold and discipline Jesus — by pulling his ear, for example — only anger the child and provoke an insolent, "Do not vex me." Containment seems to be the best that Joseph can do: "Do not let him go outside the door," he tells Mary, "for all those who provoke him die."

In this uproarious story, Joseph is just another Homer Simpson, an ineffectual father of an uncontrollable child.

History of Joseph the Carpenter *(fourth-fifth century)*

Composed in Egypt and possibly written to be read in the lit-urgy in Coptic monasteries, this work may be the oldest indirect witness to a feast in honor of St. Joseph. The entire account is presented as a discourse given by Jesus to the apostles on the Mount of Olives.

The first eleven chapters tell us about Joseph's life and draw heavily from earlier apocryphal writings while adding their own de-tails. We learn that Joseph was a carpenter from Bethlehem, that he married at forty, had two daughters and four sons, and was widowed at eighty-nine before being chosen by lot to be Mary's guard-ian. We learn, too, that after a year in Egypt, the family settled in Nazareth. Two sons married, two other sons plus Jesus stayed on in the family home, and Joseph plied his trade untouched by ill health, dimming eyesight, and even dental problems until his death at age one hundred eleven. The last twenty-one chapters recount the death of "the blessed old carpenter," which takes place when Jesus turns eighteen.

While there is much to admire here (unlike the *Infancy Gospel of Thomas*, this father-son relationship is marked by mutual love and honor), the ensemble makes for a paradoxical portrayal of the saint who is to become patron of a happy death. Though attended by Jesus and Mary, the dying Joseph is hardly at peace. He is made to speak and act "like a querulous, despairing sinner, who constantly bemoans his misfortunes," says Francis Filas. His passing is drawn-out ("tedious," Father Filas specifies) and marked by many an odd detail.

Even so, the *History of Joseph the Carpenter* includes some fine moments. Joseph's prayer to "Jesus, the deliverer of my soul" is moving, as is the picture of Jesus weeping at Joseph's bedside and preparing his body for burial. At the end, wrapped in shining cloth, Joseph's soul is carried away by angels to the abode of the pious.

Arabic Infancy Gospel *(sixth century?)*

Two of this "gospel's" three main parts take up subjects treated in the other apocryphal writings mentioned so far: Jesus' birth and his childhood wonder-workings. Again, a "superboy" presentation prevails, though in this account, Jesus is less vindictive than in the *Infancy Gospel of Thomas:* he does not kill his playmates, but changes them into goats! In the Temple he is the ultimate quiz kid who wows the teachers with his detailed knowledge of astronomy, medicine, and other sciences. In the workshop he is indispensable, not only repairing Joseph's mistakes but miraculously producing whatever is needed.

But the *Arabic Infancy Gospel* is probably best known for its fantastic stories about the Holy Family's stay in Egypt. It describes their encounter with robbers, one of whom will become the "good thief" crucified near Jesus, and with idols that turn to sand-hills as they pass. Jesus' bathwater heals lepers; the rinse water from his laundry creates a gushing spring and sweet-smelling balsam trees. This is not so much the flight into Egypt as a fantastic voyage into the Arabian Nights.

Gospel of Pseudo-Matthew *(eighth century?)*

This is the brainchild of an anonymous, enterprising editor who combined existing apocryphal writings with original additions to produce a "new improved version" of Jesus' first years. Early chapters amplify the *Protoevangelium of James*; later chapters embellish the exaggerations of the *Infancy Gospel of Thomas*.

Throughout, observes Francis Filas, *Pseudo-Matthew*'s treatment of St. Joseph "can hardly be called reverent." As in *Joseph the Carpenter*, he is not just old but ancient — a grandfather with grandchildren older than Mary. More seriously, in Father Filas's view, the sensationalistic miracles reduce Joseph and Mary to "characters in a conjurer's act," with Jesus playing magician.

Many of these conjurings take place during the journey into Egypt. Threatening dragons bend the knee and retreat at a mere look from baby Jesus. Lions and leopards mingle peacefully with the family's beasts of burden, wagging their tails and worshiping as they go. A palm tree bends to yield its fruit and is rewarded by having one of its branches carried to heaven by an angel. A thirty-day trip is miraculously compressed into one. The family enters an Egyptian temple, and three hundred sixty-five idols fall and shatter.

Despite (or perhaps because of) its flaws, *Pseudo-Matthew* became sensationally popular and exercised extraordinary influence on popular devotion, art, and literature. We feel its impact even today — whenever we admire paintings of Joseph and Mary's engagement by masters like Fra Angelico, Raphael, Rubens, and El Greco; whenever we read mystical writers like St. Bridget of Sweden and Venerable Mary of Agreda; whenever we sing Christmas carols about cherry trees bowing to give Mary their fruit. . . .

Gospel of the Nativity of Mary *(ninth century)*

St. Joseph is elderly but not widowed in this pruned remake of *Pseudo-Matthew*. And just to make his miraculous selection as Mary's husband perfectly clear, his staff bursts into bloom, and the Holy Spirit in the form of a dove descends from heaven and perches on it. In later ages this generic flower will become St. Joseph's trademark lily, symbol of his purity.

Apocryphal literature makes for intriguing, entertaining, sometimes inspiring reading. As historically accurate information about St. Joseph, though, it contains too many legendary and fantastical elements to inspire confidence.

The would-be biographer of St. Joseph who is searching for facts might move on from the apocrypha to the Church Fathers, the representative teachers of the early Church. But the Fathers did not give out much information about St. Joseph either. Justin, who was born in Palestine around the year 100, spoke of Joseph as a maker of plows and yokes. A few later Fathers seem to have pictured him as a blacksmith. He appears in patristic commentaries on scriptural episodes like the annunciation, the flight to Egypt, and the finding of Jesus in the Temple; he figures in explanations of questions surrounding Jesus' two genealogies and Mary's virginity.

Overall, however, the Fathers spoke relatively little about St. Joseph. Perhaps they thought it would be confusing and unwise to draw attention to the supposed father of Someone whose real Father was God. The rise of the great heresies, beginning in the fourth century, would have reinforced this view and focused their energies on defending Christian basics like the divinity of Christ.

Is that all there is, then? With Scripture, the apocrypha, the Fathers, and other early writers so sparing of historical detail, are there no other possible sources of factual information on St. Joseph's life? "Well, of course," some people would respond. "There are private revelations."

Private revelations are spiritual communications to an individual that apparently come from God or a heavenly messenger. Even when declared worthy of belief, though, private revelations never have the authority of *public* revelation, which must be accepted as God's complete and perfect Word as revealed in Scripture and in Jesus himself. They are not meant to improve on or complete Christ's definitive revelation, but only to serve as helps in living it out (see the *Catechism of the Catholic Church*, No. 67). No Catholic is under any obligation to accept even the best-attested private revelations — not even Mary's apparitions to St. Bernadette at Lourdes.

The question of private revelations as a source of factual information about St. Joseph arises from mystical writings that read like historical accounts of biblical scenes and events. St. Bridget of Sweden (1303-1373) dictated nine books of *Revelations* whose direct references to St. Joseph, though few, gain in impact by appearing as Mary's own statements. We learn that he was socially retiring, "dead to the world and to the flesh," and "very patient in poverty, careful in work, very meek toward scoffers, very docile in my service, my very diligent defender against those who wished to minimize my virginity. . . ."

Benedict XIV formally declared Bridget's writings to be free of anything contrary to faith and morals, but this pronouncement does not cover lesser factual errors. Of these there are many, since Bridget's portrait of Joseph was influenced by the apocrypha and legends of her day.

Venerable Mary of Agreda (1602-1665) included several portrayals of St. Joseph in her monumental biography of the Blessed Virgin, *The Mystical City of God.* One chapter, for example, reproduces Joseph's speech of contrition to Mary for his earlier decision to divorce her quietly. Another offers details about his "happy death" — nine days' bedside care by Jesus or Mary, with angels supplying music three times daily and heavenly fragrances filling the house. A twenty-four-hour ecstasy signals Joseph's imminent death: he is commissioned as Christ's messenger of coming release to the souls in limbo. Mary prepares Joseph's body for burial, which she can do with "utmost propriety" since "a wonderful light" envelops all but his face.

Never formally approved nor banned by the Church, the *Mystical City of God* sparked heated discussions, especially in view of Mary of Agreda's conviction that its every word was divinely inspired. Current assessments run the gamut from calling it a work of "high ascetical and mystical value" to "an early example of what we nowadays call automatism," in which the subconscious mind produces writings beyond an author's normal range of knowledge and ideas. Most scholars do seem to agree on at least two points: Maria of Agreda's high degree of virtue and her historically inexact rendering of New Testament events.

Another saintly nun, Maria Cecilia Baij (1694-1766), is responsible for what may be the only mystical *Life of Saint Joseph,* which was written at her confessor's request and left unpublished till 1921. Christ himself speaking within her dictated the book, she said. Even so, she never insisted on its inerrancy but humbly worried that she might have unwittingly included some "things from my head."

With all due respect to Mother Baij's piety, this seems likely.

The *Life* begins with Rachel and Jacob, a devout and childless couple whose prayer for a child is answered after a pilgrimage to the Temple. Miraculous signs follow: three bright stars indicate that Joseph is to establish "the terrestrial trinity"; angelic dreams full of "mysterious and secret facts" alert mother and father to their child's dignity. Silent and contemplative after birth, Joseph shrinks from caresses — an early indicator of his will "to preserve undiminished . . . the luster of his purity and innocence." For the same reason, having his diapers changed is embarrassing and disagreeable to him. Eight days after birth, Joseph receives the use of reason. In no time his parents are seeking his advice on all important matters.

The *Life of Joseph* carries on in this vein, embroidering on familiar episodes and creating others, until his death at age sixty-one. Says one scholar of this and Cecilia Baij's other mystical writings: it seems best to view these pious works as "meditations of a holy soul," but not as sources of reliable information.

Other mystics might be mentioned. Joseph figures occasionally in the writings of Anne Catherine Emmerich, for example. (See the source notes for a comment on Maria Valtorta's *Poem of the Man-God,* in which Joseph also appears.) But suffice it to say that no mystical writing comes with a guarantee of historical accuracy.

In fact, the "biographical" revelations contain bizarre particulars, are often demonstrably inaccurate, and contradict one another on many points. Father Herbert Thurston, who studied them extensively, concluded that it would be "impossible to name a single incident in the life of Jesus Christ or His Blessed Mother which is narrated by recipients of these revelations without manifold disagreement in matters of primary import." His inescapable conclusion: "It seems impossible to treat the visions of Anne Catherine — or, indeed, any other similar visions — as sources which can contribute reliably to our knowledge of past history."

How can saints be mistaken? Augustin Poulain, S.J., author of the landmark study *The Graces of Interior Prayer,* explains how distortions can affect even genuine revelations as they are received, interpreted, and then transmitted. Properly understood, authentic mystical "biographies" can certainly serve as aids to devotion. But, warns Father Poulain, "it is imprudent to seek to remake history by the help of the saints' revelations."

And *that* is all there is! Annoying though it may be to emerge from our search without a biography of St. Joseph, we must learn to rest content with less than our "inquiring minds" demand.

Of course, we can always react against this reality. We can become what Benedict Groeschel calls "revelation addicts," feeding our curiosity by running from one revelation or apparition to another. Or we might join another flock of "sitting ducks . . . for the possibility of deception" — for example, those who seize on the latest pseudo-historical theory about the *real* Jesus (or, in our case, the real Joseph). These are the people who send to the top of the best-seller charts dubious, "historically based" reconstructions of Jesus' life that are just as fantastical as the apocrypha, and far less reverent.

Balance is the key, as Father Groeschel points out. Openness to new ideas and private revelations can be good, but only if it is joined to healthy skepticism and does not displace Scripture and the Church's teaching as our main focus. What really satisfies spiritual hunger, says Father Groeschel, is not the "extraordinary signs" of visions and revelations, but the "reverent attentiveness" born of prayer and meditation that leads to a sense of God's presence in the ordinary experiences of life.

Likewise, as we ponder the essential core of information that Scripture gives us about St. Joseph, we can also expect to discover *his* presence in the ordinary. Perhaps we will even discover an advantage to knowing only the broad outlines of his life as spouse, parent, worker, and faithful servant of God.

Sometimes, the more details we know about particular saints, the harder it is to identify with them and to relate our experience to theirs. Few such obstacles hinder our relationship with St. Joseph! This simplicity contributes to making him the ideal patron and example for the universal Church. Joseph is, as John Paul II points out, the saint who "transcends all individual states of life and serves as a model for the entire Christian community, whatever the condition and duties of each of its members may be" (*Guardian of the Redeemer*, No. 30).

As we discover this affinity through prayerful reflection on what we *do* know about St. Joseph, our petulant "Is that all there is?" can become an exclamation of wonder, "How much there is!"

But Does He Put in Appearances?

Anyone who seeks to glean information about St. Joseph from his purported apparitions will have a hard time of it, for there do not seem to be many. Two of them are Marian apparitions, with St. Joseph playing his typical supporting role. On August 21, 1879, eighteen people in the village of *Knock, Ireland,* reported that they had seen three heavenly figures clothed in dazzling garments and apparently absorbed in silent prayer: in the center was Mary, with St. Joseph on her right and St. John the Evangelist on her left. In *Fátima, Portugal,* on October 13, 1917, St. Joseph reportedly appeared in a sort of heavenly tableau of the Holy Family. Lucy, one of the three children who saw him, wrote: "We beheld St. Joseph with the Child

117

Jesus and Our Lady robed in white with a blue mantle, beside the sun. St. Joseph and the Child Jesus appeared to bless the world, for they traced the Sign of the Cross with their hands. . . ." Invisible to the seventy thousand other spectators who were present, this scene was followed by the very visible "miracle of the sun," in which the sun whirled and plunged wildly toward the earth, throwing the crowd into a panic.

At least one European shrine preserves the memory of an apparition of St. Joseph alone, on June 7, 1660. It is near the Benedictine Priory of St. Joseph of the Fountain, in the foothills of the Alps in Provence, in southern France. Here, it is said, a shepherd named Gaspard Ricard cried out to St. Joseph for help as he lay dying of thirst. Joseph appeared to him and directed him to move a stone. Under it, the peasant found the spring that saved his life and that is still pointed out to pilgrims today.

Unmarked by shrines but enshrined in the writings of St. Teresa of Ávila are a number of her personal encounters with St. Joseph. One day, for example, as she was reflecting on her sinfulness, Teresa said she was suddenly caught up in a great "rapture" and seemed to see herself being clothed "in a white robe of shining brightness. . . . I saw our Lady at my right side and my father St. Joseph at the left, for they were putting that robe on me. I was given to understand that I was now cleansed of my sins. . . ." More typically, St. Joseph's appearances to Teresa served to guide her in practical ways.

> Once when in need, for I didn't know what to do or how to pay some workmen, St. Joseph, my true father and lord, appeared to me and revealed to me that I would not be lacking, that I should hire them. And so I did, without so much as a penny, and the Lord in ways that amazed those who heard about it provided for me.
>
> (Teresa's statements are from Jerónimo Gracián, as quoted in Joseph F. Chorpenning, *Just Man, Husband of Mary, Guardian of Christ*, Saint Joseph's University Press, 1993, pp. 243-244)

Part Three

A Friend in High Places

Joseph lives. He may seem
far away from us, but he is not.

Karl Rahner

Chapter 7

Communing with Saints

It makes a big difference
whether we think someone is dead or alive.
Luke Timothy Johnson

When one of Cheryl Scheidel's teenage sons totaled her ten-year-old van, she immediately sought help from a close friend. "St. Joseph, you know I have no way to replace this vehicle. Please provide for us." Three weeks later, a parishioner gave her a 1996 Honda Civic with only seventeen thousand miles on it. Cheryl was delighted, but not especially surprised.

"I've been turning to St. Joseph ever since I was widowed at forty-three, with eight of nine children still at home," she explains. Led into deeper prayer though her grief, Cheryl drew closer to Our Lady, and through her to St. Joseph. "As a single parent of teenage sons who needed to interact with a dad but didn't have one, I asked St. Joseph to guide and protect my family and to be a father to all the children. He has, and I have come to love him so much. As I have meditated on his life, I have been very moved by his enormous devotion to Our Lady and Jesus. I wish to love them as he does, to the best of my ability."

Visitors to Cheryl's Pennsylvania home will find evidence of her friendship with St. Joseph in the barn just behind the house. There, in a corner set aside for prayer, stands a large statue of the saint. "I got it from a warehouse of artifacts scavenged from churches that have been torn down or renovated," Cheryl explains. "It seemed right to give St. Joseph this visible place of honor as a way of representing his fatherly love and mission over my farm and family."

Why would a hard-pressed widow seek a dead man's help for her practical needs? How can a third-millennium American insist that she has a special friendship with Joseph, an "ordinary Nazorean" of first-century Palestine? Does Cheryl have strange paranormal abilities? Has she learned to combine an out-of-body experience with time-travel? Is she conjuring up the dead?

The Catholic Church has a simple explanation of experiences like Cheryl's, which have nothing to do with occultism, necromancy, or New Age weirdness, but everything to do with holiness and fullness of life. It is the vision of the Church as the Body of Christ — "a living body in which all the members are in communion with one another," explains theologian Edward O'Connor; "an organic body in which the members collaborate with one another for the good of all."

Some members of this Body — those in heaven and those who are being purified in purgatory — are no longer on earth. Yet through Christ, the head of the Body, they remain in living communion with us. Dead to the world, they are alive in Christ — and, in the case of the saints, more vibrantly alive than any earthling we will ever encounter this side of eternity. Their aliveness comes from union with the very source of life, as Father O'Connor points out: "Membership in Christ's Body attains its perfection when a person is joined with the head in glory."

And so, alive in the risen Christ and sharing in his life, Joseph lives! This first-century Palestinian who once experienced the creaturely boundaries of space and time is no longer limited by them. In Jesus and through the Holy Spirit, Joseph can become present to us, reaching out over the centuries, over the great divide of death itself. Like Jesus, Joseph is someone we can get to know personally — not just a historical figure we can only know something about, like Cleopatra or Benjamin Franklin or Elvis.

Admittedly, it can be difficult to find the simple carpenter of the Gospels in the exalted figure we now honor as St. Joseph. Sometimes devotional excesses or distortions are to blame. But perhaps another reason why it may be hard to connect the Joseph of Scripture with St. Joseph, glorious protector of the Church, is that people who have been raised to heavenly life in Christ look somewhat different from what they were on earth. They are both like and unlike their "pre-glory" selves.

"Look at my hands and my feet; see that it is I myself," Jesus has to reassure the uncertain disciples when he appears to them after his resurrection (Luke 24:39). Same uneasiness in John's Gospel. As Jesus cooks a lakeside fish breakfast, "none of the disciples dared to ask him, 'Who are you?' because they knew it was the Lord" (21:12).

Just as it took time for the disciples to grasp Jesus' identity, it can take time to grasp Joseph's. But as we move toward a fuller picture of his role in the Body of Christ, we will find it in perfect continuity with what Scripture says of him. The Joseph we honor as patron of the Church really is the same person who, as the carpenter of Nazareth, modeled obedient faith in facing challenges we can relate to — whom to marry, where to live, how to know God's will, how to earn a living, how to raise a child.

We speak of St. Joseph as patron of the universal Church, as well as patron of many other areas of life. Many of these we will explore, beginning with the next chapter. But we will benefit most from our look at "St. Joseph, patron," if we bring to it some background understanding of devotion to the saints in general: how it arose, what it is, what it is not.

What associations does the word "patron" conjure up for you? I think of scenes from the movie *The Godfather* and feel distaste for a social system where advancement is based not on personal efforts but on cultivating the good graces of a powerful, ruthless protector. But what if the protector promoted peace and the common good, not violence? And what if our highly individualistic, "pull yourself up by your bootstraps" American ideal is somewhat warped?

In the ancient Mediterranean world, where devotion to the saints developed, the patron-client system was an established and valued institution. In these ancient societies "there was not the faintest trace of human equality, whether before the law or even in some ideal equality of all males," says social scientist Bruce Malina. "The 'better' families exerted power . . . in harsh and impersonal fashion" and "without a thought to the losses of those with whom they interacted." Having a protector in this dog-eat-dog environment often made a life-and-death difference.

Though not a relationship of equals, this was a mutually satisfying arrangement. Clients had their practical needs met; patrons received honor and social approval for the good works that were expected of them. Each party had obligations. The client offered a tribute of respect, deference, and obedience, explains Father Roland Gauthier. The client was to be at the service of his patron, siding with him at all times and in all circumstances. The patron, for his part, was to view himself as his client's "official protector, in the widest sense of the word," supplying advice, influence, financial backing, protection, and even material necessities. Overall, says Father Gauthier, the patron was "to act in such a way that his protégé might in turn become a man of influence — another patron, if possible."

While we would find it demeaning to rely on someone to this extent, no one in an ancient Mediterranean society would have thought to fault it. For one thing, everyone had patrons, even the powerful (Herod, the villain of Matthew 2, was a client-king of the Roman emperor Caesar Augustus). For another, patrons and clients related to one another as family, not as transactors of coldly functional business deals — and this despite often enormous differences in status and power.

The very word "patron" points to this family feeling, deriving as it does from the Greek and Latin word for father, *pater.* It also indicated the way in which patron and clients were to relate: the former as a devoted parent, the latter as grateful and loving children.

Those who first heard Jesus call God "Father" would naturally have interpreted this in terms of the patron-client relationship they knew so well. "In the Bible, anytime anyone is called a 'father' who is not a biological father, the title refers to the role and status of a patron," explains Bruce Malina. "God is called 'father' relative to Israel as a whole (Deuteronomy 32:6) and to the Davidic king (2 Samuel 7:14)," he points out. But before Jesus, "Father" was not commonly used by individuals speaking to God of themselves and their personal concerns. The "Our Father" was thus an eye-opener, revealing God as the tender Patron par excellence, and Jesus as his representative. Malina elaborates:

> The "kingdom of heaven" proclaimed by Jesus was God's patronage and the clientele bound up in it. . . . To "enter the kingdom of heaven" meant to enjoy the patronage of God, the heavenly Patron, hence, to become a client. . . . And the introductory phrase "the kingdom of heaven is like" would come out as "the way God's patronage relates and affects his clients is like the following scenario. . . ."
>
> By taking up the task of proclaiming the kingdom (Matthew 4:17; Mark 1:15), Jesus presents himself as a broker or middleman of God's patronage. To this end he seeks other brokers to assist him in the task and outfits them with similar authorization (Matthew 10:1-16; Mark 3:13-19; Luke 6:12-16).

Patron, broker, middleman — this is not the vocabulary of close relationships in our world. Keep in mind, though, that in ancient Mediterranean societies these relationships came flavored with a strong dose of TLC.

You probably won't find the words "broker" or "middleman" in your New Testament, by the way. You probably *will* find "mediator," which describes the same role: someone who provides access to a powerful figure, a patron. St. Paul uses it in this way in speaking of Jesus, the "one mediator between God and humankind" (1 Timothy 2:5) — but one who gives other "brokers" a share in his mediating function. The disciples sent out by Jesus during his earthly ministry are the most obvious examples; the saints in heaven, whose prayers for us rise like incense before God's throne (see Revelation 8:3-4), are the most illustrious.

As we think about the saints and about the social world in which people first began to honor them, we notice that this devotion in some ways resembles the patron-client system of the times. We also observe marked differences. Reflecting on these similarities and dissimilarities can illumine our understanding of the saints in general and of St. Joseph in particular.

One immediately obvious difference is that the saints exercise their patronage unhindered by death's divide, as we saw earlier. Those of us who learned early about the communion of saints may be inclined to take this reality for granted, forgetting what revolutionary good news it proclaims. Before the coming of Christ, men and women idealized and even worshiped their deceased heroes, but without ever expecting that the dead could bring them closer to God. For otherworldly protection or favors, they might turn to a spirit, a guardian angel, or a higher, nonhuman self — never to a fellow human being.

All of this changed with the rise of devotion to the martyrs, beginning in the third century. Unanimously, the writers of the early Church insisted that "the martyrs, precisely because they had died as human beings, enjoyed close intimacy with God," observes historian Peter Brown. They were special "friends of God," and as such, especially able "to intercede for and, so, to protect their fellow mortals." Over time this understanding grew to include all saints.

Other obvious differences between the patrons of this world and those of the next have to do with the limitations and abuses that accompany any man-made system. Earthly patrons can become the stereotypical "godfathers" — grasping, corrupt, competitive, and cruel to anyone outside the in-group. At best their help is imperfect. Heavenly patrons, on the other hand, offer perfect love and care because they share in Christ's virtues and riches. They love with his love, guide with his wisdom, and dispense generously from his storehouse of gifts.

The patrons of this world seek first their own glory and power

— a priority that pits families and interest groups one against another. St. Bernadette described the opposite reality when she said, "In heaven, no one is jealous." (It was her response to a nun who had expressed surprise that Bernadette would kneel before St. Joseph's statue, but address her prayer to Mary.) Saints do not jockey for rank or position. They seek first the greater glory of the one Patron they all serve, and they direct others to do the same.

It is easy to find similarities between the earthly and the heavenly patronage systems. We notice the warmth and loyalty that characterize these freely chosen relationships, the sense of family that links client and patron. Thinking of the earthly patron as a fatherly guide and protector evokes not only "the Father, from whom every family in heaven and on earth takes its name" (Ephesians 3:14-15), but also St. Joseph, who was called by God to play a fatherly role in salvation history.

Another point of resemblance has to do with how the clients of the ancient Mediterranean world were to relate to their patrons. They were expected to approach them with requests, imitate them, and show concern for their reputation by offering public praise — "in sum, by continually adding to the name and honor of their patrons," notes Bruce Malina. On a different level, these are the very elements that are to characterize our relationship with St. Joseph and other heavenly patrons. "Veneration of the saints comprises three factors," says Father Edward O'Connor: "(1) honoring them for the life they have led; (2) taking them as models for our own life; and (3) asking them to intercede with God on our behalf."

How should St. Joseph's "clients" understand and live out these three components of devotion? What should they avoid?

HONOR • "Why honor anyone but God?" people sometimes ask. To which one might respond, "We honor athletes, astronauts, war veterans, relatives, political figures, rock stars, media personalities, cartoon characters, and even pets. Why not saints?" But, of course, the honor accorded to such figures comes in the form of parties and tickertape parades and calendar events like Secretaries' Day. Normally, it is not like the *religious* honor we offer to the saints.

One reason to honor saints, says Father O'Connor, is that God does. "Whoever serves me, the Father will honor," Jesus told the disciples (John 12:26). It makes sense to follow God's example! By doing so, we express our agreement with God's priorities for human beings and expose ourselves to the influence of specific individuals whose lives can call us on to holiness.

Three important clarifications. First, while it is religious in nature, the honor extended to a saint is not the same as the honor extended to God. We venerate the former, but adore and worship the latter. (Theologians keep this distinction clear by using two different technical terms derived from the Greek: *dulia* — honor or veneration — for saints; *latria* — adoration or worship — for God.) To worship the saints as we do God would be idolatry, an offense against the first commandment. But since it is *God's* work that we praise in the saints, honor given to them is directed to him.

Second, on the level of private devotion, honoring particular saints falls into the category of devotion, not doctrine. It is not part of the bedrock foundation of our faith, like the Creed. Certainly, we believe that those who were faithful to Christ in this life now live in glory with him in the next. But we are not therefore obliged to cultivate a special devotion to each one. Nor could we!

"We cannot, indeed, be devout without faith," remarked Cardinal John Henry Newman, "but we may believe without feeling devotion." Cardinal Newman spoke appreciatively of the wide array of devotions in the Church as providing "diversified modes of honoring God." As a convert, he said, he was struck by the fact that "the faith is everywhere one and the same," but that in matters of devotion, "a large liberty is accorded to private judgment and inclination." However, he insisted that devotion must be rooted in doctrine in order to remain healthy.

This is clarification three: devotion goes wrong when it fixates on a saint to the point of diminishing or displacing God. It goes wrong when it makes excessive claims for the saint of choice. In St. Joseph's case, says Father Francis Filas, exaggerations of this sort have included the following assertions: "that Joseph was immaculately conceived precisely like Mary; that he was the physical father of Jesus by a miraculous transfer of his sperm to Mary; that he had full miraculous knowledge of all things; that he had various miraculous visions and revelations of future and distant events in the life of Christ; or the presumption that he received all of the sacraments by anticipation."

A common distortion of doctrine assumes that St. Joseph, Mary, or other saints are somehow more merciful than any Person of the Trinity. Though in reality the saints have no mercy of their own but only a share in Christ's, they are pictured as working hard day and night to stay God's arm and assuage his wrath. In this view, God is like a volatile and irascible potentate who must be approached and handled very carefully — the "God of Holy Terror" that Phyllis McGinley describes in one of her poems.

Cardinal Newman reacted strongly against such distortions of devotion. "They seem to me like a bad dream. . . . They do but scare and confuse me." So did the Second Vatican Council. Speaking of honoring Mary, and by extension all the saints, the council warned against both "false exaggerations" and "narrowness of mind" in devotions. It urged theologians and preachers to "rightly illustrate" Mary's role and privileges as always looking to Christ, "the source of all truth, sanctity, and devotion." It directed all to "carefully refrain from whatever might by word or deed lead the separated brethren or any others whatsoever into error regarding the true doctrine of the Church" ("Dogmatic Constitution on the Church," *Lumen Gentium*, No. 67).

If we truly wish to honor St. Joseph, we must take these directives to heart.

INTERCESSION • "I pray not only for these [Jesus' first disciples], but also for those who through their teaching will come to believe in me" (John 17:20 — *New Jerusalem Bible*). "Pray for me to the Lord" (Acts 8:24). "Brothers and sisters, pray for us, so that the word of the Lord may spread" (2 Thessalonians 3:1). "I urge that supplications, prayers, intercessions, and thanksgivings be made for everyone" (1 Timothy 2:1). "Pray for one another, so that you may be healed" (James 5:16).

If you read it with an eye to intercessory prayer, the New Testament gives the impression of a vast prayer chain. And if you believe in the communion of saints, you understand that the chain's mightiest intercessors are in heaven, in the closest possible union with our great high priest. This is Jesus, whose perfect sacrifice enables him "for all time to save those who approach God through him, since he always lives to make intercession for them" (Hebrews 7:25).

Tombstone inscriptions from the first centuries after Christ offer evidence that Christians began early to pray for and to the dead. They brought their needs especially to the graves of the martyrs, because of their special closeness to God. Today we bring our needs to all the saints, who "do not cease to intercede with the Father for us" — through, with, and in the one mediator, Christ Jesus ("Dogmatic Constitution on the Church," No. 49).

Does God need the saints to inform him of our concerns? No more than he needs for my friends Cindy or Bert to let him in on the prayer request I phoned them with yesterday! Neither does the effectiveness of my prayer depend on some complicated routing system to God. I can and do address my requests to my Father, who knows what I need before I ask him (see Matthew 6:8-13). And I can and do address my requests to other Christians, whether dead or alive, because we are all members of Christ's Body and therefore called to assist one another.

Like technological advances that are directed to selfish ends, prayer to the saints can be put to wrongful use. The more we use it to seek our own way, the more superstitious it becomes. Since very few of us are characterized by the selflessness of Jesus' prayer in Gethsemane — "not my will but yours be done" (Luke 22:42) — we must be ever on guard against becoming what Father Benedict Groeschel calls "magical Christians."

"Magical Christians" approach the saints' intercession as a way of twisting God's arm, of getting control and spiritual power. "They have no thought of accepting God's will or trusting him," says Father Groeschel. "They know exactly what they want, and they are going to get it one way or another."

Distinguishing between superstition and devotion — or, to use spiritual writer Evelyn Underhill's terms, magic and mysticism — is tricky business. The two attitudes "often confuse the inquirer by using the same language, instruments, and method." But beneath the apparent similarities lies a fundamental difference, she stresses: "magic wants to get, mysticism wants to give."

Father Groeschel offers a pertinent example of outwardly identical religious behavior that, depending on a person's interior disposition, might be either "an informed devotion of piety and faith" or "simply magic."

> When affluent people who never attend church, pray, or question the moral propriety of their behavior bury statues of Saint Joseph in the garden of their expensive suburban homes in hope of selling them faster or for a better price, we are dangerously approaching magic. When the Missionaries of Charity put a medal of Saint Joseph near a building they hope to get to care for the poor, and back this act of devotion up with piety and perfect abandonment to God's will, it is not magic but an expression of devotion.

Every year an estimated two million cheap statues of St. Joseph are bought and buried to speed real estate sales. Many of the statues come in a "helpful kit" that includes instructions, a prayer, and sometimes even a waterproof "protective burial bag." There is much debate over the most foolproof burial techniques: upside-down or rightside-up and facing the house? near the "for sale" sign or in the backyard? In the end, St. Joseph goes underground, his statue interred by a wide variety of theists and atheists who simply hope "it will work."

This is magic, not devotion.

Jeanne Jugan, the saintly foundress of the Little Sisters of the Poor, put a statue of St. Joseph in her basket whenever she went out on her begging rounds. Blessed Brother André, the boarding-school porter whose simple faith God used to work many miraculous healings, prayed with people using St. Joseph's medals and oil. Dorothy Day, co-founder of the Catholic Worker Movement, liked to burn a candle before the altar of St. Joseph as she brought her needs before this "good friend."

This is not magic, but devotion.

An emphasis on technique is one reliable warning sign that our prayer to the saints is tending toward superstition. *Bury the statue just so. . . . Say this prayer to St. Joseph for nine mornings (afternoons won't work, and no other prayer will do). . . . Wear this medal at all times and you will get to heaven. . . .* This mentality bypasses the call to ongoing conversion of heart and stresses accurate performance — faith in the method, not the Maker. This is magic. As the *Catechism of the Catholic Church* explains, anyone who attributes the efficacy of prayers and sacramental signs to the way in which they are performed, independently of interior attitudes, is falling into superstition (see No. 2111).

Another indicator of magic masquerading as devotion is an emphasis on the effectiveness of certain prayers, as revealed in expressions like "results guaranteed" and "one hundred percent effective." One widely circulated prayer to St. Joseph is advertised as "never been known to fail," Francis Filas reports in his book *St. Joseph after Vatican II.* Another warns that a particular novena to St. Joseph is so powerful that "one is advised to be sure that he really wants what he asks for" before making it. (The point is illustrated by a sober moral tale.) And as "probably the ultimate in superstitious novena prayers," Father Filas proposes a final example: "The Sure-Shot Novena — If All Other Prayers

Have Failed, Say This One, and You Will Get What You Want!"

Our prayer of intercession will be healthy if we keep firmly in mind that "never been known to fail" applies only to God — not to techniques and not even to the saints themselves, who owe to God whatever merits they have.

IMITATION • Scripture urges us often to imitate those who are strong in faith (see, for example, 1 Corinthians 11:1; 1 Thessalonians 2:14; Hebrews 6:12 and 13:7). One gripping passage in the letter to the Hebrews proposes for our imitation those who died in faith: they surround us as a "cloud of witnesses," inspiring us to "run with perseverance the race that is set before us, looking to Jesus the pioneer and perfector of our faith" (12:1-2). These witnesses, the saints, form a great multitude of heavenly hosts who cheer us on as we move toward the finish line of earthly life.

The wonderful thing about a multitude is that it provides an almost limitless pool of resources. In this throng you can always find just the right role model for your own temperament, calling, and season of life. It's a bit like walking alone into a huge party and being drawn to some congenial person with whom you discover a deep and special affinity. To find a saint-friend like that is to step into a heavenly Big Brother or Big Sister program — or even, as many have said about friendship with Joseph, to find another father.

Distinguished by his fatherly welcome, St. Joseph also stands out as one of the imitable and adaptable saints at this heavenly party. He fits into every group; he demonstrates faithful obedience that can be imitated in a wide variety of situations.

Joseph is so adaptable, in fact, that he has been called "a man of contradictions." He is a model for parents and spouses, but also for single men and women who seek to live celibate lives, whether as laypeople or as consecrated religious; for workers and business people, but also for contemplatives; for travelers and pilgrims, but also for stay-at-homes. Missionaries and teachers, refugees, the poor, the sick, the dying, the persecuted, the perplexed — Joseph's example speaks to all these situations and more. Recalling St. Joseph's discretion, humility, and readiness to obey orders he didn't understand, Pope John XXIII even called him "the patron of diplomats"!

Devotional deviations that have to do with the "imitation" part of honoring the saints often involve excessive physical austerities. In their zeal for self-discipline, even saints have gone overboard.

131

Francis of Assisi referred to his body as Brother Ass and gave it many a dreadful beating — an abuse of God's gift that the saint grieved over toward the end of his life, exclaiming, "Rejoice, Brother Body, and forgive me. . . ."

Devotion to St. Joseph is blessedly free of this type of excess. Since we know so little about Joseph's spiritual life, it is difficult to misapply the details. What we do know — that his holiness had more in common with the ordinary daisy than the showy orchid — makes for a devotion that centers on the safe path of attentiveness and receptivity to the hidden workings of grace.

St. Joseph and the Mass

One of the highest liturgical honors that the Church can accord its saints is to mention them during the Mass. Before Vatican Council II, only Mary, the apostles, and a dozen early martyrs connected with the Church of Rome were so honored in the Roman rite. But on November 13, 1962, during the council's eighteenth general meeting, it was announced that St. Joseph's name would be included in the body of the Roman Canon. Therefore, what we know as Eucharistic Prayer I reads: "In union with the whole Church we honor Mary, the ever-virgin Mother of Jesus Christ our Lord and God. We honor Joseph, her husband, the apostles and martyrs Peter and Paul, Andrew. . . ."

This decision, made by Pope John XXIII on his own initiative, was greeted with joy by thousands of Catholics around the world who had for years been petitioning the Vatican for just such a move. For the council Fathers, though, the announcement came as "something of a surprise," says one history of Vatican II. It was "a bombshell," says another. Some objected, because up until then, the Canon had been preserved as "the holy arch which no one is permitted to touch," as one liturgist had put it. Adding St. Joseph's name, grumbled one observer, marks "the first time since the reign of Gregory the Great, who died in 604, that the canon of the Mass has been changed."

There were solid theological and pastoral reasons behind Pope John's action. But, as Archbishop Fulton Sheen and others liked to recount, a behind-the-scenes drama that unfolded at the council's meeting on November 10, 1962, affected the timing of his decision.

The aged Bishop Petar Cule (Mostar, Yugoslavia) put in a long plea for the inclusion of the name of St. Joseph in the canon of the mass, but as he talked on, nervously repeating himself, murmurs began to be heard and Cardinal Ruffini [who was acting as moderator] was prompted to interject: "Complete your holy and eloquent speech. We all love St. Joseph, and we hope there are many saints in Yugoslavia. . . ."

It was this cutting off of Bishop Cule that prompted Pope John to order the insertion of the name of St. Joseph in the canon of the mass. . . . This caused great astonishment, but few were aware that the pope, following the debates on closed circuit television in his apartments, knew Bishop Cule personally and also knew that his nervous manner of speaking had a tragic source: he had suffered through one of those long trials made famous by the Communists and was sentenced to four years in a concentration camp in Yugoslavia. He and other prisoners were then put on a train that was deliberately wrecked in an attempt to kill all aboard. The bishop survived, but both his hips were broken. In poor health, he had nonetheless made great effort to attend the council and speak up for St. Joseph. Thus his wish was fulfilled.

(Xavier Rynne, *Vatican Council II*, Farrar, Straus, & Giroux, 1968, pp. 75-76)

Chapter 8

A Father for the Church

If I were a Roman Catholic theologian, I would
lift St. Joseph up. He took care of the Child;
he takes care of the Church.
Karl Barth

The aroma of hot wax from ten thousand candles hits my nostrils with a rush as I tug open the heavy doors and step into the stillness. I am inside what is called the votive chapel at the Oratory of St. Joseph. Outside, towering above this lower-level complex, is the granite-and-concrete basilica where the Oratory's large solemn liturgies are celebrated. The massive basilica is a Montreal landmark. But it is the votive chapel, like the "crypt" church it adjoins, that gets the heaviest use from the approximately two and a half million people who visit this shrine every year.

The votive chapel is conducive to ambulatory personal prayer in the company of St. Joseph. It is built as a wide, open hallway with four "stations" on each side, each one evoking a different phrase from the Litany of St. Joseph. I pause before the plaque honoring St. Joseph, "Model of Workers," and light a candle for my brother, whose job situation has become impossible. Remembering a friend who is struggling to decide between marriage and lifelong celibacy, I hesitate between St. Joseph, "Guardian of Virgins," and St. Joseph, "Help of Families." Finally, I choose both, adding other names at the Spirit's prompting. "Consolation of the Afflicted" and "Patron of the Dying" prompt a host of prayer intentions, and I kneel for some time at both stops. . . .

All around me, other pilgrims follow their own private itineraries around the chapel. It is a devout but informal atmosphere. I am somehow reminded of table-hopping from one beloved group to another at some intimate gathering of family and friends. At the head table, so to speak, is St. Joseph, "patron of the universal Church." Marked out by its larger size and central placement, this station features a white marble statue of St. Joseph with a fountain at its base. Its prominence expresses visually the idea that this title of St. Joseph is on a higher level and of a different order than the others. Father Roland Gauthier, founder of the Oratory's research center,

135

explains it like this: "We should not think that St. Joseph's title of patron of the universal Church is mainly the sum total of all these particular patronage roles. . . . The *universal* patronage of St. Joseph over the Church is based first and foremost on a permanent function assigned directly by God; it is indissolubly linked to his providential mission in the history of salvation."

Official recognition of St. Joseph as patron of the universal Church came late in a devotion that developed late in the Church's life. But as Father Gauthier and others have pointed out, the foundations of this title were there from the beginning. Pope Leo XIII pinpointed them in *Quamquam Pluries,* his 1889 encyclical on devotion to St. Joseph: "There are special reasons why St. Joseph should be explicitly named the patron of the Church and why the Church in turn should expect much from his patronage and guardianship. Namely, that Joseph was the husband of Mary and the father, as was supposed, of Jesus Christ. From this arise all his dignity, grace, holiness, and glory."

If Mary had been married to the apostle Peter or Paul or, more impossible still, to Michael the Archangel, it is one of them — not St. Joseph — that we would now honor as patron of the universal Church! Fundamentally, whatever titles or sanctity Joseph possesses rest on the fact that he said yes when God singled him out to be the spouse of the God-bearer. As Pope Leo explained, this is because marriage is "the most intimate possible union and relationship," in which husband and wife each "mutually participates in the goods of the other."

We are probably most familiar with marriages where the "goods," or gifts and resources, that newlyweds offer each other are on roughly the same level. With Mary and Joseph, however, there was wild disproportion. This bride brought her unsuspecting spouse a matchless dowry that, said Pope Leo, made him "a sharer in her exalted dignity." By accepting the gift, specifies John Paul II — that is, by obeying the angel's directive to "take Mary as your wife" (Matthew 1:20) — Joseph became "a unique guardian of the mystery 'hidden for ages in God' (Ephesians 3:9)," which is the incarnation. Joseph's yes catapulted him into the heart of God's saving plan for the human race. "Together with Mary, and in relation to Mary, he shares in this final phase of God's self-revelation in Christ, and he does so from the very beginning" (*Guardian of the Redeemer,* No. 5).

Joseph's nonbiological but profound fatherhood, "a relationship that places him as close as possible to Christ," is at the heart of his special assignment. He was summoned by God "to serve the person and mission of Jesus directly through the exercise of his fatherhood" (*Guardian of the Redeemer*, Nos. 7, 8). In a sense, Joseph's fatherly role complements Mary's motherhood. The two are by no means on the same footing (how could the biological mother of the incarnate Word have a human equal?). But marriage made Joseph and Mary intimate partners in mystery and mission nonetheless.

From Joseph, "husband and father," to Joseph, "patron of the universal Church," may seem like a mysterious leap of faith, but in reality it is a logical next step. We see the connection most clearly when we reflect on the "bridge" reality that links Joseph's earthly role to his ongoing mission in the Church — namely, the Body of Christ.

At least three levels of meaning come together in this splendid metaphor. Most obviously, it refers to the individual human body of Jesus of Nazareth, who lived, died, and rose from the grave. Another meaning recalls that Jesus established a mysterious and real communion between his physical body and ours. "Those who eat my flesh and drink my blood abide in me and I in them," he assured us (John 6:56). Every time we step up to receive communion, the priest or Eucharistic minister reminds us of this meaning: "The Body of Christ."

It was especially these two aspects of the Body of Christ that Pius IX recalled in connection with St. Joseph, when he declared him patron of the universal Church.

> And so it was that Him whom countless kings and prophets had of old desired to see, Joseph not only saw but conversed with and embraced in paternal affection, and kissed, and most diligently reared — even Him whom the faithful were to receive as the bread that came down from heaven whereby they might obtain eternal life.

Implied in Pius IX's decree was the third meaning of the Body of Christ. This is the Church, that invisible organism in which the Lord's disciples from all times and places are joined together, with Jesus as their head. "In the one Spirit we were all baptized into one body," says St. Paul (1 Corinthians 12:13). "We, who are many, are one body in Christ" (Romans 12:5).

137

Alluding to scriptural statements like these, John Paul II noted that Joseph's patronage of the Church is "profoundly rooted in the revelation of the New Covenant." He explained: "The Church is in fact the Body of Christ. Wasn't it therefore logical and necessary that the one to whom the eternal Father confided his Son would also extend his protection over the Body of Christ, which, according to the apostle Paul's teaching, is the Church?" Earlier popes had also commented on the logic, with Leo XIII offering the classic statement on the subject in his 1889 encyclical:

> The divine household, which Joseph governed as with a father's authority, contained the beginnings of the new Church. Just as the most holy Virgin is the mother of Jesus Christ, she is the mother of all Christians to whom she gave birth on the mount of Calvary, amid the unspeakable sufferings of the Redeemer. Jesus Christ is, as it were, the firstborn among Christians, who are his brothers by adoption and redemption.
>
> It follows from these considerations that the blessed Patriarch [Joseph] must regard the multitude of Christians who form the Church as confided to his care in a certain special manner. This is the immense family, spread out over all the earth, over which he exercises a sort of paternal authority, because he is the husband of Mary and the father of Jesus Christ. It is therefore reasonable and in every way worthy of Blessed Joseph that just as he was once entrusted with seeing to all the needs of the family of Nazareth and guarding it with watchful care, he should now by virtue of his heavenly patronage protect and defend the Church of Christ.

Very young children normally relate to their parents on the basis of personal need or desire. If six-month-old Annie could express herself on the subject, she would tell you that Mom and Dad have just one purpose in life: attending to her wants.

I confess to feeling some affinity with little Annie as I consider my relationship with St. Joseph. It is also for personal needs that I tend to seek his fatherly help. True, I may be one step ahead of a six-month-old in that the concerns I bring him often have to do with the personal needs of others. Still, I mostly view my heavenly parent with a child's one-dimensional perception, seeing his fatherly mission as exercised primarily in terms of individuals.

Reflecting on the title "patron of the universal Church" has spurred me to reconsider. I do not plan for one moment to stop requesting St. Joseph's assistance on personal matters. But it has begun to dawn on me that our relationship is seriously incomplete if it omits or downplays his main function, which is fatherly concern for the entire Body of Christ, the Church *as a whole.*

Reading John Paul II's 1989 apostolic exhortation, *Guardian of the Redeemer,* I am struck by the pope's insistence on this universal patronage and its relevance. He urges us — as a Church and with the needs of the Church "in the first place" — to consider St. Joseph's example and intercession. He presents this patronage as "ever necessary" but especially important for us who stand at the beginning of the third millennium of the Church. He even maintains that "our prayers [to St. Joseph] and the very person of St. Joseph have renewed significance for the Church in our day in light of the Third Christian Millennium" (Nos. 30, 29, 32).

It is a rather bold assertion. Some people might even think it misguided. As an anonymous theologian observed in 1962 upon learning of a liturgical change honoring St. Joseph, "Half the world doesn't even believe in God, and we worry about St. Joseph!" But the pope, it is obvious, does not view St. Joseph's patronage as a pious frill that is unrelated to the basics of the faith. And as we will see, the fact that nonbelievers constitute "half the world" is one important reason why he is adamant about the Church's need for St. Joseph.

What can we grasp of the importance of St. Joseph for us today? God alone knows the whole story, but following John Paul's lead, we can learn something from taking a fresh look at Joseph in his traditional role as protector, intercessor, and model for the universal Church. The following reflections are offered as starters to encourage your own thinking on the matter.

St. Joseph, Protect Us!

St. Joseph's protective role stands out from the beginning of Jesus' earthly life. "Get up, take the child and his mother, and flee to Egypt," the angel warns, "for Herod is about to search for the child, to destroy him" (Matthew 2:13). The enemy is a creature of flesh and blood, but behind his scheming lie the diabolical designs of the one who was "a murderer from the beginning" (John 8:44). "To destroy the works of the devil" will be Jesus' great mission (1 John 3:8). But not yet. Until Jesus has left his vulnerable childhood years behind, Joseph will do the defending — and will do it well, as indicated by another of his titles, "Terror of Demons."

Diabolical attacks were probably not far from Pius IX's mind when he declared Joseph "Patron of the Universal Church" on December 8, 1870. Both in the Church and on the political scene, it was a time of tremendous upheaval. Nearly three months before, the troops of a uniting Italy had occupied Rome. Pius had become a virtual prisoner in the Vatican, and the First Vatican Council was interrupted, never to be reconvened. Papal infallibility was a hot topic, as was the pope's 1864 denunciation of many anti-Christian trends in a "Syllabus of Errors." All in all, "most troublous times," wrote the pope, with the Church "beset by enemies on every side" and "weighed down by calamities so heavy that ungodly men assert that the gates of hell have at last prevailed against her."

What better moment to recognize and call on a special heavenly patron?

With Pius IX blazing the way, other popes began invoking St. Joseph's help against enemies seen and unseen. Specific challenges might change from one papacy to the next, but not the basic need for his protection. The Church will always turn to Joseph, said Pope Paul VI, because it is "ever weak, always threatened, and always dramatically in danger."

Pius IX's successor, Leo XIII, certainly felt this need in dealing with the weighty issues of his day. In some major European nations, the Church faced vigorous government hostility. The intellectual climate had worsened: "Scientists everywhere were proclaiming . . . the victory of science over religion," says one commentator. Greed and materialism were rampant as the revolution of industrialization took its course, leaving a wake of social problems and challenges to pastoral care. "Hardly less calamitous" to the Church than history's darkest days, Pope Leo said of the times, and offered a sobering catalogue of woes to prove it: ". . . faith, the foundation of all Christian virtues, perishing almost everywhere; . . . charity waxing cold; youth growing up corrupted in morals and in doctrine; the Church of Jesus Christ attacked on every side with violence and rage. . . ."

Recognizing that such evils were "too great for human remedies," the pope wrote in his 1889 encyclical, he had decided to call the Church "to seek a total cure through the divine power" by a month of fervent prayer to God through the intercession of Mary and, in a special way, St. Joseph. Every day during October, each Catholic was asked to say the rosary, followed by a special prayer to the watchful guardian of the Holy Family.

The energies of Benedict XV were directed to the problems of World War I, which broke out one month before he became pope. In its aftermath, he said in 1920, materialism and anti-Christian forms of socialism were on the rise, the holiness of marriage and respect for fatherly authority were under attack, and "public morals have become more corrupt and depraved than before." His conclusion: "When we consider the calamities afflicting the human race today, it seems necessary to recommend this devotion [to St. Joseph] ever more strenuously and to spread it much more widely."

The Great War's bitter legacy continued into the pontificate of Pius XI, who foresaw great danger in what he described as a "dense fog of mutual hatreds and grievances" that polluted international politics. Extreme nationalism and totalitarian regimes, both fascist and Communist, he condemned as false promises of "the ancient tempter" who has never ceased to deceive. Against Communism Pius XI directed an entire encyclical, issuing it in 1937 on the feast of St. Joseph. In concluding the document, he made this noteworthy declaration: "To hasten the advance of that 'peace of Christ in the kingdom of Christ' so ardently desired by all, we place the vast campaign of the Church against world Communism under the standard of St. Joseph, her mighty protector." In 1955 Pius XII continued this thrust by establishing the feast of St. Joseph the Worker on May 1, as the Church's response to Communist May Day celebrations.

Looking back now on the astonishing fall of the Iron Curtain in 1989, it is at the very least interesting to reflect on this relatively little-known connection between St. Joseph and the Church's resistance to Communism. Many Catholics have seen the collapse of the Soviet system as a response to the faithful prayers of those who heeded the Blessed Mother's Fátima call to "pray for the conversion of Russia." I do not doubt that Mary had a hand in this historic undoing. At the same time, I wonder, might it not have been something of a joint effort, with Joseph, patron of the Church's anti-Communist activity, playing his usual discreet role alongside Mary?

And what of us? We, too, need St. Joseph's protection, John Paul II insists, and so the Church still commends to him "all her cares, including those dangers which threaten the human family" (*Guardian of the Redeemer*, No. 31).

Perhaps the most blatant present-day danger threatening the Church is persecution. "Mounting evidence indicates a worldwide trend of anti-Christian persecution based on two political ideologies — Communism and militant, politicized Islam," writes Nina Shea, an activist in a religious freedom watchdog organization. In many countries, she says, Christians are experiencing "not just discrimination but real terror."

Christianity is completely banned in Saudia Arabia, where the Muslim religious police raid private homes for evidence of religious services, Bibles, rosaries, and the like. Thousands are in prison — among them some of the foreign workers who comprise a quarter of the country's population. In the Sudan, Shea reports, non-Muslims are subjected to truly unbelievable atrocities. The large Christian population in the south is being starved, tortured, and sold into slavery. In countries like North Korea, Vietnam, and China (whose patron, by the way, is St. Joseph), Communism is far from dead. There, Catholics and other Christians who practice their faith are routinely harassed, tortured, imprisoned, and even killed.

Though it gets sparse media attention, the persecuted Church is producing record numbers of martyrs and confessors of the faith. As we invoke St. Joseph's protection for the Church today, these brothers and sisters in Christ have special claim to our prayers.

In Western countries, where Christians face social pressures rather than persecution, St. Joseph's patronage is equally urgent. While physical death or harm is usually not the issue, we experience the pull of powerful secular trends that can lure us off the narrow way that leads to life.

Often we need help to see where we are drifting along with the culture and away from Christ; then we need help to change direction. *St. Joseph, I ask your protection especially against the spirit of . . . consumerism? selfish individualism? apathy? hedonism? . . .* The blanks are ours to fill in. But with the Spirit's guidance and St. Joseph's protection, we can identify areas where Herod is out "searching for the child to destroy him" — that is, searching to destroy our souls — and find refuge in the loving arms of God.

St. Joseph, Pray for Us!

Who has the higher place in heaven — St. Joseph or the angels? What human being, after Mary, wields the most intercessory clout — John the Baptist? the apostles? Joseph?

Not a few spiritual writers have gone in for this sort of speculation about St. Joseph's rank and privilege. Refreshingly, Teresa of

Ávila was not among them. But she did hold definite views about the spiritual influence of her favorite saint:

> For with other saints it seems the Lord has given them grace to be of help in one need, whereas with this glorious saint I have experience that he helps in all our needs and that the Lord wants us to understand that just as he was subject to St. Joseph on earth — for since bearing the title of father, being the Lord's tutor, Joseph could give the Child commands — so in heaven God does whatever he commands.

St. Teresa hardly intends us to picture Joseph striding about the heavenly courts and ordering God around! She is drawing the parallel for effect, to stress St. Joseph's unique role.

Teresa's confident trust in St. Joseph was rooted in her experience of miraculous healing from a mysterious, debilitating illness when she was twenty-one. St. Joseph, "being who he is, brought it about that I could rise and walk and not be crippled," she explained in her autobiography. Gradually, as Teresa found her place of service in the Church and began her reform of the Carmelite Order, her interactive relationship with this "true father" broadened outward and took on a mission orientation.

As Teresa saw it, her contribution to the Church consisted in founding reformed monasteries where Carmelites could devote themselves to ardent, undistracted prayer for God's people. "The purpose of this prayer was apostolic and missionary," says Father Joseph Chorpenning; "it was for the Church that was being attacked by Protestant reformers and for the millions of souls in the New World that were being lost for want of Christian instruction." In collaboration with St. Joseph, Teresa founded seventeen of these "prayer power" centers — underscoring Joseph's key role by placing his statue in each monastery and naming twelve of them after him. Indeed, Father Chorpenning observes, Teresa relied so obviously on St. Joseph's help that the whole reformed Carmel came to regard him as its founding father.

It was three centuries after St. Teresa's death that St. Joseph became officially honored as patron of the universal Church. Nonetheless, she was forward-looking in her affectionate, trusting recourse to Joseph not just for personal intentions but for the Church's greater needs.

Teresa's example still speaks to us today. First of all, it encourages us to ask the patron of the Church for help in finding our special role of service in the Body of Christ. This is no optional extra. Participating in Christ's saving mission is "the responsibility of each and every member of the Church," says John Paul II, one in which Joseph can be "an exceptional teacher" and guide. With his help, the Church as a whole and we as individual members of it can hope "to discover ever anew . . . [our] identity within this redemptive plan, which is founded on the mystery of the Incarnation" (*Guardian of the Redeemer*, Nos. 32, 1).

Teresa's example also suggests specific prayer requests that we can bring to St. Joseph on the Church's behalf. Missionary work and Church renewal, two of her main concerns, are also crucial today. To underscore their timeliness and their connection with St. Joseph, we might focus these intentions as *implementing Vatican II* and *evangelization.*

VATICAN II • St. Joseph's connection with the Second Vatican Council came about through Pope John XXIII's deep devotion to the patron of the Church. "I love him very much," he used to say, and liked to add that his baptismal name was Angelo Giuseppe ("Angel Joseph" in Italian). He would have chosen to go down in history as Pope Joseph I, he confided, but was concerned that the name might seem too great a break with tradition.

Pope John's devotion found magnificent public outlet on March 19, 1961, when he issued an apostolic letter proclaiming St. Joseph patron of the Second Vatican Council, which was to open in October 1962. In view of the need "to obtain from heaven that divine power by which it seems destined to mark an epoch in the history of the Church," wrote the pope, the event "could not be entrusted to a better heavenly protector than St. Joseph, the venerable head of the family of Nazareth and protector of Holy Church." Pope John could hardly contain his enthusiasm at the thought: "Oh! prayer to St. Joseph! Oh! devotion to St. Joseph for the protection of the Second Ecumenical Council of the Vatican!" It was the first of many urgent requests that every member of the Church join in a campaign of prayer to St. Joseph for the council's success.

Cynics today might question how well "St. Joseph, protector of Vatican II" fulfilled his mission. In countries like the United States, they might point to numerous signs that the council ushered in not renewal but erosion: empty confessionals, falling attendance at Sunday Mass, a sharp decline in religious life and the priesthood, widespread questioning and rejection of Church teaching on sexuality.

Vatican II was indeed "an epoch in the history of the Church," Catholics agree. But they are divided over whether it was for good or ill. Some wish we could simply turn the page and forget the whole thing. This is not the mind of the Church, however. As John Paul II explained in 1985 when he convoked a special synod of bishops to review and affirm the council documents: "Vatican II remains the fundamental event in the life of the modern Church: fundamental for examining the riches entrusted to her by Christ, . . . fundamental for fruitful contact with the modern world for the purpose of evangelization and dialogue on all levels and with people of upright conscience."

It seems obvious that St. Joseph's work of overseeing Vatican II is far from over. With the Church still in a follow-through period of implementing council directives, we stand in great need of his guidance to find our way.

St. Joseph's help "could not be more timely," observed Cardinal John Wright, who attended the council. Writing in 1971, he recalled one reason why Pope John had put Vatican II in his care: "St. Joseph is the model of serenity," the pope had said. "The lovable, amiable, sublime serenity that shines forth from the man thought to be the father of Jesus is what draws me to come ever closer to him with holy confidence that in his silence lies the answer to the noisy questions, . . . the agitation of the hour."

Today the noise is loudest and St. Joseph's help most vital in one key area. Notre Dame professor Ralph McInerny singles it out as "the one issue that gives life to so many of the other controversies swirling around the council and the Church today: the crisis of authority. . . . Where does authority in the Church really reside?"

Before the council, it was generally understood that the Church's teaching authority is exercised by the pope and the college of bishops in union with him. Vatican I had focused on papal primacy; without altering this teaching, Vatican II also spoke of the authority of all the bishops together, their "collegiality," in union with the pope. Since Vatican II, however, the Church has been torn by widespread public rebellion against its teaching authority, especially as vested in the papacy.

Ralph McInerny makes a thought-provoking connection between these attacks and a vision received by Jacinta, one of the children to whom the Blessed Virgin appeared at Fátima in 1917.

145

Jacinta said she saw the Holy Father in a large house, kneeling and crying with his head in his hands, while a crowd outside threw rocks and shouted curses. "Has anyone described better the beleaguered picture of the state of the Papacy and the Magisterium of the Church since Vatican II?" he asks. After examining some of the details of this sorry picture, he concludes, "It will be by following Mary's wishes as expressed to the children at Fátima that the promise of Vatican II will be fulfilled. She advised prayer and fasting."

To which Pope John XXIII and other fans of St. Joseph might add: *Not forgetting prayer to the special patron of the council!* (And of collegiality, Cardinal Wright would also add.)

St. Teresa of Ávila would have liked the idea of Joseph and Mary together as special intercessors for the Church's renewal. It was an image that Our Lord had given her in a directive regarding her first reformed monastery: "He said it should be called St. Joseph and that this saint would keep watch over us at one door, and our Lady at the other, so that Christ would remain with us." This is the picture evoked by Cardinal Wright's observation about Vatican II.

> As Pope John at the beginning of the council placed the council under the patronage of St. Joseph, so Pope Paul at the end of the council declared Mary to be the mother of the Church. . . . Thus as a result, we find the total Church, of which you and I are the children, under the protection of Mary and Joseph to do the work of Jesus.

EVANGELIZATION • St. Joseph's patronage is "ever necessary for the Church, not only as a defense against all dangers, but also, and indeed primarily, as an impetus for her renewed commitment to evangelization in the world and to re-evangelization. . ." (*Guardian of the Redeemer,* No. 29). Apparently, John Paul II sees nothing strange in asking a saint who was a homebody for ninety-nine percent of his life to be the special intercessor for the Church's missionary and apostolic work! (Interestingly, another homebody saint, Thérèse of Lisieux, is patroness of the missions.)

Some Church Fathers also thought "missionary" when they reflected on how Joseph carried the child Jesus into Egypt. They saw the incident as pointing ahead to the spread of the Gospel to the whole world. "Joseph represents the apostles to whom the protection and promotion of Christ is entrusted," St. Hilary wrote in the fourth century.

At least one missionary order has drawn inspiration and focus from Hilary's observation. Its founder was Father (later Cardinal) Herbert Vaughan, who was known for his absolute confidence in St. Joseph. Just before he died, he reiterated his founding insights, asking his priests to look upon his comments as the last words of a loving father.

> St. Joseph's Society for Foreign Missions [popularly known in England as the Mill Hill Fathers and its American offshoot as the Josephites] cultivates a special devotion to the foster father of Our Lord, who carried Jesus and Mary [into Egypt]. . . . He represents the whole college of the apostles in his own person and office. And for his most intimate association during thirty years with the Mother and Divine Child, he is the first and most powerful patron to be invoked and deserves to be chosen as the father of apostolic men, especially of those sent into foreign lands.

St. Joseph can thus be seen as a type of those missionaries, lay or religious, who go to foreign lands in service to the "first evangelization" to peoples who have never heard the Good News. At the same time, Joseph's many rooted years of tending the Word in Nazareth make him a special patron for stay-at-home evangelizers. These may participate in the Church's missionary work through their everyday witness, prayers, and financial help. Many of them are called to the "new evangelization" — that is, the reevangelization of once Christian areas where the Gospel is now neglected and even unfamiliar.

One way or another, St. Joseph's help is relevant for each of us. As John Paul II has made clear, "no believer in Christ can avoid this supreme duty: to proclaim Christ to all peoples. . . . Today all Christians . . . are called to have the same courage that inspired the missionaries of the past, and the same readiness to listen to the voice of the Spirit" (*Redemptoris Missio,* Nos. 3.4, 30.1). Joseph, who always listened to God's voice and responded courageously to his call, can show us how to do the same. After all, said Paul VI, Joseph and we have the same basic call. Wherever we are, whatever we do, "the mission of St. Joseph becomes our own: to protect Christ and allow him to grow in us and around us."

We who live in the Americas — North, Central, or South — have an extra reason for counting on St. Joseph's help in spreading the Gospel in whatever ways we can. He is the special patron of the

New World — of that "first evangelization" through which the Christian faith made its initial appearance in our countries.

Devotion to St. Joseph came earliest to New Spain (present-day Mexico, Central America, and the Philippines), largely through the efforts of a small band of Flemish Franciscans who arrived in Mexico in 1523, on the heels of Cortés. Their preaching, their schools, and especially the inspired labors of a lay brother named Pedro de Gante caused St. Joseph to become widely revered by the Amerindians as both a role model and a loving father. In 1555 New Spain became the first territory ever to take St. Joseph as its special patron. Later missionaries, notably Blessed Junípero Serra, brought Christianity and devotion to St. Joseph to present-day California and left proof of it in a string of missions honoring their patron San José.

New France, a vast territory extending from present-day Canada to the Gulf of Mexico, named St. Joseph its patron in 1624, thanks to the influence of the Franciscan (Recollect) Fathers in Quebec. Its later evangelizers were also characterized by a deep personal relationship with St. Joseph — among them, Blessed Marie of the Incarnation, the intrepid French Ursuline whose zeal led her to become the first woman missionary, and the North American martyr St. Jean de Brébeuf and his fellow Jesuits.

By this time, it will perhaps come as no surprise to discover that the evangelization of the Americas has taken place under the joint banner of St. Joseph and his holy spouse.

We think immediately of Our Lady of Guadalupe, whose appearance to the pious Aztec Christian Juan Diego touched off an evangelistic explosion. In the seven years after Mary's 1531 apparition, eight million Aztecs were received into the Church — a pastoral challenge that kept missionaries like Pedro de Gante incredibly busy. (He alone reportedly baptized "with his own hands" over one million Amerindians!)

To a people left devastated by the Spanish conquest, Mary's revelation of herself as "Mother of the True God" and "your merciful mother" pointed to a loving God who called them to himself. It also paved the way for their welcoming her spouse as their own father. According to Father Chorpenning, a sizable segment of the population were *mestizos,* children of Amerindian mothers and Spanish fathers whom they did not know. With the Franciscans' encouragement, "Joseph . . . became the father of this conquered and oppressed people who would protect and shelter them."

In New France, the pioneering figures' strong devotion to the Holy Family gives an impression of Our Lady and St. Joseph working hand in hand for the spread of the Gospel there. One example among many comes from the life of Mother Marie of the Incarnation.

One night, in her convent in France, she had a prophetic dream of a silent, beautiful land where the Madonna and Child sat enthroned over a vast expanse of fog-shrouded mountains and valleys; at its entrance was a man in white, clothed "as painters depict the apostles." Over a year later, while praying before the Blessed Sacrament, Mother Marie was given to understand her mysterious dream and her mission: the land was Canada, and she was to go there to "build a house for Jesus and Mary." Two or three months later, Mother Marie received another important insight: the man in white was St. Joseph, "the guardian of this great land," and in her house, God would be adored and praised "in company with Jesus and Mary — along with St. Joseph who should never be separated from them."

In this and many other ways, "Jesus, Mary, Joseph" became the hallmark of missionary work in New France. Centuries after this "first evangelization," thousands of Catholic parochial schoolchildren like myself would bear unwitting witness to its impact each time we began a new sheet of paper and followed instructions to "always write *JMJ* at the top."

JMJ — a good standard, too, under which to do our thinking and praying about evangelization.

St. Joseph, May We Be Like You!

"It's not enough to pray to him," said Paul VI; "we must also imitate him."

Much has been said about what it is that we should imitate in St. Joseph. " 'Just man' means adorned with every virtue," held John Chrysostom and others who then went on to expand on those qualities at some length. We will focus here, however, on the one virtue that makes Joseph an especially good model for the Church as a whole: his faith.

Quoting one of the Vatican II documents, John Paul II emphasized that "the basic attitude of the entire Church must be 'hearing the word of God with reverence,' an absolute readiness to serve faithfully God's salvific will revealed in Jesus." And just what might this ready obedience of faith look like? We have not been left in the dark, said the pope. "Already at the beginning of human redemption, after Mary, we find the model of obedience made incarnate in St. Joseph, the man known for having faithfully carried out God's commands" (*Guardian of the Redeemer*, No. 30).

It is Matthew's Gospel, especially, that showcases Joseph's free and full assent to God's revelation. Three times, we are told there, he believed and obeyed God's word received in a dream (1:24; 2:14, 21). John Chrysostom raised an interesting question: Why did the angel appear as Joseph slept? "Why not openly, in the manner that he appeared to the shepherds and to Zechariah, as well as to the Virgin?" Chrysostom's answer to his rhetorical question accentuates Joseph's faith: "This man was so ready to believe that he did not require such a manifestation." Risky business, believing and acting on dreams — but Joseph's discernment and faith were up to the challenge.

Any writer faced with a large chunk of material to communicate must make decisions about how to present it — what to emphasize, what to trim, what structure to adopt. Guided by the Spirit, Matthew made some of those decisions in a way that highlighted themes related to the Church and discipleship.

You might call Matthew's Gospel the Church-building Gospel. Jesus as founder of a new community, Peter as its base, expectations for leadership and church life in general — Matthew more than any other evangelist put these issues front and center. We might ask whether his Gospel also puts forward someone who embodies the life of the Church that he shows Jesus founding. Who exemplifies the response to his call to discipleship that Jesus desires?

It is not Peter: Matthew recounts Peter's denial of Jesus but does not include the later lakeside scene where Peter indicates his repentance (but see John 21:15-19). It is not the other apostles: three verses from the end of Matthew, some are still doubting (28:17). And in Matthew there is no beloved disciple standing faithfully at the foot of the cross. Nor does Matthew replicate Luke's portrayal of Mary as the model follower of Jesus: where Luke focuses on her pondering God's word and persisting in faith, Matthew mentions Mary hardly at all.

Instead, Matthew gives us an opening series of stories whose hero hears and obeys, like the wise man — was he a carpenter? — who builds his house on rock (Matthew 7:24). Who more than Joseph exemplifies the response of faith that builds the Church? By

150

placing his example at the very beginning of his Gospel, Matthew offers Joseph as the prototype of the ready trust and obedience that Jesus awaits from each of us.

Let us make this our daily prayer: "St. Joseph, model member and universal patron of the Church, be with us on our journey of faith!"

Devotion to St. Joseph: The Popes Take Action!

1479 • Sixtus IV introduces the feast of St. Joseph to be celebrated locally, in Rome.

1726 • Benedict XIII inserts St. Joseph's name into the Litany of the Saints.

1870 • Pius IX declares St. Joseph Patron of the Universal Church.

1889 • Leo XIII issues an encyclical on devotion to St. Joseph, *Quamquam Pluries.*

1909 • Pius X approves the Litany of St. Joseph.

1911 • Pius X declares March 19 a solemn feast in honor of St. Joseph, husband of Mary.

1937 • Pius XI selects St. Joseph as patron of the Church's fight against atheistic Communism.

1955 • Pius XII announces the feast of St. Joseph the Worker on May 1.

1961 • John XXIII declares St. Joseph the heavenly protector of the Second Vatican Council.

1962 • John XXIII announces the insertion of St. Joseph's name into the Canon of the Mass.

1989 • John Paul II issues *Guardian of the Redeemer,* an apostolic exhortation "on the person and mission of Saint Joseph in the life of Christ and of the Church."

Chapter 9

Her Most Chaste Spouse

How wonderful the bond between two believers,
now one in hope, one in desire, one in discipline,
one in the same service!

Tertullian

Steve Wood, founder of the men's organization St. Joseph's Covenant Keepers, was riding with a trucker one day, when a radio announcer reported John Paul II's reaffirmation of the Church's teaching on birth control. The trucker greeted the news with sarcasm, expletives, and a dismissive, "What the hell does that old pope know about sex, anyway?"

His reaction — minus the belligerence — may not be so far removed from our own response to the idea of St. Joseph as patron of married couples. "How can he be a model of conjugal love?" we wonder, zooming in on what society would have us see as the indispensable condition of happiness: "He and Mary never had sex!"

As anyone who has ever benefited from a support group knows, there is indeed a special kind of help that we receive from people who have learned something from experience. On the other hand, it would be a mistake to assume, as the truck driver did, that experience is always indispensable for speaking knowledgeably and authoritatively. This is especially true when the subject is marriage, that "intimate partnership" of life and love that "has been established by the Creator and endowed by him with its own proper laws" ("Pastoral Constitution on the Church in the Modern World," *Gaudium et Spes*, No. 48). To be fully understood, marriage must be illumined by the wisdom from on high that God has given the Church. Human experience and understanding alone will not suffice.

"While this may come as a big surprise to that truck driver," Steve Wood can therefore conclude, "Pope John Paul II knows approximately ten thousand times more about marital sexuality than the average American male, including the so-called love experts."

And what of St. Joseph, who lived under the same roof with Christ, "the wisdom of God" (1 Corinthians 1:24), and who now lives united with the Author of marriage? How much *he* must know!

As it happens, St. Joseph has both God's wisdom on marriage

and the personal experience we look for in the experts we consult. Although his relationship with Mary did not include the physical expression of marital love, it was in every other way a marriage. Joseph and Mary were truly husband and wife, not an odd guardian-ward duo masquerading as a couple.

"But was it a *real* marriage?" people sometimes ask, thinking of the couple's virginity. The early Fathers of the Church were skittish on the subject. Insisting on the marriage might undermine belief in Jesus' divine sonship and Mary's virginity, they seemed to reason — and with *good* reason, in a climate where heresies were springing up like dandelions. Instead, the Fathers stressed the nonphysical nature of Mary and Joseph's relationship and also speculated about God's purposes for it. Why, they asked, did God bring Joseph into the picture? Granted, God's fatherhood of Jesus meant that Mary had to be a virgin. But why a *married* virgin? Why not a holy single mother?

With characteristic clarity and focus, St. Thomas Aquinas gathered up twelve centuries' worth of reflections and distilled the best of them into the section of his *Summa* that deals with Mary and Joseph's relationship. He distinguished twelve reasons for their marriage, which he divided into three groups according to their prime beneficiary. The marriage was *for Jesus' sake*: it gave him a home and a legal ancestry; it protected him against charges of illegitimacy and against premature exposure to the devil's evil designs. It was *for Mary's sake*: marriage spared her from being punished as an adulteress, protected her reputation, and gave her a husband's support. It was *for our sakes*: among other things, the marriage secured Joseph as an impeccable witness to Mary's virginal motherhood, and it ensured that both virginity and marriage would be honored in the Church.

Aquinas did not mention it, but we should not overlook the fact that the marriage was *for Joseph's sake,* too. "God, by giving Joseph to the Virgin, did not give him to her only as a companion for life, a witness of her virginity, and protector of her honor," wrote Pope Leo XIII; "he also gave Joseph to Mary in order that he might share, through the marriage pact, in her own sublime greatness."

God did not carry out his saving plan for the world at Joseph's expense. Unlike the strapped Third World doctor who must make hard decisions about which patients to treat and which to ignore, God has a wealth of benefits for everyone who comes to him. To Joseph he offered a match made in heaven. "When God finished creating the world, he began creating marriages," goes an old rabbinic saying that applies nicely to Joseph's marital situation. By stepping into the marriage God had arranged for him, Joseph embraced radical sacrifice and, through it, radical joy and holiness. Looking at his life, we learn anew that serving God's larger plan does not cost us our happiness. Rather, it guarantees it.

The Church Fathers' tendency to tiptoe around the reality of Joseph and Mary's marriage was definitively reversed in the late fourth century, with St. Augustine's declaration that "every good of marriage was fulfilled in the parents of Christ: offspring, loyalty, and the sacrament." Helping us to understand these three "goods" in light of Vatican II's teaching on marriage is canon lawyer Father Bernard Siegle:

> 1. *Offspring* means "the right to intimate sexual union having openness to fecundity — the capacity to be responsible parents, not only procreating, but properly rearing and educating a family."
>
> 2. *Loyalty* is "the right to a marital love special to this exclusive and lifelong union — the possibility of loving and being beloved as the 'only one.'"
>
> 3. *The sacrament* is "that Christian love which signifies and partakes of the mystery of that unity and fruitful love which exists between Christ and the Church. . . ."

No question that goods two and three shine out in Joseph and Mary's marriage. But offspring? Once again, Thomas Aquinas is helpful here. A marriage is genuine, he explains, by reason of its attaining two perfections. First is perfection of "form," which is the thing that makes marriage what it is. The "form" of marriage is the "inseparable union of souls by which husband and wife are pledged to each other with a bond of mutual affection that cannot be broken."

The second perfection of marriage concerns its "operation," says Aquinas, by which he means its attainment of the goal of begetting and raising children. Though Mary and Joseph never conceived a child, their marriage "had its second perfection in the upbringing of the Child," he says. In this they are like married couples who are unable to have their own children: their conjugal love finds fruition in other ways of serving Jesus.

"It's a good thing you can't see into the future when you're getting married," a friend remarked to me recently as we prayed for an acquaintance whose son had just committed suicide. "Good thing," I echoed, thinking of another friend's loving care of his wife, who became mentally ill a few years into their twenty-year marriage. "You might not have the courage to do it."

No bride and groom standing at the altar know what lies ahead as they pledge fidelity "for better, for worse, for richer, for poorer, in sickness and in health, until death." They have no way to predict and certainly no way to control future events, no guarantee that the easy will outweigh the difficult. They simply love — and hope for happiness.

Joseph, too, was hoping for happiness as he awaited the day when the woman he loved would come to live with him. How long that traditional one-year interval between betrothal and marriage must have seemed to him! Mary's pregnancy must have taken him completely by surprise. It certainly precipitated a major crisis in what was looking to be a very short marriage! And then, after learning from an angel in a dream that it was none other than God who had disrupted his life, Joseph faced additional weighty questions.

God had taken possession of what Joseph held most dear. Mary was bearing God's Son, and Joseph was being asked to take mother and child under his protection. What would *look* like a normal family situation would be anything but. Father to God's child, husband to a woman consecrated to God in a unique way — in a sense, Joseph would be living as a man with nothing to call his own. Furthermore, as head of the house, he would be exercising authority over two people who, it had become clear, far surpassed him in virtue. What a humbling position!

Could Joseph put aside his hopes and dreams for the future? Legitimate, healthy desires they had been, too — not fantasies or crass ambitions or indulgences like a weekly trip to the casino. Could he accept the sacrifice?

Another weighty question for Joseph: *Could he surrender his rights to marital intercourse?* Whether he realized it immediately upon hearing that Mary's child was "from the Holy Spirit" (Matthew 1:20) or whether the conviction came from deliberations with Mary, Joseph understood that sexual relations would not be part of this marriage. We should not imagine him greeting this realization with a "No sweat!" There is every reason to think that Joseph had the normal desires of a man who looks forward to married life with the woman of his dreams. Joseph loved Mary, and love seeks union with the beloved. Would Joseph accept a marriage marked by deep union, but without its normal physical expression?

For love of God and love of Mary, Joseph said yes to the whole unique ensemble. He made a total gift of self, the highest and fullest expression of human love. And thanks to the unrepeatable circumstances of his calling, Joseph's absolute surrender made him a model and patron for both states in life in which human beings can seek holiness: marriage and celibacy.

St. Joseph is the patron of women and men who have consecrated themselves to celibacy for Jesus' sake. Especially, says one spiritual writer, he is the patron of priests: like Joseph, who was the first man to hold Jesus in his arms, "the priest is privileged to touch and reverently handle Him who was born of Mary."

Even more broadly, St. Joseph stands ready to serve as "guardian of virgins" for anyone who must avoid sexual intercourse, for whatever reason. The following groups alone provide a multitude of candidates:

• Young people contending with tremendous pressure — beginning in grade school and communicated via peer groups, the media, and the overall culture — to lose their virginity as quickly as possible. According to one recent report, more than half the number of girls in the U.S. have sexual intercourse by age seventeen.

• Single people who choose *not* to live together outside marriage. Theirs is not a comfortable stand. By the end of 1998, an estimated six million couples were cohabitating in the U.S. Furthermore, about fifty-five percent of the population — including forty-five percent of regular churchgoers — think that "trial marriage" is a good idea. (Never mind the hard evidence that it results in a higher divorce rate: forty-six percent higher for couples who have lived together than for those who haven't, says one 1999 study.)

• Men and women who struggle with homosexual or lesbian tendencies but want to live chastely.

• Married couples who must abstain from intercourse for a time: one partner is ill . . . a pregnancy would be imprudent . . . husband or wife is away on business or military duty. . . .

• Catholics who are in an "irregular situation" — that is, who have divorced and remarried, with their previous marriage still considered valid by the Church. Their special challenge was summarized in a headline to a newspaper article about guidelines issued by the Vatican's Pontifical Council on the Family: "Divorced Catholics Who Remarry Should Shun Sex." Responding to a questioner who wondered how realistic this directive might be, New York Cardinal John O'Connor wrote:

> Is it possible for a married couple to live as celibates? . . . With God's grace, *all* things are possible. Is it possible for someone who is divorced and remarried to live in what we used to call a "brother and sister relationship" with a second or third spouse — hence, live as a celibate? With God's grace, all things are possible.

On the basis of his own experience, St. Joseph would thoroughly agree.

What makes a successful marriage? I look at my parents, happily married for fifty-five years. What they did at the altar of St. Rita's Church in Oakland Beach, Rhode Island, where they exchanged vows, I see them doing today: they are saying yes. "Yes, I will make you lunch (for the twenty-thousandth time). Yes, I will go to that event (though I would prefer to stay home). Yes, I will make the effort to tell you what's on my mind. . . ."

Yes is the indispensable beginning of each couple's journey together. Every marriage is rooted in "the contract of its partners, that is, in their irrevocable personal consent" (*The Church in the Modern World,* No. 48). Given over and over again in a myriad of ways and settings, that loving yes opens into a union and intimacy so deep that it defies math: one plus one equals one. In his jewel of a book, *Marriage, A Great Sacrament,* Canon Jacques Leclercq describes this unity as coming to encompass everything about the husband and wife — "their whole life, their whole soul, their whole personality." Keep Joseph and Mary in mind as you read his description: they exemplify it best.

> [Marriage is] a complete union, as radical as it can be between human beings, a union which must go down as deep as the human person possesses depth, as far as sharing the same sacrament, as far as being one before God, as far as having the most intimate, the most delicate elements of the interior life and of the supernatural life in common. There is no limit to married intimacy as Christians understand it, and everything in Christian marriage . . . only finds its meaning in a married intimacy which truly brings about the most harmonious and the most

complete unity in the partners, the image of the union of Christ and His Church.

Joseph and Mary gave their full and free consent to God and to one another. Mary, being sinless, surrendered herself completely; Joseph, being a good match for her, must have come as close to total surrender as a non-immaculately conceived human being possibly can.

As Joseph — sure now that God was calling him to this love — chose for the second time to marry Mary, the Spirit who had overshadowed her moved into their relationship as a couple. "Are we not to suppose that [Joseph's] love as a man was also given new birth by the Spirit?" asks Pope John Paul. Every human love is molded to perfection by the love of God "poured into our hearts through the Holy Spirit," he explains (see Romans 5:5). "This love of God also molds — in a completely unique way — the love of husband and wife, deepening within it everything of human worth and beauty . . ." (*Guardian of the Redeemer*, No. 19). Are we not to think that Joseph and Mary knew this deep, united love from the moment of their consent?

Then too, their common mission drew them together as no other couple has ever experienced. By believing what Mary had already accepted about her pregnancy, Joseph was united to her "in an altogether special way." He was "the first to share in the faith of the Mother of God," supporting his spouse "in the faith of the divine annunciation." This made Joseph, together with Mary, "the first guardian of this divine mystery" (*Guardian of the Redeemer*, Nos. 5, 4).

Another aspect of their unity: every couple who enters into the sacrament of marriage can count on the grace of God's special presence in their life together. "Just as of old God encountered his people with a covenant of love and fidelity, so our Savior, the spouse of the Church, now encounters Christian spouses through the sacrament of marriage. He abides with them. . . ." ("Pastoral Constitution on the Church in the Modern World," No. 48). As Jacques Leclercq puts it, "God becomes as it were a third party in the intimacy of married life."

An unseen third party in other marriages, God took visible, human form in Joseph and Mary's. "And the Word became flesh and lived among us" (John 1:14), they might have said after Jesus' birth — and with a nuance of meaning unshared by anyone else in history. They had received the Spirit, the Giver of Life (see John 6:63) who effects the deep spiritual closeness arising from marriage. In this Spirit, says Pope John Paul, Joseph found "the source of love, the conjugal love which he experienced as a man." No wonder that "this love proved to be greater than this 'just man' could ever have experienced within the limits of his human heart" (*Guardian of the Redeemer*, No. 19)!

But Joseph's consent won far more than the happiest, most successful marriage of all time. It is not overstating things to say that by agreeing to God's surprising plan for his life, Joseph advanced God's saving plan for the whole world. Because of him, Jesus was received into a loving home and mothered by a woman we hail as Ever-Virgin. This could not have happened without Joseph's complete self-sacrifice.

Mary, after all, was not a free-as-a-bird single woman at the time of the annunciation. "We must stop imagining the Virgin as a cloistered nun or a young girl living like a hermit," Father Roland Gauthier points out. Since Mary was legally Joseph's wife when she conceived, it was crucial that he, too, consent to a virginal marriage.

How can any of us guess what God might do with our faithful obedience to difficult invitations? As for Joseph's generous response, it enriched the very institution of marriage for all generations to come. John Paul II, in his 1994 "Letter to Families," points out that "thanks also to Joseph, the mystery of the Incarnation and, together with it, the mystery of the Holy Family, come to be profoundly inscribed in the spousal love of husband and wife and, in an indirect way, in the genealogy of every human family. . . . The family truly takes its place at the very heart of the new covenant" (No. 20).

In union with Mary's *fiat*, Joseph's yes changed the world.

But how much the world still needs changing! More than ever, it seems. "For Better or Worse, Marriage Hits a New Low," announced a front-page headline in a recent edition of the *Washington Post*. The accompanying article — about a July 1999 report by Rutgers University's National Marriage Project — does not make for cheery reading. We are informed that "the nation's marriage rate has dipped by 43 percent in the last four decades," a historical low that the report attributes to a trend toward cohabitation and later marriages. Later, a *New York Times* article took issue with the percentage, while also admitting, "Yes, marriage bonds are weaker than ever."

This decline might not be such bad news if it meant fewer

marital breakups, says sociologist David Popenoe in his study of fatherlessness in America, but this has hardly been the case. "The divorce rate has climbed to an historically high level and stayed there." In the United States, which has "by far" the highest divorce rate in the industrialized world, "the chance that a first marriage occurring today will end in divorce stands at around 50 percent — by some estimates as high as 60 percent."

We are caught up in a vast, unprecedented, and disastrous social experiment in which every traditional element of marriage is being challenged and dismissed. Small wonder that the *Post* article speaks of people's increasing pessimism and "dramatically altered attitudes" about marriage as an institution.

One aspect of the change, according to marriage counselor Frederic Flach, is "a curious and widespread assumption that few people can find happiness in marriage because the bond itself ruins any excitement and whatever love may have been there at the start." Instead of being seen as "the natural outcome of romance and the legitimate ambition of every college senior," he says, "marriage is more likely to be viewed now as a tricky and often dangerous obstacle course leading to disenchantment, boredom, or . . . private warfare. . . ."

Not only that, notes David Blankenhorn, author of *Fatherless America*: marriage is increasingly viewed as stodgy and same-old, same-old. Divorce is what's considered cutting-edge and fulfilling now, outranking marriage as "an authentic, interesting, and culturally authoritative experience." Why, it can even be "a metaphor for adult birth and renewal"!

Perhaps you have noticed, as Blankenhorn points out, that "better divorce" and not "better marriage" is the message of many movies, TV programs, and magazines. Bookstores, too, bulge with information on how to divorce in a good, civilized, creative, constructive, self-affirming, and, yes, even pleasant sort of way. "Just as we must learn to part and say goodbye," coos one author, "we must also learn how to move on. We must learn to say Yes to others, to new possibilities, and to ourselves." Once we learn to see loss and gain as "the very nature of the universe," we are assured, "we will become available to new people and situations effortlessly."

And, presumably, available to new divorces as well.

G. K. Chesterton titled one of his commentaries on social and moral issues *What's Wrong with the World?* Accusing and deploring is not what Chesterton did in this thoughtful book, as is obvious from its opener, one of the funniest dedications ever written. (Sample: "As far as literature goes, this book is what is wrong, and no mistake.") Neither should a point-and-condemn attitude sum up our own approach to the present marriage crisis. After all, even staunch defenders of matrimony are unconsciously affected by the very trends they bemoan. To some degree all of us have bought into the egocentric attitudes that undermine marriage. We are so shortsighted, so easily deceived and influenced by whatever panders to our weaknesses that, to some extent, *we* are what's wrong with the world!

The solution? "Only a continuous, permanent conversion" will do, John Paul II reminds us. We must all set ourselves in opposition to certain aspects of modern culture "through a conversion of mind and heart, following Christ Crucified by denying our own selfishness: such a conversion cannot fail to have a beneficial and renewing influence even on the structures of society" ("The Role of the Christian Family in the Modern World," *Familiaris Consortio,* No. 9).

For incentives to conversion, it's hard to beat an examination of conscience. I know, because under St. Joseph's gentle tutelage, I have been rethinking my own experience of married love and my response to it. True, every marriage is different. "Love can take as many forms as there are couples," says Jacques Leclercq. And some unions seem more marked by the cross than by the Song of Songs. Still, others' thoughts are sometimes helpful prods to personal soul-searching. If you are married, then, your own experience will fill out the following reflections, drawn from the only conscience that I am able to examine. If you are not married, you might adapt these three points to refer to your relationship with Jesus, the Spouse we all serve regardless of our marital status.

Am I guarding the vision? "He's a good man," said my friend when I confided that Kevin and I were thinking of marriage. "Just one thing. Can you live with that laugh?"

It came as a bit of a shock to realize that not everyone was as charmed as I by Kevin's distinctive laugh (loud, frequent, and, when prolonged, three-pitched). Was it a case of love is deaf? I thought not, and I found ammunition for my position in another jewel of a book on marriage, this one by the philosopher Dietrich von Hildebrand.

"Nothing is more mistaken than the adage, 'Love is blind,' " I read. "Love is that which *gives us sight. . . .*" The conjugal kind of love reveals the beloved's faults and quirks, "but also the particular charm of his individuality as a whole, which permeates everything [even a laugh!] and characterizes the essence of his being. . . ."

In a way, marital love is a privileged glimpse of the beloved as God sees her or him. It is what Alice von Hildebrand, Dietrich's wife, calls a "Tabor vision." Like the disciples who saw Jesus transfigured (see Mark 9:2-8), spouses are given an intense look at one another's true face and unique beauty. "Trust this bright Tabor vision," she advises in her own insightful book on marriage. "Daily rekindle it in your heart. Let it nurture your love."

This is where my daily battle lies. Routine, laziness, dullness, self-preoccupation, irritability — left unchecked, these and so many other sins and weaknesses would not only cloud my Tabor vision of Kevin but quench it. Heaven forbid that my "only one" would ever become "just anyone," someone I no longer see from within! Even without adultery or divorce, this betrayal of the initial vision would already be unfaithfulness.

"We must fight against a weakening of this love, against this 'falling asleep,' " Dietrich von Hildebrand emphasizes, "just as we must always strive — in an incomparably higher sphere — to keep our love for Jesus unfailingly awake."

So I fight, enlisting the special help of Joseph and Mary, who surely lived in Tabor's bright light, faithful guardians of the vision they had received.

And yes, I am still charmed by my husband's laugh.

Am I giving myself completely? "Stop wasting your time with a relationship that is draining your life rather than enhancing it. Get rid of him: Life is too short for it not to be special."

"Well, that's blunt," I muttered, flipping through the pages of a bestseller in the bookstore's "self-help" section. And I wondered how we would all be faring now if Joseph had followed such advice, had chosen to "get rid of her" because marriage to Mary, as redefined by God, didn't look to be personally fulfilling for him.

Some people, struggling in marriages that are truly difficult, are vulnerable to blatant encouragements to walk away without a fight. For many of us who are happily married, the temptation comes in those subtle, incessant urges to take back bits of what we gave away at the altar. We will give *of* ourselves but not our whole selves. *Oh no, do I have to listen to that story again? . . . So what if it's the last beer in the fridge? I'm thirsty! . . .Tell your relatives they can't come over. I'm tired and they're so boring. . . . What about me? When am I going to have some fun? . . . That's your problem. I'm not doing it. . . .*

Being married does not mean accepting abuse or dysfunctionally ignoring problems that need resolving, but it does require that I put my spouse's good above my own. In this, I am not helped by the current societal climate, where an inordinate emphasis on self-fulfillment compounds the universal human tendency to selfishness. I must ruefully admit that I am not unaffected by this trend.

The following guideline from Jacques Leclercq points me back to the narrow path I really want to walk: "Learning to love is learning how to give oneself. Whoever gets married undertakes responsibility for the happiness of another. The husband must provide the happiness of his wife, the wife that of her husband."

This is what Joseph did for Mary. "Through his complete self-sacrifice, Joseph expressed his generous love for the Mother of God, and gave her a husband's 'gift of self.' . . . [He] took Mary into his home, while respecting the fact that she belonged exclusively to God" (*Guardian of the Redeemer,* No. 20).

Joseph discovered the way in which God was calling him to make his gift of self in marriage. Every day I must discover mine.

Am I trusting God? Seven habits, four guidelines, six principles, three easy steps. Contemporary wisdom conveys the message that success in marriage depends largely on mastering techniques. Granted, it can be helpful to know something about conflict resolution and the differences between "Mars" and "Venus" ways of communicating. But unless I place my trust in God first, I will "labor in vain" to build the house of my marriage (see Psalm 127).

Technology will not work to build the "house" of Christian marriage, because marriage is not merely a natural human institution. For Christians, God has stepped in and made it a sacrament, an instrument of grace. Because of this, marriage is above all a means of sanctification. Every day Kevin and I must help each other to holiness: for this, we have no "method" other than turning to God and throwing ourselves on his mercy.

Ten commandments, six precepts of the Church, twelve works of mercy, eight beatitudes. . . . There are certain lists that must be heeded by any Catholic who answers God's call to holiness. None of them, however, represents a technique for achieving it. We plant, till, and water, but it is "only God who gives the growth" (1 Corinthians 3:7).

Countless couples have walked the road to holiness before us. "But where are they acknowledged in the Church?" Kevin and I sometimes ask. Many of the married people who have been canonized seem to have attained holiness after the death of a spouse and their entrance into religious life. Others, who dealt with difficult or indifferent spouses, achieved holiness *despite* their spouses, not *with* them, as a flowering of conjugal love.

But sometimes I wonder: Is it that there are objectively fewer married saints? Or is it that they are harder to spot? Perhaps the very nature of Christian marriage — the only human institution become a sacrament — makes for a more hidden, less heroic-looking holiness. "Nothing, in one way, is so human as the conjugal union," observed Jacques Leclercq:

> No activity of man is so spontaneously natural, so immediately derived from nature, as the love of married people and the communal life which results from it. Now it is that which God transforms by the sacrament; all the simple everyday things that make up the conjugal life are sanctified and become, through the sacrament of marriage, the instruments and manifestations of the divine life in the soul.

Simple, ordinary-looking, holy, and "perhaps the most radical consequence of the Incarnation," Christian marriage is God-with-us in the everyday. That's the way it was in Nazareth, where a young couple made a loving home for God's Son. May it be that way, too, in St. Paul, Minnesota, where a middle-aged couple seeks to put aside its baby-boomer tendencies to make way for Emmanuel.

St. Joseph's Covenant Keepers

A number of Catholic movements and organizations are springing up in response to the current crisis of marriage and family life and also to John Paul II's call to bring the world back to Christ through the family. One of them is the Family Life Center International, founded by Steve Wood one year after he attended the 1991 pro-life summit sponsored in Rome by the Pontifical Council for the Family. Moved by the event, Wood launched the apostolate with a view to providing solid Christian literature and other supports for families worldwide. "The heart of our mission," he explains, "is

to cooperate in building a civilization of love that protects all innocent human life by restoring the sanctity of the marriage covenant."

Two years later, on the Feast of the Holy Family 1994, Wood
began a complementary organization inspired by the Promise Keepers movement. Aimed specifically at Catholic husbands and fathers, St. Joseph's Covenant Keepers is "an informal international
network of Christian men, under the patronage of St. Joseph."
Through conferences, small group meetings, newsletters, a website
(www.dads.org), and other means, members help one another to
commit and stick to eight promises:

1. Affirming Christ's lordship over our families.
2. Following St. Joseph, the loving leader and head of the Holy
   Family.
3. Loving our wives all our lives.
4. Turning our hearts toward our children.
5. Educating our children in the discipline and instruction of
   the Lord.
6. Protecting our families.
7. Providing for our families.
8. Building our marriages and families on the "Rock."

St. Joseph plays a key role in both organizations, acting as
provider as well as patron. Steve realized this one day as he stood
agonizing over the survival of the Family Life Center. Growth having far outpaced donations, "I was facing the prospect of closing
the ministry and having no job" (no small problem: he and his wife,
Karen, have eight children). His two-year-old daughter's trusting
request for a drink of water triggered a chain of thought that led
Steve to see St. Joseph as a mighty intercessor — the epitome of
the "righteous," or "just," man of James 5:16 whose prayer is "powerful and effective." Wood's conclusion and encouragement to the
anxious: "St. Joseph is better than a friend who can merely relate to
our financial difficulties; he can do something about it!"

(Information is from Stephen Wood and James Burnham's *Christian Fatherhood,* Family Life Center Publications, P.O. Box 6060,
Port Charlotte, Florida 33949)

166

Chapter 10

Jesus Called Him Dad

St. Joseph helped God be a man.

Ernie

L'Arche, Clinton, Iowa

Sociologists looking for popular indicators of social change might do well to consult the greeting card counter. If they choose their destination carefully and do their exploring in the spring, they will hit upon cards that exclaim *Happy Father's Day, Mom!* and *Happy Mother's Day, Dad!*

"Parenthood is changing," such greetings tell us. "Family" can now mean something other than a man, a woman, and their biological children. "Daddies can make good mommies," many radical feminists contend. "Mommies can make good daddies" is the message to our rapidly swelling population of single mothers.

In this era of seismic social change — or rather, social confusion — about marriage and family life, no one is taking more hits than the traditional father. "Does a mother need a husband?" people are wondering. Or is it true that, in Gloria Steinem's catchy phrase, "a woman without a man is like a fish without a bicycle"? What is a father anyway? What does he do, beyond conception? Can't someone else fill in for him?

It strikes me that St. Joseph is just the right patron for a society that has lost its moorings with regard to parenthood in general and fatherhood in particular. Joseph was the perfect father — "the luminous, discreet image of the heavenly Father's care," said Pope Paul VI — but he fulfilled this role in a society where family life was undergoing great change, and in a family where his position was unusual, to say the least.

Considered objectively, Joseph's fatherhood was ambiguous, and uniquely so: he played absolutely no physical part in the conception of Jesus. Where today's father is being judged superfluous once a child is conceived, Joseph was in a way superfluous for that bottom-line function itself. He might have drawn back, miffed or puzzled at how to relate to Jesus. He might have adopted the hands-off "strategy of disengagement" so often recommended to stepparents. Instead, Joseph embraced his calling so fully that everyone in

Nazareth thought of Jesus as "the carpenter's son" (Matthew 13:55).

"What do I call him?" Unlike older children who puzzle over how to address a stepfather, Jesus would have gotten Joseph's attention with the simple Aramaic word he would later teach his disciples to use in the Our Father (see Luke 11:2; Matthew 6:9). "Abba," he would have said: translation "Father," "Dad," or, when he was very young, "Daddy." ("Emma," he would have called Mary.)

Though it apparently never posed a problem for Jesus — or for Mary, who referred to Joseph as "your father" (Luke 2:48) — the question of what to call St. Joseph has proved something of an intellectual challenge for others who have tried to describe his unique fatherly role. "Father," they have called him, but with various adjectival prefixes: so-called, putative, adoptive, foster, matrimonial, vicarious, virginal, legal. Behind the names are varying conceptions of the role.

As with Joseph's marriage to Mary, some early Church Fathers took a deliberately minimalist view of his relationship with Jesus. Writing in the third century, with heretical attacks on Jesus' divinity in mind, Origen suggested that perhaps Joseph's role was purely functional, and not fatherhood in a real sense. But starting with Ephrem of Syria in the fourth century and continuing on with John Chrysostom, Augustine, Thomas Aquinas, and others, Church writers came to see Joseph's fatherhood as real, though not biological. Among their conclusions:

• Joseph was married to Mary when she conceived: Jesus was thus given to their marriage — to Joseph and Mary both. "On account of this loyal marriage," said St. Augustine, "both merited to be called the parents of Christ, and not only she as mother but he as his father and as her husband."

• Jesus was actually the fruit of Joseph and Mary's marriage. Every newlywed is called to be open to new life. Joseph was no exception. But his marriage to Mary was designed with just one precious Life in mind. It was "specially ordained for this purpose," said Thomas Aquinas, "that the Child should be received and brought up within it." By receiving Jesus, therefore, Joseph and Mary's union attained the unique fruitfulness that God had designed it for.

• Joseph was charged with naming Jesus — a father's task, as John Chrysostom indicated by picturing the angel of Joseph's first dream speaking the following words:

> Mary will bring forth a son, and you will call his name Jesus.
> For you must not think that because he is of the Holy Spirit you

are therefore excluded from cooperating in this plan. Even though you contributed nothing to his generation and the Virgin remained inviolate, nevertheless, what belongs to a father without destroying the dignity of virginity, that I bestow on you, that you name the Child.

• Joseph contributed to Jesus' conception — not in the usual way but by supporting Mary's virginity, which was necessary for it. Jean Gerson, the influential fifteenth-century preacher and theologian who seems to have had this insight first, wrote: "The procreation of the Child Jesus occurred in you, Mary, by the Holy Spirit, with the true or interpretative consent of your husband Joseph. For he wished that the will of God should be accomplished in all things, 'being a just man.'"

Over time, such arguments added up to a general consensus in favor of Joseph's genuine fatherhood. Some of them figured among the ten reasons — based on "the offices that he discharged as father" — that appeared in a watershed book by Jerónimo Gracián, Teresa of Ávila's closest friend and fellow-worker. Written in 1597 at the request of a group of Roman carpenters, his *Summary of the Excellencies of St. Joseph* was a thoughtful, creative culling from earlier writers that quickly became the most widely circulated book on St. Joseph in Europe. "Within the first decade of its publication," says Father Joseph Chorpenning, who recently provided a first-ever translation of the *Summary* into English, "there was a surge in devotion to Joseph in Italy and Spain." It was accompanied, no doubt, by a surge of appreciation for the reality of Joseph's fatherhood.

The Church has reaffirmed this appreciation over the centuries, most recently in Pope John Paul II's *Guardian of the Redeemer.* This is "a true fatherhood," the pope insists. "In this family, Joseph is the father: his fatherhood is not one that derives from begetting offspring; but neither is it an 'apparent' or merely 'substitute' fatherhood. Rather, it is one that fully shares in authentic human fatherhood and the mission of a father in the family" (No. 21).

For some of us, it is not only Joseph's fatherhood that needs rethinking but also his family life. Was the social unit headed by Joseph in that simple Nazareth house an authentic family? For a long time, I for one saw it more as the prototype of the monastery, with St. Joseph as a sort of novice master watching over the first nun and the first priest. Mine was a holy-card image of a pale, haloed trio who lived in silence behind drawn blinds and shunned contact with the outside world. It was in some ways an attractive picture of unbroken mystical contemplation far removed from everyday cares and concerns. But it related not at all to anything I saw in my family, other families I knew, or even the leaven-in-society, "domestic Church" family described by Vatican II ("Decree on the Apostolate of Lay People," *Apostolicam Actuositatem,* No. 11).

Without denying that Joseph, Mary, and Jesus can serve as models for religious life, it is important to understand that they were first and foremost a normal-looking family. Their deep spiritual life did not develop within a monastic enclosure specially dedicated to a permanent observance of "great silence." Its setting was a first-century village with narrow streets, houses built one against another, and shared courtyards. Social interaction in Nazareth was intense and ongoing to a degree that many of us — with our privacy fences, caller I.D., get-away cabins, and other ways of screening out the world — would find unsettling. Looking at archeological excavations of first-century Galilean villages — in Capernaum, for example — more than one American suburbanite has experienced claustrophobia!

Every day the Holy Family interacted with the less holy and the unholy families around them. Jesus played games and ran about in courtyards with the other boys. Mary joined the groups of women making their daily runs to the well and maybe the village oven. Joseph had friends and business contacts; perhaps he received some of them at home, with Mary waiting on them as Peter's mother-in-law would one day wait on Jesus and his disciples (see Mark 1:31).

Then too, if Jesus' "brothers and sisters" lived with the family, Joseph's household itself was livelier than we usually imagine. As we saw in chapter four, it is not unreasonable or sacrilegious to think that Joseph may have had more than two other mouths to feed. And even if these "brothers and sisters" were relatives who did not live under Joseph's roof, their presence in the Gospels directs us away from seeing Jesus, Mary, and Joseph as ivory-tower recluses. They appear instead as members of a larger extended family, a kinship group that was especially strong and tightly knit in first-century Mediterranean societies.

One way or another, other relatives figured in the life of the Holy Family. Their exact relationship is unclear, but Mary's various appearances in the company of Jesus' "brothers" (presumably after Joseph's death; see Matthew 12:46-50; Mark 3:31-35; Luke 8:19-21; John 2:12) give the impression that it was close.

Relating to Joseph and his household as a real family is also facilitated by gaining a realistic picture of the society in which they lived. As noted in chapter five, the Galilee of Joseph's day was experiencing a crisis of family life. Biblical scholar Ben Witherington describes it as "the breaking down of the extended family into more nuclear family units, caused by the rapid growth of the population." Parental authority was not being undermined in the drastic way it is today, but it was weakened as sons moved away from the family homestead and took up occupations different from those of their fathers.

Ours, too, is a time of crisis for families, with Western society tripping gaily into a brave new world of never-been-tried approaches. In the U.S., traditional precedents have been overturned. Marriage rates are low and falling — not yet at their lowest ever, says sociologist David Popenoe, but rapidly approaching "uncharted territory." The other side of the coin is that nonmarital cohabitation, out-of-wedlock births, and marital dissolution are at historic highs. Even more strongly, scholar Dana Mack contends that we are living in an increasingly "family-hating culture" that sabotages parents' efforts to raise their children and, in fact, considers parenthood "the repository of brutality, tyranny, and incompetence."

The modern development that past societies would have considered most difficult to comprehend, though, is our violation of what prominent anthropologist Bronislaw Malinowski called a "universal sociological law" and "the most important moral and legal rule" concerning birth: "that no child should be brought into the world without a man — and one man at that — assuming the role of sociological father, that is, of guardian and protector, the male link between the child and the rest of the community."

Past generations would recoil at our society's growing acceptance of the conditions that have led to this breakdown — divorce, unmarried parenting, nonmarital births, and sperm-donor technologies. It all adds up to a historical first. Says David Popenoe, "We are seeing the emergence of an extreme form of fatherlessness in which the father is permanently absent, unknown, and often unknowable from the moment of conception." The ancients would not have been surprised at the consequences: a "human carnage" that takes its toll on everyone, and especially children.

How is St. Joseph's example relevant to the revolutionary changes we are seeing in marriage and family life? Does he model any approaches that might help us face these new challenges? We might start to consider the question by looking at what Joseph did in first-century Palestine.

ACCEPTING • The first thing Joseph offered Jesus was the vital social connection that Bronislaw Malinowski mentions above: a legitimate place in society. By obeying God's directive to give Jesus his name, Joseph acknowledged the child as his own and took legal responsibility for his welfare.

"Maternity is a fact, paternity is a matter of opinion," a Roman jurist named Baius once observed. For Joseph, though, non-paternity was a fact too: he knew without a doubt that he had not fathered the child in Mary's womb. To accept Jesus nonetheless was to take a difficult, highly countercultural stand.

Joseph's society sought a high degree of "paternity confidence." It prized a woman's chastity, hedging it about with many laws and sanctions, because it prized legal offspring. Before becoming invested in a child, a man wanted assurance that he was really the father.

This is still an up-front expectation in many societies. It came home to me forcefully in a recent article about the plight of ethnic Albanian women who face rejection by their husbands and families if they admit to having been raped during the 1999 Serbian campaign to drive Albanians out of Kosovo. One thinks also of Muslim countries where unchaste daughters and unfaithful wives are occasionally executed — sometimes by the government, sometimes by the family's shamed menfolk.

To modern Americans, this concern for legitimacy seems excessive — which indeed it is when it fosters cruelty, abuse, and a double standard for women. But our culture has swung to the other extreme by no longer considering it important to know who a child's father is. Nonmarital births are generally accepted; their number has increased "600 percent in just three decades," according to David Popenoe. This development has the advantage of not stigmatizing children by branding them "illegitimate."

And yet, for all our blasé acceptance of children entering the world without a socially recognized and responsible father, paternity confidence remains an important behind-the-scenes issue for us too. "If paternity confidence is on the wane, which certainly seems

172

to be the case," Popenoe observes, "it helps to explain today's downward spiral of fatherhood." In other words, even in the "tolerant" U.S., the less certain a man is that a child is his, the less likely he is to stick around and assume responsibility.

St. Joseph, who took a countercultural stand in accepting Jesus, can help today's fathers buck their own culture. For biological fathers who are tempted to shirk responsibility for the children they have helped bring into this world, Joseph models acceptance of God-given responsibility. For men who are called to some kind of nonbiological paternity — stepfathers, adoptive fathers, and even spiritual fathers — Joseph models generous, accepting love.

Joseph could have said no to paternity. "Well, gee, I'm not really equipped for this," he might have protested. "Raising God's Son! Who needs that kind of responsibility?" Instead, "from the beginning, Joseph accepted with the 'obedience of faith' his human fatherhood over Jesus. And thus, . . . he certainly came to discover more fully the indescribable gift that was his human fatherhood" (*Guardian of the Redeemer*, No. 21).

Every father who follows Joseph's example of obedient faith can expect the same.

PROVIDING • The liturgy for the feast of St. Joseph (March 19) refers to him as "the faithful and prudent steward whom the Lord has set over his household" (see Luke 12:42). Like the other faithful provider with whom he is often compared — the Old Testament Joseph, appointed by Pharaoh to take Egypt through a time of famine (see Genesis 41) — St. Joseph was specially chosen for an important task. God made him "lord and chief of His household and possessions, the guardian of His choicest treasures," said Pius IX. "By his labor," Leo XIII specified, Joseph "regularly provided for [Jesus and Mary] such necessities of life as food and clothing."

Joseph the carpenter of Nazareth worked hard to meet the physical needs of his family. "I can see him planing, then drying his forehead from time to time," Thérèse of Lisieux imagined in a moment of realism. "How many troubles, disappointments! How many times did others make complaints to good St. Joseph? How many times did they refuse to pay him for his work!"

"Labor of love" is the phrase that comes to mind when I think of Joseph on the job. Whether crafting tables or lugging roof timbers, he turned every project into an expression of deep love for God — an attitude that St. Thérèse, too, recommended as part of

173

her "little way" of holiness. This was Joseph's approach to his entire life, as Pope Paul VI explained:

> He made his life a service, a sacrifice to the mystery of the Incarnation and to the redemptive mission connected with it; in having used the legal authority which was his over the Holy Family in order to make a total gift of self, of his life and work; in having turned his human vocation to domestic love into a superhuman oblation of self, an oblation of his heart and all his abilities into love placed at the service of the Messiah growing up in his house.

St. Joseph is, of course, the prime model of the diligent breadwinner who assumes responsibility for the needs of others. He is the perfect patron for every household provider.

PROTECTING • The second chapter of Matthew introduces a Joseph who is savior to the Savior. He preserves Jesus' life by whisking him and Mary out of Herod's range and into the safety of Egypt.

Those who have experienced the trauma of leaving their people and their homeland can guess something of what it must have cost Joseph to lead his little family into the unknown. "Oh, it is so wrong to picture the flight into Egypt as a nice, smooth hike with angels on all sides ministering to them," wrote Maria von Trapp, remembering her own experience of fleeing over the Austrian Alps to escape the Nazis in 1938. There is the constant fear of pursuit, she said, the tedium and difficulty of travel, and finally the challenge of being "poor refugees" in a foreign country. For Joseph, who had grown up in an area where people did not relocate at the drop of a hat, the displacement must have been difficult. But the guardian of the Redeemer did what comes naturally to a father: he made sacrifices to protect his child.

Pope John Paul finds "a certain prophetic eloquence" in the fact that Jesus, the "sign of contradiction," faced threats and dangers from his very birth. "Prophetically eloquent also," he says, "is the tragedy of the innocent children of Bethlehem, slaughtered at Herod's command." Life proclaimed, life threatened, life snuffed out — it is a drama that the pope views in connection with "the gravity of all attempts on the life of a child in the womb of its mother" ("Letter to Families," No. 21).

In our world, many newly conceived children need protection

not from cruel tyrants but from their own parents, as well as counselors, doctors, and other health care professionals who may even think they are doing good. In the U.S. alone, an estimated thirty-five million unborn babies were put to death between 1973 and 1996. Some died because their mothers yielded to powerful social pressures. Some were victims of society's emphasis on self, convenience, and technology. There are countless other victims too — for example, all the "spare" embryos discarded in pursuit of artificial reproduction, genetic engineering, cloning and embryo research, and some forms of contraception.

Today scientific and technological breakthroughs are giving rise to "new forms of attacks on the dignity of the human being," John Paul II warned in his 1995 encyclical, *The Gospel of Life*. "A new cultural climate is developing and taking hold, which gives crimes against life a new and — if possible — even more sinister character" (No. 4).

A culture in which so many fathers and mothers have abandoned their natural roles as protectors is sinister indeed. When parents betray life, society as a whole loses its sense of solidarity with other human beings and becomes indifferent to suffering, injustice, and the dignity of the person. It becomes a culture of death.

St. Joseph, who was the man of the hour when Jesus' life was imperiled, is in a special way the "saint of the hour" for a society where millions of defenseless human beings are in jeopardy. His example of fatherly protection teaches us to cherish life and resist compromises with our death-dealing culture. It speaks of protecting our children — and ourselves — from societal influences that lead to spiritual death. His special intercession can make a vital difference: for the conversion of our society . . . for help to see and change whatever in us opposes life . . . for today's "holy innocents," young and old . . . for help to build a culture of life.

TEACHING • "Parents are the first and most important educators of their own children, and they also possess a fundamental competence in this area: they are educators because they are parents" ("Letter to Families," No. 16).

We are reminded that "the place and task of the father in and for the family is of unique and irreplaceable importance" ("The Role of the Christian Family in the Modern World," *Familiaris Consortio*, No. 25).

Not so long ago, most Americans would have seen these statements as ever-so-obvious truisms. Hard to live up to, yes — especially that call to fatherly involvement — but the right ideals to aim for. Today Americans agree far less on these ideals and expend relatively little energy to achieve them.

Fewer fathers are teaching their children, because fewer fathers are living with them. Other men are absentee fathers because of work demands. Driven by economic pressures or led like lemmings down the path of least resistance, many parents have surrendered significant portions of their teaching responsibilities to schools, TV, social-service agencies, child-care providers, and even their children's peer groups. In many cases, the keys have been handed to teaching authorities who subvert parental authority and undermine traditional values.

Christian parents who seek moral and spiritual support for opposing these trends and taking charge of their children's education — especially their moral training — should reflect on Joseph and Mary. Scripture does not describe exactly how they trained Jesus. But what it shows of the result permits some assumptions about their dedication and competence. Scripture scholar John Meier remarks:

> If we glance ahead to Jesus' activities during his public ministry, . . . we can make some reasonable extrapolations about the boyhood that produced such an adult. If we take into account that . . . he is presented . . . as engaging in learned disputes over Scripture . . . with students of the Law, that he was accorded the respectful . . . title of rabbi or teacher, that . . . Gospel tradition presents him preaching or teaching in the synagogues . . . and that . . . his teaching was strongly imbued with the outlook and language of the sacred texts of Israel, it is reasonable to suppose that Jesus' religious formation in his family was intense and profound, and included instruction in reading biblical Hebrew.

In Old Testament times, says Father Roland de Vaux, and probably still into Jesus' day, "it was the mother who gave her children the first rudiments of education, especially of their moral formation." Both parents set an example of prayer and visits to the local synagogue and the Temple in Jerusalem. As a boy grew beyond infancy — after his third birthday, some scholars think — his father took over the primary responsibility for his training, especially for teaching him the Jewish faith. This was mainly word-of-mouth catechesis centered on the Torah, the ensemble of God's instructions and revelations to Israel.

Did Joseph carry out Jesus' instruction by himself? Did he hire a learned teacher to provide additional formation in Scripture? Did he send Jesus to the local synagogue school? (*Was* there a synagogue in Nazareth? No one knows for sure.) Somehow, Joseph made it possible for Jesus to learn Hebrew and thus acquire deeper knowledge of the Scriptures.

This would not have been run-of-the-mill training for a Jewish boy from the lower social echelons, one scholar points out. It indicates a devout and devoted father. Even though Hebrew was the language of Scripture, many Jews did not know it. When Scripture was read aloud in the synagogue, they waited for the accompanying Aramaic translations and homilies to understand what they had heard. Jesus, on the other hand, developed what Father Meier calls a "scribal literacy" that typically came from higher studies at some urban center — "the ability to read sophisticated theological and literary works and comment on them."

As God's Son, Jesus had access to unsuspected "higher learning" that would later astound his hearers (see John 7:15). But it was as "Joseph's son" that he got his start.

The four most dreadful things on earth, goes one Japanese saying, are "fires, earthquakes, thunderbolts, and fathers."

What lies behind the adage, I don't know. Does it refer to overbearing, authoritarian, abusive domestic despots? Life is bitter in the homes of these "macho" men, whose wrongful claim to male superiority and prerogatives "humiliates women and inhibits the development of healthy family relationships" ("The Role of the Christian Family in the Modern World," No. 25).

Or is the Japanese adage an expression of healthy respect for the discipline and authority of a loving father? Modern propaganda to the contrary, families do not thrive without this kind of authority. David Blankenhorn and other professional observers of the American family cite studies that show "a clear correlation between family dysfunction and weak or passive fathers." Children especially suffer, their growth to maturity stunted by the absence of wisely imposed parental values, guidelines, limits, and restrictions.

Even Jesus, who acknowledged Joseph and Mary's authority by obeying it, needed parental direction as he "increased in wisdom and in years" (Luke 2:51-52). In St. Joseph, says French bishop Albert de Monléon, "Jesus found this fatherhood which allowed him to grow. He found protection and refuge. . . . Through this very deep relationship with his adoptive father, Jesus found that extraordinary human balance which he had and which is apparent throughout the Gospels. The peace, security, authority and majesty of Jesus were strengthened and nourished by St. Joseph's secure and loving presence."

In his Angelus message on March 21, 1999, Pope John Paul had a suggestion for anyone seeking some timely spiritual reading: his 1989 apostolic exhortation on St. Joseph, *Guardian of the Redeemer*. Since "this last year of preparation for the Great Jubilee is dedicated precisely to God the Father," he said, it would be especially fitting to reflect on Joseph, who was "called to be the earthly father of the incarnate Word." In him, "the divine fatherhood is reflected in a most extraordinary way." All of this suggests perennial themes for meditation.

What is the Father like? In the Old Testament, one Hebrew word — *hesed* — sums it up. It takes more words to describe it in English, since we have no exact equivalent for it: "unswerving faithfulness in personal relationships; unfailing readiness to show mercy." As my husband, Kevin, has written, the Father's *hesed* "is one of the most relevant things the Bible has to say to us about parenting. Simply, we fathers and mothers should be men and women of unwavering faithfulness, of inexhaustible kindness."

"Who is sufficient for these things?" St. Paul exclaimed about the task of evangelizing (2 Corinthians 2:16). Kevin would be the first to make the same exclamation about the task of parenting. "Who is sufficient for raising children?" every parent wonders. "Not me. I don't have the patience, the love, the wisdom. . . ."

It is easy to imagine Joseph feeling similarly inadequate. With heroic faith, however, he accepted the daunting challenge of raising God's only Son — and met it so well that he merits to be called the "mirror" or "shadow" of the Father. Quite simply, Joseph trusted that God, who had called him to a unique fatherhood, would give him the gifts to carry it out. He acted on the basis of a principle that St. Thomas Aquinas articulated in reference to Mary: "Those whom God chooses for an office, he prepares and disposes in such a way that they become suited to it."

Here is hope for every parent! If we put our faith in God, he will equip us to care for the children he has entrusted to us. If we allow him, he will fill our hearts to overflowing with that *hesed* which is the essence of fatherly and motherly care.

More good news: Joseph shows us that *biological* parenthood is not the prerequisite for receiving this love. Adoptive parents, step-parents, and others who have assumed responsibility for someone else's children can expect it too. To whatever degree is appropriate for the situation, so can single people, men and women religious, counselors, teachers, and caregivers of all kinds.

This love, too, can be deep and life-giving. Some of us experienced it growing up, through the solicitous attentions of unmarried aunts (Mary and Leone, mine were called). But it finds a multitude of outlets. "You have been a real father to me," Scripture scholar and Marianist priest George Montague was told by a member-in-training of his religious order, whose father had recently died. Father Montague knew what the young man meant: "I could say the same about many others who have fathered me into life as Joseph did for Jesus," he says.

Still more good news: St. Joseph's fatherly love is directly available to us through our mutual connection in the communion of saints. This was Teresa of Ávila's groundbreaking insight, notes spiritual writer André Doze; she spoke of Joseph as her father "in ways no human being under the sun had ever done before."

Others, too, have experienced Joseph's paternal care. For St. Bernadette, he stepped in to fill the gap left by the death of her natural father, François Soubirous, in March 1871. Grief-stricken at the loss of "the most precious thing we had in this world, our dear and beloved father," Bernadette could nonetheless say with a smile the following year, "Don't you know that now my father is St. Joseph?"

But you don't have to be a saint to know the love of the father who keeps loving watch over the Body of Christ. Shirley Bachmeier, of San Diego, California, discovered this one day while attending a charismatic conference. At the time, she says, her relationship with St. Joseph was "sporadic and aloof." Still, when a priest who was leading a conference session on inner healing invited participants to think of either Joseph or Mary as prayer companions for the exercise, Shirley felt strongly drawn to choose St. Joseph. Unaware of any particular need, she closed her eyes and began to pray anyway. All unexpectedly, she found herself in Joseph's presence.

179

In my mind's eye, I saw myself as an infant being rocked back and forth by St. Joseph. He was holding me high in the air, singing of the wonder of my birth and my being — words of praise and love pouring out for *me*.

I watched in total amazement, hardly breathing. Such words I had never heard from either one of my parents. When I was born, they had been totally overwhelmed with responsibilities and absorbed in their own problems. They had not had the capacity to heap love and affection on their children.

But Joseph did! And now I realized how much I had longed to know that I was not accidental, unwanted, and ordinary, but loved and cherished. As Joseph lifted me to the Father in dedication and thanksgiving, God's unconditional love washed me clean and gave me new birth.

What God did for Shirley through St. Joseph, he stands ready to do for others. "Go to Joseph," Pharaoh told all the Egyptians who wanted food to carry them through the famine (Genesis 41:55). It is still good advice, as Steve Wood stresses:

> To the thousands of men deprived of a healthy relationship with their fathers: Go to St. Joseph! To those seeking to overcome a negative father image: Go to St. Joseph! To the millions of children in fatherless families: Go to St. Joseph!

To anyone in need of a saintly father's attention (and who is not?), go to Joseph! And as you do, go in confidence. The father you are turning to, said Paul VI, is the living "illustration of the cry . . . that sums up Christ's loving tenderness for us: 'Come to me, all you who are weary and burdened, and I will comfort you' " (see Matthew 11:28).

Protector of the Unborn

Many Catholics see St. Joseph as the logical patron of children in the womb. At the Shrine of St. Joseph, Guardian of the Redeemer, in Santa Cruz, California, plans are under way for an outdoor statue that will focus on this special patronage. The statue will depict St. Joseph cradling an unborn child of seven months or so. The following article about this timely aspect of St. Joseph's fatherly care is taken from the magazine published at the shrine.

In the Gospel of Matthew (1:18-25), St. Joseph was told by the angel to take Mary as his wife when she was pregnant with Jesus. This makes him the protector of Jesus even before he was born. Therefore, St. Joseph can be considered as an intercessor for the protection of the unborn, as a model for fathers of unborn children, and as a model for our whole society of someone who valued the unborn life of a human child. If God entrusted his unborn Son to the care of St. Joseph, it seems likely that he would do the same for other unborn children. . . .

Though the circumstances of Jesus' birth were difficult, Joseph trusted that God would provide, and he did the best he could with what God did provide. He did not feel that it would be better for the child not to be born than to be born in poverty — a refrain we hear often in our day. He knew that the decision about whether or not to have the child had already been made, when the child was conceived in Mary's womb. . . .

In a world which too easily decides to kill an unborn child for convenience or financial considerations, St. Joseph serves as a model of one who truly respects and cherishes the unborn human life present in the womb. He is a protector who will do all that is necessary to make sure that the life of that unborn child is allowed to continue and grow until birth. May St. Joseph inspire us all to do all that we can to protect and care for the unborn children in our society.

(Adapted and used with permission from *Guardian of the Redeemer Magazine,* 544 West Cliff Drive, Santa Cruz, California 95060 / (831) 457-1868)

Chapter 11

Patron of What We Do All Day

What's cool about St. Joseph is he didn't perform any
miracles. He just stayed home and worked.

Jack Boyle, age ten

Staying home and working is not most people's idea of cool. Right this minute, I assure you, it isn't mine. On this sunny Minnesota day, here I sit in our basement office with yet another blank computer screen daring me to fill it. Thoughts and ideas flutter about elusively. Only a few go gently onto that blue screen. Most are a defiant, unruly bunch whose "I will not serve!" will yield to nothing less than my strenuous, ongoing efforts — if they yield at all.

Today, for sure, I'D RATHER BE FISHING, as thousands of bumper stickers in this "land of ten thousand lakes" proclaim. And I don't even fish.

Escape from toil, escape from routine — whatever daily work we do — isn't this what most of us long for, at least much of the time? "One minute to five is the moment of triumph," says a receptionist in *Working*, reporter Studs Terkel's classic collection of interviews about jobs and job attitudes. "TGIF," we hear at the end of each workweek. "Vacation getaway" ads lure us with promises of adventure and relaxation. So does the new American dream of early retirement followed by happy golden years of travel, golf, fine dining, and other carefree pursuits.

In our spiritual lives, too, we favor the exciting, the exceptional, the routine-breaking. We tend to view "Ordinary Time" as a mere filler in the liturgical year. Our taste runs to miracles and drama — to Joan of Arc and Francis of Assisi rather than to Brother Benildus, the nineteenth-century French schoolteacher whom Pius XI dubbed "the Saint of the Daily Grind." Spiritual highs appeal to us, as do spiritual breakthroughs that demand little or no effort. "We yearn for those special transcendent experiences that will take us out of the tedium of sitting at a computer terminal, chasing children, washing dishes, and driving on crowded highways," observes Gregory F. Augustine Pierce, former president of the National Center for the Laity. "It seems that what we really want is to touch God."

But how do we "touch God"? If it is only in our peak spiritual moments — those divine encounters experienced on retreats or before the Blessed Sacrament or at some critical life junction — then we have a problem. "Either we learn to find God in ordinary, everyday life, or else we shall never find him," warned Josemaría Escrivá de Balaguer, who founded Opus Dei precisely to help Christians encounter Christ in their daily tasks. For, try as we may, we cannot live on mountaintops far removed from toil and tedium. Mostly, our lives are routine, commonplace, full of tiring, trivial tasks endlessly repeated. Full of that activity we call work.

St. Joseph, whose life can be summed up in the word "carpenter," knew the challenges of the daily grind. But as someone who was privileged to literally touch God in his labors, he offers assurance that holiness is not incompatible with the humble and mundane. He testifies that "what is crucially important here is the sanctification of daily life" (*Guardian of the Redeemer*, Nos. 22, 24).

In fact, Joseph stands before us as perhaps the prime example of everyday workaday living as the high road to holiness. In the ensemble of his life, as in the hidden years of Jesus, seeming opposites are reconciled: prayer and work come together, contemplation and action, sacred and secular. It is another aspect of the incarnation — God affirming and sanctifying the ordinary, Emmanuel learning and working alongside a simple carpenter.

Joseph's on-the-job time with Jesus makes him the outstanding patron for anyone who works. He models an accessible path to holiness, which is why Monsignor Escrivá chose him as Opus Dei's special patron: "It is not given to everyone to imitate Teresa of Ávila or Vincent de Paul, but each of us can easily follow St. Joseph."

While teaching and exercising his trade, Joseph himself was schooled in holiness. As a result, "the spirit of the Gospel" characterized him to an exceptional degree," said Pius XII in announcing the feast of St. Joseph the Worker, on May 1, 1955. "No worker was ever more completely and profoundly penetrated by [this spirit] than the foster father of Jesus, who lived with him in closest intimacy and community of family life and work. Thus, if you wish to be close to Christ, we again today repeat, '*Ite ad Joseph* — Go to Joseph' (Genesis 41:55)."

Larry Briskey, of Shelby Township, Michigan, was just a boy when he started reflecting on how to "go to Joseph." His friendship with the saint — which, he says, has brought "great peace to my forty-nine years of marriage and to my family" — was sparked by a twelve-inch statue of St. Joseph holding the Christ child: "My mother had it on a pedestal in our hallway, and it made a great impression on me." Without quite knowing how to address Joseph, Larry started thinking and reading about him. "Over the years, I developed a great love and respect for his holiness and dedication." And when Larry did begin to pray to St. Joseph, it felt most natural to begin with work-related issues:

> In my everyday maintenance or building projects, I learned to always pray to St. Joseph for help, especially when I had difficult or even impossible problems in my mechanical tasks. He was always there for me, assisting me. Now I am retired and work with wood as a pastime and hobby. I build furniture, mostly. Not having any formal training in cabinetmaking, I depend entirely on St. Joseph and pray for his guidance and assistance. Now there is a demand for my work, and I am very proud and thankful to St. Joseph.

It is easy to understand why woodworkers like Larry would feel an affinity with the carpenter from Nazareth. But as we saw in chapter five, those who work with any hard and lasting material might also legitimately claim Joseph as their special patron. *Tekton,* the Greek word for his trade (used in Matthew 13:55 and Mark 6:3), could refer to a bricklayer, stonemason, or even a chiseler of marble.

At least one Church Father thought of Joseph as a goldsmith. A few others described him as a blacksmith — an idea that Jerónimo Gracián, for one, pooh-poohed on a number of grounds, including its unseemliness: "It cannot be believed," he maintained, that Mary and Jesus "would walk about amid coal and coal dust" with their "conversation about heavenly matters" constantly interrupted "because of the noise of the forge and hammer blows and because of the sparks that constantly fly from the anvil." More convincingly, Francis Filas argued that Church Fathers like Hilary, Ambrose, and Peter Chrysologus had been speaking allegorically — about God the Father, fire-wielding fashioner of the world — in statements that were misinterpreted as referring to "Joseph the blacksmith."

Did Joseph work with iron? Probably not. Did he work with stone as well as wood? It seems likely. Nazareth being too small to support more than one *tekton* establishment, Joseph would have possessed general construction skills, as well as more specialized knowledge of furniture-making and carpentry. To satisfy the needs of clients who came calling at the workshop door, Joseph had to be prepared for a wide range of tasks — everything from wrestling foundation stones into place to fixing broken knife handles.

This broad job description indicates that Joseph was not a physical wimp! In his book of Scripture commentaries, *God's Word,* George Martin tells of a recent visit to an archaeological dig in Israel, excavating first-century Bethsaida. Watching a group of young, muscular workmen moving a stone from the wall of a house, he reflected that, as a *tekton,* Jesus might have strained with similar stones. Joseph might have too, of course, and George Martin's conclusion applies to him as well as to Jesus: "I therefore think that Jesus was a rather rugged man, with heavily callused hands and well-developed muscles. I don't know whether he was stocky or lanky, but he was strong. He could put in a full day of hard manual work, day after day."

Was Joseph the kind of workman you could trust to do the job right? None of his handiwork has survived that we know of, so we cannot judge by the product. Neither do the evangelists report anything about his level of competency. Apocryphal writers, as always, offered their opinions. The *Protoevangelium of James,* where Joseph makes his first appearance holding an adze, gives the impression that he is a successful and, presumably, competent contractor. "I leave you in my house and go away to build my buildings," he tells Mary as he embarks on a six-month business trip. The *History of Joseph the Carpenter,* which presents Joseph as a priest "well instructed with wisdom and learning," gets more explicit about his expertise: "He was, also, skilful in his trade, which was that of a carpenter."

But here end the positive job evaluations. In the *Infancy Gospel of Thomas,* as you may remember (see pages 110-111), Jesus' miraculous powers come to the rescue when Joseph's skills are insufficient for constructing a bed. The story reappears in the *Arabic Infancy Gospel,* with the added information that this is not the first time Jesus has bailed Joseph out: "Jesus lengthens or shortens beams which Joseph had cut wrongly: for he was not clever at his trade."

Given that the apocryphal writers were intent on emphasizing Jesus' divinity (at Joseph's expense, it turns out), their assessments are more than dubious. Paul Hanly Furfey is on more solid ground when, after an interesting review of first-century woodworking tools, techniques, and materials, he concludes: "The most plausible guess is that the work [done in the shop at Nazareth] covered the whole range of wooden objects current at that time and place, and this range was probably broad enough to include at least some very skillful and fairly elaborate work." To which we might add the more philosophical pronouncement of scholar and novelist Dorothy Sayers:

> No crooked table-legs or ill-fitting drawers ever, I dare swear, came out of the carpenter's shop at Nazareth. Nor, if they did, could any one believe that they were made by the same hand that made heaven and earth. No piety in the worker will compensate for work that is not true to itself; for any work that is untrue to its own technique is a living lie.

Nor can we easily believe that the carpenter who guided the "hand that made heaven and earth" would have flunked quality control!

"I figured out what to do," my husband announced triumphantly one busy workday. I was surprised to see his grin and the glint in his eye. Things hadn't been so cheery earlier, as he struggled to get a new modem to work properly on his laptop computer. And since these technical difficulties had a way of swallowing up large chunks of the workday, a happy resolution seemed premature.

"So how did you figure it out?" I inquired dutifully.

"I prayed to St. Joseph," Kevin answered in dramatic tones. "Remember when I was having that terrible time with the fax machine yesterday? Well, once I thought of asking St. Joseph to help, I saw what to do. Same thing happened today."

St. Joseph, office technician? Sometimes it feels like a bit of a stretch to connect St. Joseph's overall patronage of work and the kinds of work that so many of us do — jobs that first-century Nazoreans couldn't have begun to imagine. That my uncle Donat and his family would ask St. Joseph's help with their dairy farm and bean fields seems entirely reasonable. After all, Joseph lived in a rural setting; he probably had a vegetable garden and kept a few chickens, goats, and maybe a donkey. And if my cousin Bob, the stonemason, does the same, that's a good fit, too. But what about my cousin Pierre, on Wall Street? or Tom, the TV scriptwriter? What about computer programmers, bus drivers, marketing analysts, social workers, CEOs, neurosurgeons, fast-food employees, rocket scientists, and electricians? What about writers and editors working with E-mail, scanners, and sometimes-working fax machines?

Joseph is your patron, too, Pope John Paul II wants us to know. Though we connect him especially with manual labor, he said during a visit to Madagascar on May 1, 1989, St. Joseph is the patron "of human work and of all those who carry out this work in varied ways and varied professions."

The general experience of work, not the similarities of our specific job descriptions, is what we share in common with our patron. Joseph knew the challenges of working to support oneself and others. He experienced the tiring monotony of the workweek. He faced on-the-job pressures — difficult projects, fussy customers, late payments. He shared in the universal experience of toil — a suffering and discipline known to every profession, no matter how white-collar. As our Holy Father explains in his encyclical "On Human Work," *Laborem Exercens* (No. 9.2):

> [Toil] is familiar to those doing physical work under sometimes exceptionally laborious conditions. It is familiar not only to agricultural workers, but also to those who work in mines and quarries, to steelworkers at their blast-furnaces, to those who work in builders' yards and in construction work, often in danger of injury or death. It is likewise familiar to those at an intellectual workbench; to scientists; to those who bear the burden of grave responsibility for decisions that will have a vast impact on society. It is familiar to doctors and nurses, who spend days and nights at their patients' bedsides. It is familiar to women, who, sometimes without proper recognition on the part of society and even of their own families, bear the daily burden and responsibility for their homes and the upbringing of their children. It is familiar to all workers, and, since work is a universal calling, it is familiar to everyone.

Fundamentally, then, St. Joseph is the model and intercessor *par excellence* for anyone who works.

The first lesson we can learn from Joseph has to do with the essential dignity of work. "By choosing a carpenter as his 'putative father,' and by becoming a carpenter himself, Christ enriched human work with an incomparable dignity," John Paul II told workers and managers at an Olivetti factory on March 19, 1980. "From now on, the one who works knows that he is accomplishing something of the divine, something that can be linked to the initial work of the Creator."

We can begin to appreciate this "initial work of the Creator" by giving the first chapter of Genesis an attentive reading. What we see there, says Jesuit theologian John Haughey, is "a very energetic and resourceful God . . . inventive, committed, busy, and productive." Here is a God who derives immense enjoyment in bringing order out of chaos, in calling forth an earth-full of plants and creatures "of every kind" (verses 11-12, 21, 24).

After creating a world that pulses with life, God fashions two creatures who resemble him — one male and one female, made "in our image, according to our likeness" (1:26). Genesis doesn't leave us guessing about how this likeness is to be demonstrated, says Father Haughey: "The God who works creates a man and woman who are to be chips off the old block. They, too, will playfully work." They will "pick up with their productivity where God left off." This they do by obeying God's command to "be fruitful and multiply, and fill the earth and subdue it; and have dominion . . . over every living thing that moves upon the earth" (Genesis 1:28).

This stewardship begins simply, with agriculture and animal husbandry (see Genesis 4:2). Today we also exercise it by means of the whole set of instruments lumped together in the term *technology* — "the world of machinery which is the fruit of the work of the human intellect and a historical confirmation of man's dominion over nature" ("On Human Work," Nos. 5.4, 5.5).

Most days, sitting dully at my intellectual workbench, it is hard to connect with the exalted view of work presented in Genesis 1. And this, despite the fact that I like what I do. So did my mother, a high-school home-ec teacher. But how exhilarating was the kind of day-to-day "dominion" she had to exercise to keep order in her classes?

How ennobled by their work does any ordinary trainload or busload of commuters appear to be, as they travel together in glum silence? What about people who are trapped in unpleasant, low-paying jobs — like the chicken eviscerators I worked the night shift with at a processing plant one summer? Difficult bosses and working conditions, downsizing, slippery ethical questions, low wages and no benefits, stress — to say nothing of the horrific realities of sweatshops and slave labor. . . . Where, in all this, do we find God's original plan of a happy, industrious, co-creating people?

It is still there, but colored now by toil and trouble because of what happened between Genesis 1 and Genesis 4. Adam and Eve's act of disobedience lost for us the ease and unalloyed gladness that we were to have experienced in our work. "By the sweat of your face" (Genesis 3:19) was not part of God's original plan! Even so, the plan itself still stands. It "was not withdrawn or canceled out. . . . Work is still the means by which man subdues the earth" ("On Human Work," No. 9.2). Not only that: work remains "a good thing" — not just by virtue of its practical benefits, but most importantly because through it, each of us "achieves fulfillment as a human being and indeed, in a sense, becomes 'more a human being' " ("On Human Work," No. 9.3).

Which is not to say that every *job* is a good thing. Some employments degrade. Some lower a worker's dignity by exalting the bottom line and the finished product. Others transgress the moral law. No drug pusher, abortion provider, pornography distributor, or slum landlord is becoming "more a human being" through work.

In the first centuries of the Church, Tertullian and other leaders identified professions that could not be practiced by Christians. Acting was one of them (the theater of the day was notoriously immoral), as was astrology and training gladiators. Selling incense was forbidden, too, because it contributed to idol worship.

Since every society gives rise to new occupations and puts a different spin on old ones, Christians must stand ready to evaluate their jobs against Gospel standards. "Is this the type of work that a 'just man' might conceivably do?" we could ask.

Some answers will be obvious. It would be impossible to imagine a "just" person — someone who seeks God's glory in all things — doing sexy commercials or developing video games that promote violence. Other situations may be more ambiguous. Should you accept that position at the nuclear power plant? the cigarette factory? the company that does business in countries notorious for civil rights abuses? Should you stay in a telemarketing job that increasingly requires you to put more pressure on people than you feel comfortable with?

Christian job-seekers must sift through many important considerations. *Will I make enough? Do I have the gifts for it? What are the hours?* . . . But the fundamental question — *Is it honest work?* — is the one we must ask ourselves and answer truthfully. If the answer is yes, then no matter what the job or its difficulty, we can take heart from the truth that it really is a participation in our Creator's activity. It even has redemptive possibilities: "By enduring the toil of work in union with Christ crucified, man in a way collaborates with the Son of God for the redemption of humanity.

He shows himself a true disciple of Christ by carrying the cross every day in the activity that he is called upon to perform" ("On Human Work," No. 27.3)

In part, we have St. Joseph to thank for the fact that our work "has been taken up in the mystery of the Incarnation" and "redeemed in a special way," says John Paul II. "At the workbench where he plied his trade together with Jesus, Joseph brought human work closer to the mystery of the Redemption" (*Guardian of the Redeemer,* No. 22). He worked side by side with Jesus, who, by devoting "most of the years of his life on earth to manual work at a carpenter's bench" revealed the sources of the dignity of work — "not primarily the kind of work being done but the fact that the one who is doing it is a person" ("On Human Work," No. 6.5).

For Christians, therefore, a self-deprecating "just a housewife" or "just a secretary" or "just a janitor" is *not* a right response to "what do you do?"! In fact, disdaining certain types of honest work as beneath us may be a holdover attitude from pagan Greece and Rome. Philosophers like Plato and Aristotle placed the highest value on performing civic duties and achieving intellectual and physical fitness. Since these were full-time pursuits, anything that interfered — which meant pretty much every type of paying work — was considered degrading and vulgar.

Around the year 200, Clement of Alexandria took it upon himself to correct this attitude and instill a respect for physical labor among the wealthy converts attending his catechetical school. For this he wrote the *Paedagogus,* a book of instruction buttressed by biblical examples, common sense, and theological reasoning. Even for Clement, who had considerable persuasive powers, it must have been a hard sell. In his milieu, writes Arthur Geoghegan, "it was fashionable for a prosperous man in robust health to feign weakness when walking and to require the assistance of his slaves to mount the slightest incline." That Clement should not only praise but urge this pampered group to work themselves "is a clear indication of the important place of labor in the Christian pattern of life," says Geoghegan. (And a clear message to *today's* slackers!)

Unlike the Christians of Alexandria, William Diehl never had a problem with the idea of work. And as manager of sales for Bethlehem Steel for thirty-two years, he probably never felt tempted to belittle his job either. "But there was a problem: a major problem," he says. Although he was a committed Lutheran whose service within his

191

church had even earned him a "dedicated layperson" award, Diehl was unable to bring the basic elements of his faith into his experience of everyday life and the workplace. "My Sunday experience had no connection to my Monday world. . . . I lived in two worlds, the Sunday world of religion and the Monday world of secular life."

Unfortunately, most of us can probably relate to Diehl's dilemma. Without even realizing it, we divide life into "sacred" and "secular" — a compartmentalizing that not only hinders our relationship with Christ but also neutralizes our ability to bring him to others. "To contribute to the sanctification of the world, as from within like leaven, by fulfilling their own particular duties . . . [to] manifest Christ to others — this is our mission as laypeople in the Church," Vatican II emphasized ("Dogmatic Constitution on the Church," No. 31). How can we pursue it?

Reading books like William Diehl's *The Monday Connection*, which describes and offers solutions for the Sunday-Monday problem, can help. But as a first step, what about turning to St. Joseph, patron of workers? This is, after all, a "spirituality" problem: we need a viable spirituality of work and the everyday. And, as Teresa of Ávila stressed, in St. Joseph we have the best of spiritual directors. "Anyone who cannot find a master to teach him prayer should take this glorious saint for his master, and he will not go astray," she said.

If we ask him, St. Joseph, who is patron of both the interior life and the working life, will help us to experience the connection between these two areas. As a superb spiritual director, he can guide us to a more spiritual understanding of work-related issues — money and time, for instance.

MONEY MATTERS • "Jesus in Nazareth was insufferably ordinary," Father John Meier observes, by which he means that God's own Son fitted into the routine rhythm of life in the village. "Insufferably ordinary," too, was *Joseph* in Nazareth, whose main vocation was the mundane task known to household heads down through the ages: providing for his family.

How much did Joseph earn? The vineyard workers in Jesus' parable (see Matthew 20:1-15) received a laborer's daily pay of one denarius. What this is worth in American currency is hard to say, but you might think of it as minimum wage or less. Because Joseph was a skilled and self-employed *tekton*, though, he "might have earned a little more than a laborer," thinks Paul Hanly Furfey. Consequently, he says, "there seems no reason to believe that the Holy

Family was conspicuously in want, as judged by working-class standards of first-century Palestine."

Nor, however, were they relatively well-to-do, as some scholars have proposed, in a scenario that pictures Joseph and Jesus as master builders earning great wages in cities like Sepphoris! "Pure hypotheses, unsupported by the New Testament text," is Father Meier's pronouncement on such theories. The Holy Family was poor, though not on the rock-bottom poverty level. "Somewhere at the lower end of the vague middle" of the socioeconomic ladder is where a Nazareth woodworker would rank, says Father Meier. This is "perhaps equivalent — if we may use a hazy analogy — to a blue-collar worker in lower-middle-class America."

Did Joseph ever have to fight anxiety as he sought to provide for his family? Lacking safety nets like Medicare, Social Security, and pensions, ordinary workers like him lived a more precarious existence than most of us do. But perhaps Joseph modeled the kind of trust in God that Jesus later proposed to us: "Do not worry about your life, what you will eat, or about your body, what you will wear" (Luke 12:22). Perhaps Jesus first saw this trust lived out by the man he called *abba*.

Besides asking St. Joseph to help us deal with our financial worries, we should also seek his guidance for how to live in a consumer culture. In a country where two-thirds of the households have three TVs or more and where nonstop advertising leaves us feeling deprived if we cannot afford the latest movies, clothes, and gadgets, it can be hard to assess our true needs. No doubt about it, says Dana Mack, we are "battling a culture in which material acquisition has become the very definition of the good life." With St. Joseph, we can step back and ask some hard questions about whether our lifestyle expresses our response to God's call.

Am I earning enough? . . . Should I look for another job or try to make ends meet on this one? . . . Should I stop wandering through the mall on my lunch breaks? . . . Am I giving generously to the church and to charity? . . . What about my credit card purchases? . . . How am I trying to heed Jesus' warning: "Be on your guard against all kinds of greed; for one's life does not consist in the abundance of possessions" (Luke 12:15)? . . .

Good questions for a heavenly spiritual director!

TIME CRUNCH • The median income of American households is rising, the Census Bureau announces periodically. But as many a worker could affirm and as a *New York Times* article reports, "It is not higher wages but extra time on the job that is the main source of the rising household income."

Are we becoming a nation of workaholics? Are our materialistic desires to blame for schedules that are becoming more and more frenzied? Not necessarily.

As the *Times* reporter points out, some of us are working more now because we fear lean times ahead: "Like bears gorging themselves in anticipation of winter, American workers are taking on work in these good times to offset the bad years they have been conditioned to expect." Others put in long hours because it is the only way they can keep groceries on the table. Job insecurity motivates many people, especially hard-charging professionals who know that others stand ready to displace them on the corporate ladder if they fail to work sixty-hour weeks and put career before all else.

Ken Canfield, founder and president of the National Center for Fathering, points out the consequences: "I have searched for the CEO of a publicly traded company who would say he is strongly committed to both family and his company, and I have found none." The same could be said of many non-CEOs with demanding jobs.

Long hours at work mean short hours at home, which means a further erosion of family life. Wives and husbands follow their separate tracks. Adolescents and teenagers go without the parental contact and supervision they desperately need. Young children spend more time with child-care workers than with their parents.

All over the U.S., we see day-care services mushrooming. Some of them are financed by corporate giants whose goal, says Dana Mack, is "to trap parents in the workplace for as long as possible each day." In my area, a recent company-sponsored training session for child-care directors was described as designed "to help employees worry less about their preschool children and focus more on their work." More well-off families hire nannies. The affluent go in for personalized, all-around domestic services that a *New Yorker* magazine article humorously described as "dial-a-wife." But no family thrives when its time together ebbs away.

Telecommuting, home businesses, flex time, making do with one income — with a little creative thinking and readiness to change, we may discover that options like these can work for us. Or they may not. Either way, the important thing is to talk over the situation with God. Always ready to facilitate this conversation is St.

Joseph, whom John Paul II called "patron of the world of laypeople" and "patron of the close link between work and family."

And while we're on the subject of time and work, how about asking St. Joseph to help us keep Sunday holy?

God our Father,
creator and ruler of the universe,
in every age you call man
to develop and use his gifts for the good of others.
With Saint Joseph as our example and guide,
help us to do the work you have asked
and come to the rewards you have promised.
(From the Liturgy of the Hours morning and
evening prayer for May 1, honoring Joseph
the Worker)

St. Joseph and Catholic Workers

St. Joseph's patronage, Catholic social teaching, and the theme of work combine in the life and labors of Dorothy Day (1897-1980). Determined to change the world by fighting against poverty, Dorothy had aligned herself with anarchists, Socialists, and Communists. After her 1927 conversion to Catholicism, though, her social involvement diminished as she puzzled over how to pursue her commitment to the poor as a Catholic.

In 1932 Dorothy discovered a series of new friends who gave her the guidance she needed and influenced the rest of her life. One was St. Teresa of Ávila, in whose writings Dorothy found everything she herself wished to be. Through Teresa, Dorothy met St. Joseph. She soon considered him "both her banker and householder, a confidence which lasted for the duration of her active years" (Bridget O'Shea Merriman, O.S.F., *Searching for Christ: The Spirituality of Dorothy Day*, University of Notre Dame Press, 1994, p. 186). Then on December 8, after an anguished morning of prayer for direction at the Shrine of the Immaculate Conception, in Washington, D.C., Dorothy had her first encounter with a key earthly friend, Peter Maurin. Through him, she was introduced to Catholic social teaching in the encyclicals of Leo XIII and Pius XI.

"Our job is to make the encyclicals click," Peter told Dorothy — to bring their teaching alive and make it practical and understandable to the working public, and to work for a more just social order. With this ideal in mind the two launched the Catholic Worker movement and weekly newspaper of the same name — all under St. Joseph's special protection.

As Dorothy Day's example suggests, devotion to St. Joseph and commitment to Catholic social teaching are complementary callings. With St. Joseph's encouragement, then, we might explore the popes' social encyclicals for ourselves. Some suggestions:

✓ Leo XIII: *Rerum Novarum*, 1891 — a groundbreaking document on the relation between capital and labor.

✓ Pius IX: *Quadragesimo Anno*, 1931, on the reconstruction of the social order.

✓ John XXIII: *Mater et Magistra*, 1961 — on Christianity and social progress.

✓ John XXIII: *Pacem in Terris*, 1963 — on the establishment of world peace.

✓ Paul VI: *Populorum Progressio*, 1967 — on the development of peoples, an application of the teachings of Vatican II.

✓ John Paul II: *Laborem Exercens*, 1981 — on the struggle between capital and labor, solidarity, and the human person as worker.

✓ John Paul II: *Sollicitudo Rei Socialis*, 1987 — on social concerns: a rereading of *Populorum Progressio* that provides a survey and theological reading of modern problems and stresses the importance of the Church's social doctrine.

✓ John Paul II: *Centesimus Annus*, 1991 — Leo XIII's *Rerum Novarum* honored and reconsidered on its centenary.

Chapter 12

Assisted Living, Assisted Dying

"What particular grace did you ask St. Joseph for?"
"I asked him for the grace of a good death."

St. Bernadette to her confessor on
March 19, 1879, less than a month before she died

How and where do you want to die? British medical historian Roy Porter says he wants to die quickly, while gardening. "I quite like the idea of being conscious of dying," he says, "but actually in the middle of doing something at the same time, rather than going through a long process." Dame Cicely Saunders, founder of the modern hospice movement, holds the opposite view. "Everybody else says they want to die suddenly, but I say I'd like to die of cancer, because it gives me time to say I'm sorry, and thank you, and goodbye."

A friend of mine, as full of "good works and acts of charity" as any Tabitha (see Acts 9:36), always said she wanted to die with her boots on. She did, quite literally, at age seventy-seven, after bundling up to step out into a chill winter evening. In her coat pocket was a prayer card identifying her as a member of the Pious Union of St. Joseph, an association whose members intercede daily for those who are dying.

We disagree over how to achieve it, but not about the goal itself: everyone wants the happy death, the good death, the peaceful death, death with dignity. Just the kind of death that St. Joseph must have experienced.

We have no particulars about how or when Joseph died. As we saw in chapter three when we looked at the Gospel of Luke, he simply fades from the scene after the finding of Jesus in the Temple. Luke does seem to imply, however, that when the twelve-year-old Jesus returned obediently to Nazareth with his parents, he was settling in for the long haul — for "years" (Luke 2:52) of increasing in wisdom and grace under both Joseph and Mary's supervision.

Did Joseph die before Jesus' public ministry? With the possible exception of Ambrose and John Chrysostom, the Church Fathers and later writers thought so. Why else would Mary alone be mentioned among the relatives who came looking for Jesus (Matthew 12:46-50; Mark 3:31-35; Luke 8:19-21; John 2:12)? And, Jerónimo Gracián and others reasoned most sensibly, if Joseph were not dead, he would surely have attended the wedding feast at Cana. He "would have been present when the Redeemer died on the cross . . . nor would Christ have entrusted his mother to the beloved disciple" (see John 2:1-10; 19:26-27).

What was the cause of Joseph's death? Was it old age? Did he fall sick? Was he mortally injured on the job? How satisfying it would be if we could read an obituary notice! But even the apocryphal *History of Joseph the Carpenter,* so imaginatively expansive about Joseph's deathbed conversation, says only that his death "drew near" and that Joseph sensed it. For St. Francis de Sales, on the other hand, the reason for Joseph's death was eminently obvious:

> A saint who had loved so much in this life could not die except from love. His soul could not sufficiently love his own dear Jesus amid all the distractions of this life, and he had already performed the services required of him during the childhood of Jesus. What remained, then, but for him to say to the eternal Father, "O Father, I have accomplished the work which you have given me to do," and then to the Son, "O my Child, as your heavenly Father placed your tender body in my hands on the day you came into the world, so do I now place my spirit in your hands on this day of my departure from this world."

Unlike the cause, the circumstances of Joseph's dying seem never to have been contested. The *History of Joseph the Carpenter* indulges in a fanciful presentation of end-of-life fear and anguish, but it nonetheless shows Joseph expiring peacefully, with Mary at his feet and Jesus at his head, praying for the protection of his soul. It is the best of good deaths. "No man or woman ever had such a privilege as that of dying in the company of Jesus and Mary," says Francis Filas. "No deathbed scene could ever have been attended by witnesses who were more consoling."

Consoling for Joseph, the deathbed farewell must have been wrenching for Jesus and Mary. Surrendered though they were to the Father's will, losing Joseph had to be a blow. "How they must have grieved at his death!" says Alice von Hildebrand. Besides being their guardian and protector, St. Joseph was the only person in the whole world who had shared in the stupendous events of the annunciation, the incarnation, the nativity. . . .

How challenging for Mary especially, who before long would also see Jesus leave home. "The most blessed among women was also a widow, who lost her husband before she lost her beloved son," reflects Alice von Hildebrand, whose own husband died in 1977. "I can now turn to the Holy Virgin as the exemplary widow — a model for those who weep over the deaths of their spouses, yet fully accept God's will."

And after Joseph's death, what? Today, when someone passes away, the immediate family is caught up in a whirlwind of activity and decision-making. Contacting funeral home and cemetery, arranging wake and funeral, choosing among a myriad of options (burial or cremation? top-of-the-line or economy coffin? open or closed casket? fancy monument or simple marker? funeral flowers or "donations preferred"?) — like it or not, this is part of what muckraking journalist Jessica Mitford called the "American way of death."

Not surprisingly, the first-century "Palestinian way of death" was quicker and simpler. Not that we know every detail. The Old Testament contains descriptions of burial and funeral rites, and various customs are mentioned in a collection of rabbinic laws collected around A.D. 200. There is no way to ascertain, however, whether all these practices were customary in Joseph's day.

At the very least, the New Testament indicates, Joseph's body would have been washed (see Acts 9:37), anointed with fragrant oil (see Matthew 26:12), and wrapped with "spices in linen cloths, according to the burial custom of the Jews" (John 19:40). (The *History of Joseph the Carpenter* imagines Jesus performing the first two tasks, with angels taking over for the shrouding!) Joseph's body was certainly not embalmed, as this was never the practice in Israel, nor was it cremated: with the puzzling exception of King Saul and his sons (1 Samuel 31:12), says Father Roland de Vaux, "to burn a body was an outrage, inflicted only on notorious criminals."

If Joseph's burial followed the usual pattern, it probably took place on the very day he died. Relatives and friends gathered at his home, placed his body on a wooden stretcher (Joseph and Jesus had probably filled orders for many a bier in their workshop), and carried it to a gravesite outside the village. Vocal lamentation being very much a part of this culture, it was surely not a quiet crowd. Funeral etiquette involved wailing, weeping, and singing dirges. (See Acts 8:2, where Stephen is buried to the accompaniment of "loud lamentation," and Matthew 9:23, where professional mourners and

199

the crowd are "making a commotion" over the death of the synagogue leader's little girl.) Joseph's funeral procession was just the
kind that Jesus would later encounter and be moved by in the town
of Nain (Luke 7:11-14).

Were any priests present? What official prayers, eulogies, and
blessings were said along the way and at the burial place? We cannot really say. With only later rabbinic tradition to go by, all we can
reasonably hold is that some sort of praying took place and that
Jesus played the key part in this and other aspects of the burial, as
would befit a "firstborn son." In this culture, ensuring a proper
burial for his parents was a son's special responsibility (see Tobit
6:15). We may not know exactly what services this entailed, but we
can be sure that Jesus performed them for Joseph with the greatest love.

No one knows where St. Joseph was buried. A cave discovered
in 1889 is occasionally advanced as the site, but without any evidence of authenticity. Joseph is as hidden in death as he was in life.

Joseph's body was laid to rest in the earth or in a natural cave
or tomb hewn out of rock. Either way, no coffin was used. Burial in
the ground was a straightforward procedure, as it has always been,
but burial in a family cave or tomb was a two-step process. First, the
corpse was placed on one of the ledges or niches built around the
inside of the tomb chamber; or it was slid head first into a body-size
shaft cut horizontally into the wall. Then, once the body had decom-
posed, the bones were gathered up and placed in an ossuary, a small
box usually made of limestone and often decorated and inscribed.

Interestingly, ossuaries were used in Jewish tombs for only
about a hundred years, up until the Roman destruction of Jerusalem in A.D. 70. Before then, bones had simply been heaped up together in a corner of the burial chamber. In Joseph's day, ossuaries
seem to have been "both popular and common," Léonie Archer reports, "having been found in all types of graves both elaborate and
simple, and apparently used by all levels of society." (If ever you
visit the Israel Museum in Jerusalem, you can see a number of
ossuaries. One of them, it is virtually certain, contained the bones
of Caiaphas, the high priest who interrogated Jesus and handed
him over to Pilate — John 18:14, 24, 28.)

It should be noted here that St. Francis de Sales, among others, would have considered the whole discussion of Joseph's resting place entirely beside the point. He held it as certain that St.

Joseph was carried bodily into heaven on the day of Christ's ascension. "How could we doubt that Our Lord raised glorious St. Joseph up into heaven, body and soul? For he had the honor and grace of carrying him so often in his blessed arms, arms in which Our Lord took so much pleasure. . . . St. Joseph is therefore in heaven body and soul, without a doubt."

That Jesus prepared for Joseph a very special "dwelling place" in his Father's house we can well believe (John 14:2-3). That Joseph was bodily assumed into it remains a question mark, St. Francis' conviction notwithstanding!

Consoled at death, tenderly cared for after it, welcomed into heaven with a "well done, good and faithful servant" — is it any wonder that St. Joseph has become patron of the happy death? He is "justly regarded as the most efficacious protector of the dying," said Pope Benedict XV in a 1920 message that also encouraged bishops to "assist in every possible manner" all pious associations dedicated to praying for the suffering and the dying.

By extension, St. Joseph is the "solace of the afflicted" and "hope of the sick," as the litany in his honor calls him. Members of religious orders dedicated to nursing and other types of health care have long considered him their special patron (witness the numerous Catholic hospitals that have borne his name). All caregivers might do well to imitate them — perhaps especially those called into service as life spans lengthen and America grays.

In chapter ten, we considered St. Joseph as the saint of the hour for our culture-of-death society, whose technological expertise and esteem for the expedient puts its weakest members at risk. These risks are greatest at both the very beginning and the very end of life — seasons that are in a special way under St. Joseph's patronage. Having reflected on his role as protector of the first season, let us now explore his significance for the second.

Not so long ago, due to a trend with roots in the nineteenth century, death was a taboo subject in many Western societies. For centuries up until the mid-1800s, death had been very much a part of life — a feared but familiar passage that most people faced with the help of family, friends, and faith in God. By the 1930s, though, the new trend was shaping up into what French historian Philippe Ariès calls "a brutal revolution in traditional ideas and feelings. . . . Death, so omnipresent in the past that it was familiar, would be effaced, would disappear. It would become shameful and forbidden." As the deathbed moved from bedroom to hospital room, death was "furtively pushed out of the world of familiar things."

By 1955, British sociologist Geoffrey Gorer was making a persuasive case for the fact that death had become the new pornography, replacing sex as society's main forbidden subject. Apparently, this was still the case ten years later, as Elisabeth Kübler-Ross sought to find and interview people who were facing death. "Dying? But there are no dying here!" she heard again and again from offended directors of clinics and hospitals. To say otherwise would have been to admit the failure of medical science.

But another cultural revolution was in the offing. Thanks to literature like *On Death and Dying*, the 1969 book that emerged out of Kübler-Ross's research and interviews, it became suddenly acceptable to discuss death and death-related issues — death with dignity, pain management and palliative care, the hospice movement, and other alternatives to isolated dying in a hospital. More than thirty years later, the discussion continues, but now with the sinister twists introduced by society's growing acceptance of euthanasia and physician-assisted suicide.

Far from repressing thoughts of death, Americans today seem obsessed with it. "A cosmic paradox," *New York Times* writer Tom Kuntz says of this phenomenon. "At the height of its global ascendancy, supposedly optimistic and youth-obsessed America is now also increasingly fixated on death."

Celebrity deaths fascinate — Diana, Marilyn, Elvis, both John Kennedys. . . . Instruction books abound with information about "home deathing," "the true work of dying," "reshaping the end of life," "how we die," and even how we decompose. Hollywood serves up tearjerkers, fluffy New Age flicks about death and afterlife, and movies that combine the old and new pornographies, sex and death.

Our discussions are fueled by impressive scientific breakthroughs in treating illness and extending life. "The utopian vision of current Western medicine is that of a person who drops painlessly dead on the golf course at eighty-five after a disease-free life," writes Bryan Appleyard in a recent book about genetic advances. "Some now talk of using genetics to increase that optimum age to one hundred twenty-five."

Biologists have identified genes that slow the rate of aging. Human cells in the test tube have been made to grow beyond their usual life span. Genetic engineers discuss the possibility of cloning or growing new organs as old ones wear out. For some time, cryonics specialists have been freezing corpses in anticipation of the day when science will call them back to life.

"If cells can be made to live indefinitely, can people too be made immortal?" wonders science writer Nicholas Wade. "It takes a pinch of hubris even to ask the question."

You bet it does! But hubris seems to be in great supply these days. Speaking about physicians, Dr. Sherwin B. Nuland, who teaches surgery at Yale, recognizes that in the past, "doctors were far more willing to recognize the signs of defeat and far less arrogant about denying them. . . . The greater humility that should have come with greater knowledge is instead replaced by medical hubris: Since we can do so much, there is no limit to what should be attempted. . . ."

Besides trying to push the limits of mortality to an infinite remove, our culture has also been promoting engineered dying as an answer to a wide range of problems. This prideful approach to death has become an idol, observes Vigen Guroian, professor of ethics and theology:

> As with all things we fashion into gods, we have managed to overcome our fear of death enough to seek to manipulate it for our own purposes, to summon it to provide a solution for our personal and social problems. We have overcome our aversion to death enough to get comfortable with using it to get rid of criminals, to end unwanted pregnancies, and, increasingly, to relieve the misery of illness and injury. Through our own choices and predilections, we have fashioned a culture of death.

Has our society, then, so tamed and manipulated death that there remains no obvious role for a patron like St. Joseph to help us through it? Hardly. Scratch the surface, and it becomes evident that our manipulation of death has not removed our fear of it.

We flirt with death as an answer to problems, we approach it technologically, and we focus on engineering its details. But our solutions have only added to our dread.

Who wants to die alone in a hospital (eighty percent of American deaths now occur there), their last moments guided by medical personnel, rather than loved ones? Who is not reluctant to surrender oneself to the potentially dehumanizing machinery of modern medicine? Ironically, our ability to extend life has become one of the factors driving the movement for the right to end it. Comments John

J. Paris, professor of bioethics at Boston College: "The demand for active euthanasia is, in part, a response to the fear of [a] . . . seemingly uncaring world of medicine" — a response to overly aggressive medical treatment that, by refusing to accept its limits, violates the dignity of the dying.

We are still scared to death of death. Look at death directly? at our own death? at the possibility of having our life snuffed out in a plane crash or drawn out in a losing battle with cancer or Alzheimer's? We are more intent on forgetting anything that reminds us of our fragility.

This is especially true of baby boomers, the oldest of whom are quickly approaching retirement age. Marketing experts, noting their distaste for aging, are responding with a wide range of easy-to-use "sheep's clothing" products, said a recent news article — items specifically designed and subtly marketed to "a population that refuses to acknowledge the prospect of failing eyesight, hearing and dexterity." Confided one associate product manager: "We don't mention the age word."

But baby boomers are not the only Americans who are uncomfortable with their mortality. How many of us are prepared to look at death as Catholics did in days past, when it was customary to meditate regularly on "the four last things" — death, judgment, hell, heaven? How many would approach death with the confident eagerness of St. John Fischer, who, upon seeing the scaffold where he was to be executed, exclaimed, "Walk swiftly, feet, we are not far from paradise!"?

We are more like the old woman that a medical student described to Evangelical writer Joseph Bayly: "She knows she has only a few weeks, a month or so to live. . . . But do you know what she does? Reads from a pile of love and screen magazines every waking moment"!

Conquering apathy or unhealthy fear, finding meaning where we see none, acknowledging and trusting God as the Author and Giver of life from beginning to end — for all of this and more, we need the help of the Holy Spirit. And today, perhaps more than ever before, we also stand in special need of an end-of-life guide and intercessor. St. Joseph, patron of a happy death, stands ready to meet that need. If we ask him, he will help us to see past the cultural confusion that surrounds us and discover what it really means to die well. He will help us to face death in a way that gives glory to God.

Here are just a few of the graces we can expect as we turn to St. Joseph. You will surely think of more.

PEACE • As many a spiritual writer has pointed out, there is a healthy and an unhealthy fear of death. The unhealthy kind is what most of us would most likely develop if we followed techniques like the following, taken from a manual of piety for schoolchildren in eighteenth-century France: "As you climb between the sheets, reflect: this linen may one day form my shroud. . . ." Also not usually helpful in this regard are certain types of moral tales — like the story of the young person who, on the one day he forgets to wear his scapular, commits a mortal sin and is killed in a car crash!

"There is a kind of good fear which, if handled properly, leads to confidence in God and not to panic," says Dom Hubert van Zeller. With grace, he says, our "cowardly fear of death" can be changed into a higher "humble fear of punishment for sin," and then into a "fear of offending God" by not offering him our total trust. At that point, says Dom van Zeller, "we find we are not really afraid of death at all. Why not? Simply because we are now leaving the question of our death to him. That is trust. And trust, like love (of which it is an absolutely essential part), casts out fear."

St. Joseph, patron of the peaceful death, pray for us.

MEANING • "I wouldn't ever do it, but let me tell you: seeing somebody die in so much pain makes you think about calling 'Dr. Death' " (Jack Kevorkian, the most visible and controversial activist in the crusade to legalize euthanasia). The speaker was one of the mechanics who service our cars: first his mother, then his father had undergone a slow, painful death from cancer. "It makes you think. . . ."

In every time and place, human beings have grappled with the mystery of suffering. But until the twentieth century, no society has ever decided to resolve the problem by cutting it off at the root — that is, by legalizing or tolerating euthanasia and physician-assisted suicide. "Might not life be too sacred for extended suffering?" asks one author, representing the "pro-euthanasiast" position. "Is there no sanctity in relieving the suffering of others?"

Yes, when that "relief" means providing painkillers and sedatives and other forms of palliative care for those who suffer. No, when it means deliberately eliminating the sufferer! As Pope John

Paul II explained in his 1995 encyclical: "True compassion leads to sharing another's pain; it does not kill the person whose suffering we cannot bear" ("On the Value and Inviolability of Human Life," *Evangelium Vitae,* No. 66.2).

In the Christian view, suffering does not diminish the value and dignity of human life. On the contrary: because Jesus won our salvation through an agonizing death on the cross, suffering and death itself have been redeemed. Futile and senseless apart from God, they become meaningful and beneficial — for the sufferer and even for others — when united with the Passion of Christ. Choosing to suffer with Jesus under the sign of the cross does not eliminate the pain or the mystery; rather, it is the path to peace and to the hope that does not disappoint. "We suffer *in communion with the Lord,*" Cardinal Joseph Bernardin affirmed during his fight with the pancreatic cancer that finally claimed his life in 1996. "And that makes all the difference in the world!"

Examples abound of people who have found meaning in their suffering by accepting it in a context of sacrifice and offering to God. Cardinal Bernardin is one of them. Perhaps you know others. Judie Brown, president of the American Life League, saw this drama unfold in the life of her mother, who died of "a terrible case of rheumatoid arthritis compounded by ulcers and other conditions that left her bedridden for five years." Early on, "well before the worst years of her suffering had even begun," Judie's mother tried to kill herself with a drug overdose.

> As she slowly came out of her deep sleep, she told my father and me that while she was lingering in life, so close to death, God had spoken to her. He told her that he would give her one more chance to live the rest of her life as he would have her live it, rather than face the awful hell to which her suicide would surely bring her.
>
> In her agony and her recovery from attempted suicide I saw the divine meaning of compassion. . . . It has everything to do with absolute, unconditional love and a total surrender of self during times of excruciating pain and helplessness.

St. Joseph, patron of the suffering, pray for us.

HUMILITY • "You will not die," the serpent assured Eve. Eat this forbidden fruit and "you will be like God" (Genesis 3:4, 5).

The sin of our first parents, the desire to usurp authority over our own lives that belongs to God, afflicts us still. A "certain Promethean attitude," John Paul II called it — a mindset that "leads people to think that they can control life and death by taking the decisions about them into their own hands" ("On the Value and Inviolability of Human Life," No. 15.3).

Doctors and scientists may be especially vulnerable to this pride, as we saw above, but in our society it is all-pervasive. You can see it even in the rapidly growing body of secular literature about how to prepare for death. Being in control is an important theme there. One author provides tips and techniques for "cutting death down to size," creating end-of-life "rituals and myths," and even "planning your eternal future." ("Of course, some will say your afterlife plan is pure fantasy. Tell them that your present life is too, yours and theirs. After all, our lives, our health, our feelings, our dreams and longings are all products of our thoughts.") Another author suggests that heaven and hell are human constructs ("we create them from our own image and likeness").

We delude ourselves if we fall for such fictions. We must have the humility to see ourselves as creatures. O Lord, "you have power over life and death," not I (Wisdom 16:13). "Eternal punishment" and "eternal life" are realities over which you reign (Matthew 25:46). It takes faith to be humble — to surrender our illusion of control over life-and-death matters and to trust that God is loving and merciful to those who turn to him.

"The one who is righteous will live by faith," wrote St. Paul (Romans 1:17). And will die by faith, too, he might have added!

St. Joseph, you who lived and died by faith, pray for us.

END-OF-LIFE ASSISTANCE • "St. Joseph is very special to me and my family," says Jo Mabou, of Deville, Louisiana. "Most important" among the many reasons she cites: "My dad was baptized on his deathbed in the hospital" — an answer to years of prayer by members of his family. Jo didn't know it at the time, but a niece in Tennessee and her friend had just finished a thirty-day novena to St. Joseph for her father's baptism. St. Joseph was very present in that hospital room, says Jo, who with her husband served as godparent. "As Father Chris was talking to Daddy and explaining that he should choose a saint's name for confirmation, I heard 'St. Joseph' in my mind. Without my saying anything, this was the name he chose. When I heard Father Chris say, 'I confirm you Elmer Joseph,' I almost fell under the bed! Truly, my dad's death was a miracle of grace."

In a different way, a small group of people who often pray together also experienced St. Joseph's presence at the bedside of a dying person. Lesley Vaitekunas, of Coconut Creek, Florida, tells the story.

> We were praying over a man who was dying of cancer, a young father of two. As we prayed, one of us had a mental image of St. Joseph watching over this man's two little girls and also helping his wife. This image was shared with the couple, and it seemed to comfort both of them.
>
> The person who had received the image also had a sense that the number 19 was significant but, not knowing exactly what it meant, did not share it with the couple. "Perhaps it means that this young man will die on the nineteenth of this month," we thought. But one month passed, then another. By the third month, we had forgotten all about it. Well, that was the month and day on which this young man died: on March 19, St. Joseph's feast day!

St. Joseph, help of the dying, pray for us.

"The thought of death, perhaps very near, certainly not far away, brings me back to my beloved St. Joseph." Pope John XXIII was eighty when he made this entry in his spiritual journal in 1961. It was not the first time he had thought about death, nor the first time he had considered it in the company of St. Joseph, his "first and beloved protector."

Saints and spiritual writers agree: preparation for a happy death begins long before we arrive at death's door. God will provide all we need for that moment, wrote Dom Hubert van Zeller. Will we accept it? Yes, he says, if we have prepared by learning "to make use of the graces he sends long before we are faced with the problem of dying. God is helping us now, and he will be helping us then. If we want to make certain of being full of grace then, we must do our best to be full of grace now."

As Pope John's experience reveals, the patron of the good death stands ready to help us with this assignment. Under St. Joseph's gentle direction, learning to live with our mortality in mind will not be a grim, fearful duty. He will help us to approach it in the spirit that writer Henri Nouwen recommended to his friend Cardinal Bernardin: "People of faith, who believe that death is the transition from this life to eternal life, should see it as a friend."

St. Joseph, patron of the good death, help us to live well so that we may die well!

Praying for a Happy Death

St. Alphonsus Liguori, whose devotional works include a meditation on the death of St. Joseph, once wrote: "The work of aiding the dying to die well is a work of charity most dear to God and very efficacious for the salvation of souls." Outstanding for his embrace of this important work of mercy was Blessed Louis Guanella (1842-1915), who spent most of his life assisting those he called God's "favorites" — orphans, the abandoned elderly, people with physical or mental handicaps or chronic illnesses. To serve them, he founded two congregations, the Servants of Charity and the Daughters of Mary, proposing St. Joseph to each as the model of religious life and naming many of his institutions after him. "There is not a single chapter of the Regulations that does not mention the name of his dear St. Joseph," says one of Guanella's biographers. "Devotion to this saint is an integral part of his spirituality and charism."

Convinced that the congregations' work was in vain unless the people they served died in the Lord, Blessed Guanella designated a section within his homes to serve as a hospice for the dying. "There is need of living well, but there is even more need of dying well," he used to say. "A good death is everything — especially today when people think only of temporal things and enjoyment here on earth, rejecting eternity."

Not surprisingly, Blessed Guanella was especially devoted to St. Joseph as patron of the dying. When Pius X invited him to build a church in the Trionfale quarter of Rome, near the Vatican, the priest dedicated it to the death of St. Joseph. Consecrated on March 19, 1912, after four years of planning and construction, the church represented "a constant prayer in order to obtain a happy death," Guanella said. "Oh, how I desire that [this church] may be a center of prayer and a heart of spiritual charity to obtain the good death of all, not only in Rome but throughout the entire world."

Today *San Giuseppe al Trionfale* still serves as home base for the international association of intercessors for the dying begun there by Blessed Guanella. Launched in 1913 with the blessing and encouragement of Pius X, who enrolled as its first member, the Pious Union of St. Joseph includes nearly a million registered members worldwide. Their daily prayer for the dying revolves around this invocation to the patron of a happy death: *O St. Joseph, foster father of Jesus Christ and true spouse of the Virgin Mary, pray for us and for those who will die this day (or night).*

The U.S. branch of the Pious Union was begun by a retired Servant of Charity priest, Germano Pegoraro. Depressed and aimless after years of serving the handicapped in America, Father Pegoraro was tempted to simply return to his native Italy and await death. Then, inspired by doing an oil painting of the death of St. Joseph and also by memories of his first assignment as assistant pastor of the Roman church built by Blessed Guanella, Father Pegoraro felt called to establish his founder's outreach to the dying in the U.S.

In 1987 he presented his painting to the local bishop, then Kenneth Povish of the diocese of Lansing, Michigan, along with a request to begin the Pious Union. Bishop Povish said yes and asked to become its first member. With his encouragement, Father Pegoraro drew up plans for a national shrine of St. Joseph, Patron of the Dying, which is now in development in Grass Lake, Michigan, a few miles west of Ann Arbor.

(Information from the Pious Union of St. Joseph, 971 East Michigan Avenue, Grass Lake, Michigan 49240-9210 / (517) 522-8017 / PiousUnion@aol.com)

210

Afterword

In the Family Portrait

I don't know how one can think about the Queen of Angels
and about when she went through so much with the Infant
Jesus without giving thanks to St. Joseph. . . .
St. Teresa of Ávila

Every now and then, our friend Jim shows up alone for the Sunday liturgy. Usually he attends with an entourage — his wife, Linda, and their five children. "It feels strange to be here alone," he comments whenever he comes solo.

It seems strange to us, too. Not that we fail to appreciate Jim as a person in his own right! It is just that we are used to seeing him in context, with his wife and family. Same thing when Nick, Stan, Robert, Mark, Gary, or any of the other fathers in the parish appears by himself: something important about him is missing from the picture.

St. Joseph is like that too. Important as it is to get to know him on an individual basis, we miss something crucial if we fail to situate him with Jesus and Mary. More than that, our devotion to him will go wrong if examining him close-up does not lead us to a deeper appreciation of his family portrait.

St. Joseph's most devoted and enthusiastic cheerleaders have known this. Blessed Brother André Bessette, who saw himself as "St. Joseph's little dog," had such confidence in the saint's fatherly intercession that he counseled everyone to turn to him for every kind of healing and help. But Brother André taught, too, that devotion to St. Joseph should never be separated from devotion to Our Lord and the Blessed Virgin. For Francis de Sales, who also had a special love for Joseph, the members of the Holy Family were inseparable. Speaking to Mary, he said, "It is impossible not to picture beside you, in a place of honor, one whom your Son in his love for you so often graced with the title of father." Same insistence in the writings of Teresa of Ávila, whose innovative way of relating to St. Joseph as her father marked a milestone in the history of devotion to him. More recently, John Paul II has sounded the theme: "Just as we cannot speak of Jesus without referring to his Most Holy Mother, so we cannot speak of Jesus and Mary without recalling him who, through an authentic, although very particular, form of 'paternity,' had the task of serving as 'father' to the Son of God."

Imagine paging through a photo album and finding a family picture in which one member is blurry, faded, or just barely in view. Imagine, too, that the blurriness is symbolic — that it represents your lack of knowledge about the person in question. How much easier it would be to appreciate the group as a whole if you knew the identity and character of the mysterious personage. The interplay of individual personalities is such an important factor in determining the unique quality and flavor of a family's life. How much more you would appreciate that flavor if you were acquainted with each member of the family and knew something of how they all related to one another.

For quite some time in the history of the Church, the picture of the Holy Family was like that incomplete photo in the family album. From the first, Jesus stood out in bold relief. Relatively quickly, his light illumined Mary, revealing her singular dignity as Mother of God. But until the late Middle Ages, the earthly head of this remarkable family was just a dim, peripheral figure. And because Joseph was hidden in the shadows, devotion to the family as a whole was also slow to develop. "The image of St. Joseph as an active, full-fledged participant in the Holy Family had to be established before it was possible to consider Jesus, Mary, and Joseph as forming an integral and credible family unit," explains Father Joseph Chorpenning.

Credit for this restoration goes first to Jean Gerson (1363-1429), energetic and influential chancellor of the University of Paris. Reacting against the apocryphal portrayal of Joseph as doddering caretaker, Gerson insisted instead on his youth, vigor, and importance in exercising the role of husband and father within the Holy Family.

As various writers have noted, this recapturing of St. Joseph's true significance — along with the accompanying development of devotion to the Holy Family — unfolded during a historical period when the ordinary family was especially at risk. Plague, war, famine, economic distress — in the face of such dangers, it made sense to turn to the Holy Family, and especially to its protector and provider, St. Joseph.

In the modern era, too, the same dynamic is noticeable: heightened appreciation for St. Joseph goes hand in hand with heightened devotion to the Holy Family. And both devotions are a response to challenges facing the family. As we saw in chapter eight, both flourished during the social upheavals occasioned by the colonization of New France and New Spain in the sixteenth and seventeenth centuries.

Devotion to the Holy Family burst into bloom in the nineteenth century, at another period of crisis for families, says Father Chorpenning. Economic activity was shifting away from the home and into the factory; new laws and a new individualism were undermining the family as an institution.

Leo XIII, who encouraged devotion to St. Joseph in his 1889 encyclical (see pages 138 and 140), followed up with some of the first papal encouragements of devotion to the Holy Family. An apostolic letter he wrote in 1892 has been called "the *magna carta* of the Holy Family devotion in modern times." The following year Pope Leo instituted the feast of the Holy Family, which we now celebrate on the Sunday after Christmas (or on December 30, if Christmas falls on a Sunday). Similarly, Benedict XV reacted to new attacks against the family with renewed stress on the importance of St. Joseph and the Holy Family. In his 1920 statement about St. Joseph, he encouraged imitation of the Holy Family as the primary means to the healthy family life on which the future of society depends.

The latest series of papal encouragements to devotion to St. Joseph and the Holy Family come, of course, from John Paul II. This, too, is an age of family crisis, as he notes in his 1994 "Letter to Families" (No. 5):

> Various programs backed by very powerful resources nowadays seem to aim at the breakdown of the family. At times it appears that concerted efforts are being made to present as "normal" and attractive, and even to glamorize, situations which are in fact "irregular." Indeed, they contradict "the truth and love" which should inspire and guide relationships between men and women, thus causing tensions and divisions in families, with grave consequences especially for children. The moral conscience becomes darkened; what is true, good, and beautiful is deformed; and freedom is replaced by what is actually enslavement.

Pope John Paul's "Letter to Families" contrasts the forces that now threaten the family with "the civilization of love" — that communion of persons in Christ that characterizes the Church above all (No. 15). Elsewhere, the pope takes up one of the themes of Vatican II, affirming that "the Christian family constitutes a specific revelation and realization of ecclesial communion, and for this reason it can and should be called a *domestic church*" ("The Role of the Christian Family in the Modern World," *Familiaris Consortio*, No. 21).

Like the Trinity, like the Church, the family is above all a communion of persons. It is meant to be a sign and image of the loving relationship that unites Father, Son, and Holy Spirit.

If you were told to find a concrete way to depict that goal, you could hardly do better than to draw a portrait of the Holy Family. In fact, some spiritual writers did this by explicitly presenting Joseph, Jesus, and Mary as a sort of "earthly trinity" representing the mystery of Father, Son, and Holy Spirit. As evidenced by numerous paintings of "the heavenly and earthly trinities" in the religious art of Canada, Latin America, and Europe, artists also found this idea congenial. In their images, Father Chorpenning explains, "the pictorial space is divided into a heavenly realm, where God the Father, the dove of the Holy Spirit, and angels dwell, and an earthly realm, where the Christ Child stands in the center, flanked by Mary and Joseph. The vertical and horizontal trinities intersect in the God-man Jesus, who unites heaven and earth."

Perhaps more in the spirit of the incarnation, however, are those representations of the Holy Family in which the heavenlies remain veiled. It is an ordinary scene: one husband, one wife, one child. But for Maria von Trapp and others, this is the portrait with power to amaze:

> Men have founded orders, congregations, and organizations; God's own foundation is the Christian family. A real mother, a real father, and a real Child, living, loving, suffering — not symbols, but people like us. . . . That means that instead of having a "devotion to the Holy Family," we must treat the Holy Family in a way as our next-door neighbors, become acquainted with them, go visiting, invite them over, watch them all the while, and ponder about them in our hearts.

Whenever St. Teresa of Ávila looked at the Holy Family, she saw herself as part of the portrait. What could be more natural for someone who had taken Mary as her mother (after her own mother's death) and Joseph as her father (after her healing from a crippling illness)? As André Doze commented, Teresa rediscovered "the incarnation of the Infant Jesus, of Mary, of Joseph, as living human beings, with whom one could speak on familiar terms, who answered you, who were interested in you."

The same discovery is ours to make as well. The Holy Family is near us, too. In fact, it is even closer than the family next door, for Baptism has made us members of it. Like St. Teresa, we have only to see and experience this reality for ourselves.

Perhaps, then, there are *two* images to be recaptured as we ponder the portrait of the Holy Family. There is St. Joseph, whose profile, it is to be hoped, is emerging more clearly as we come to the end of this book. "And there is me," each of us must discover. "I'm in this picture, too!"

Jesus, Mary, Joseph — and me, and you, and all who enjoy the communion of life and love in the Body of Christ. Look at it closely and the portrait of the Holy Family is not just an image of three persons: it is a miniature of the entire Church.

A Prayer to the Family for Families

O Jesus, our most loving Redeemer, you came to enlighten the world with your teaching and example, and you willed to pass the greater part of your life humbly and in subjection to Mary and Joseph in the poor home of Nazareth. You thus sanctified the Family that was to be an example for all Christian families.

Graciously take to yourself our family, as it dedicates and consecrates itself to you this day. Defend us, guard us, and establish among us your holy fear, true peace, and harmony in Christian love. Help us to conform ourselves to the divine pattern of your family, so that all of us without exception may be able to attain to eternal happiness.

Mary, dear mother of Jesus and our mother, by your kindly intercession make this, our humble offering, acceptable in the light of Jesus and obtain for us his graces and blessings.

O St. Joseph, most holy guardian of Jesus and Mary, help us by your prayers in all our spiritual and temporal necessities, that we may be enabled to praise our divine Savior, Jesus, together with Mary and you for all eternity. Amen.

(Francis L. Filas, S.J., *The Family for Families,* The Bruce Publishing Co., 1947)

Source Notes

*(This section indicates the sources of material quoted in
the text. Numbers on the left refer to pages in the text.)*

Chapter 1
Joseph the Silent?

19 *Prayers and Meditations of Thérèse of Lisieux*, ed. Cindy Cavnar
(Ann Arbor, Mich.: Servant Publications, 1992), p. 105.

19 Romano Guardini, *The Lord*, trans. Elinor Castendyk Briefs
(Chicago: Henry Regnery Co., 1954), p. 13.

20 Jacques-Bénigne Bossuet, "Premier panégyrique de saint Joseph," quoted in *Saint Joseph: Textes anciens*, ed. Henri Rondet,
S.J. (Paris: P. Lethielleux, 1953), p. 121.

23 Luke Timothy Johnson, *The Gospel of Luke*, Sacra Pagina
Series (Collegeville, Minn.: The Liturgical Press, 1991), p. xii.

23 George Martin, *Reading Scripture as the Word of God* (Ann
Arbor, Mich.: Servant Publications, 1998), p. 26.

Chapter 2
Matthew's Portrait: Joseph the Hero

27 On the Church Fathers' approach to St. Joseph, see also the
following, which appeared too late to be cited in this book:
Joseph Lienhard, S.J., *Saint Joseph in Early Christianity* (Philadelphia: Saint Joseph's University Press, 1999).

27 Raymond E. Brown, S.S., *A Coming Christ in Advent*
(Collegeville, Minn.: The Liturgical Press, 1988). pp. 17, 19.

29 René Laurentin, *The Truth of Christmas Beyond the Myths*,
trans. Michael J. Wrenn and associates (Petersham, Mass.: St.
Bede's Publications, 1986), p. 263.

30 Joseph A. Fitzmyer, S.J., *Saint Joseph in Matthew's Gospel*,
Saint Joseph's Day Lecture, March 21, 1997 (Philadelphia:
Saint Joseph's University Press, 1997), pp. 2, 4.

32 *Basil the Great, Pseudo Origen:* Quoted in Francis L. Filas,
S.J., *Joseph: The Man Closest to Jesus* (Boston: St. Paul Edi-
tions, 1962), p. 145.

32 *early commentator:* Pseudo-Chrysostom. Quoted in Filas, p. 144.

32 *Jerome:* Quoted in Filas, p. 144.

35 *Jewish law code, on paternity:* From the Mishnah *Baba Bathra*
(8:6). Quoted in Brown, p. 34.

36 *greater identity:* Brown, p. 35.

36 *no clear evidence:* "There is not a scrap of evidence to show that pre-Christian Jews understood Is. 7:14 as foretelling a virgin birth; in the words of Paul Billerbeck . . . 'Mt. 1:18 represents something absolutely new to Jewish thought.'" Quoted from John McHugh, *The Mother of Jesus in the New Testament* (London: Darton, Longman & Todd, 1975), p. 282.

38 *reed:* John P. Meier, *A Marginal Jew* 1, Anchor Bible Reference Library (New York: Doubleday, 1991), p. 321.

39 *secretiveness:* Laurentin, pp. 272-273.

39 Léonie Archer, *Her Price Is Beyond Rubies: The Jewish Woman in Graeco-Roman Palestine* (Sheffield: JSOT Press, 1990), pp. 248, 249.

40 *hospitality:* Bruce Malina, *Windows on the World of Jesus* (Louisville: Westminster/John Knox Press, 1993), p. 57.

40 *queen mother:* Roland de Vaux, O.P., *Ancient Israel*, trans. John McHugh (New York: McGraw-Hill, 1961), pp. 117-119. Quoted by Raymond E. Brown, S.S., *The Birth of the Messiah*, Anchor Bible Reference Library (New York: Doubleday, updated edition, 1993), p. 192.

41 *Herod's character:* William J. Gross, *Herod the Great* (Baltimore: Helicon Press, 1962), p. 350.

41 *Herod in old age:* Stewart Perowne, *The Life and Times of Herod the Great* (London: Hodder and Stoughton, 1957), pp. 185-186.

41 *John Chrysostom:* Quoted in Filas, pp. 385-386.

42 *apocrypha and popular traditions:* Otto Meinardus, *The Holy Family in Egypt* (Cairo: The American University in Cairo Press, 1986).

44 *sixth-century monk:* E. P. Sanders, *The Historical Figure of Jesus* (New York: Penguin Books, 1993), pp. 11-12.

44 *paidion:* Meier, p. 376.

44 *Archelaus:* F. F. Bruce, *New Testament History* (Garden City, N.Y.: Anchor Books/Doubleday, 1972), p. 24.

45 *Bernard of Clairvaux:* Quoted in Rondet, *Textes anciens*, p. 72.

47 Brown, *Coming Christ*, p. 39.

47 *hallmark of Matthew's Gospel:* Donald Senior, *Matthew*, Abingdon New Testament Commentaries (Nashville: Abingdon Press, 1998), p. 40.

Chapter 3
Luke's Portrait: Joseph the Hidden

49 Luke Timothy Johnson, p. 39.

49 Georgina Sabat-Rivers, *Sor Juana Inés de la Cruz and Sor Marcela de San Félix: Their Devotion to St. Joseph as the Antithesis of Patriarchal Authoritarianism*, Saint Joseph's Day Lecture, March 21, 1996 (Philadelphia: Saint Joseph's University Press, 1997), p. 18.

50 Kevin Perrotta, "Luke: Chapters 1 to 14," *God's Word Today* (January 1998), p. 15.

51 Laurentin, p. 15.

52 *Mary and social prestige:* Johnson, p. 39.

53 Joseph A. Fitzmyer, S.J., *The Gospel according to Luke, I-IX*, The Anchor Bible (New York: Doubleday, 1970), p. 337.

53 *"Son of God":* Fitzmyer, *Luke,* pp. 205-206.

55 *vow of virginity:* Fitzmyer, *Luke,* p. 349.

55 *childlessness:* Brown, *Messiah,* p. 304.

55 Karl Rahner, *Recherches de Science Religieuse* 42 (1954), p. 517, n. 73. Quoted in McHugh, p.184.

56 *God's extraordinary action:* Brown, *Messiah,* pp. 300-301, 530-531.

56 *Bernard of Clairvaux:* Quoted in McHugh, p. 66.

57 *Isidore of Isolano and Francis de Sales:* Edward Healy Thompson, *The Life and Glories of St. Joseph* (Rockford, Ill.: Tan Books, 1980), pp. 181-182.

59 *census:* Sanders, p. 86.

60 Fitzmyer, *Luke,* p. 394.

60 Brown, *Messiah,* p. 415.

60 Laurentin, p. 174.

61 *firstborn:* Fitzmyer, *Luke,* pp. 407-408.

61 Eugene LaVerdiere, S.S.S. *Luke,* New Testament Message (Wilmington, Del.: Michael Glazier, 1980), p. 31.

61 de Vaux, p. 43.

62 Fitzmyer, *Luke,* p. 394.

63 Michael Baily, C.SS.R., "The Crib and Exegesis of Luke 2, 1-20," *Irish Ecclesiastical Record* 100 (1963), pp. 361, 366.

65 *circumcision:* de Vaux, p. 46.

65 *name:* de Vaux, p. 43.

65 *names:* Meier, pp. 207, 208, 350.

69 *Passover:* Sanders, p. 249.

69 *Jerusalem population and crowds:* Rami Arav and John J.

Rousseau, *Jesus and His World* (Minneapolis: Augsburg Fortress, 1995), p. 163. While suggesting a permanent population of one hundred fifty thousand, these authors cite another scholar's estimate of thirty thousand as an indicator that estimates vary widely. Under fifty thousand is the more usual figure.

70 Fitzmyer, *Luke*, p. 437.

70 Laurentin, p. 211.

71 *mothers and sons:* Malina, p. 82.

71 *Bede:* Quoted in Edmund F. Sutcliffe, "Our Lady and the Divinity of Christ," *The Month* 180 (1944), p. 347.

72 Sutcliffe, p. 348.

72 *Augustine:* Quoted in Filas, p. 193.

72 *Origen:* Quoted in Guy-M. Bertrand, C.S.C., *Saint Joseph dans les écrits des Pères* (Montreal: Fides, 1966), p. 146.

72 *Augustine on Jesus' explanation:* Quoted in Filas, p. 186.

73 *Jesus' obedience:* Brown, *Messiah*, p. 493.

73 *Pierre d'Ailly:* Quoted in Filas, p. 224.

73 Leo XIII, *Quamquam Pluries*, August 15, 1889, *The Catholic Mind* XLI, no. 963 (March 1943), p. 3.

73 Archer, p. 45.

73 *Origen:* Quoted in Bertrand, p. 146.

75 Raymond E. Brown, S.S. *An Adult Christ at Christmas* (Collegeville, Minn.: The Liturgical Press, 1977), p. 24.

Chapter 4
Inquiring Minds Want to Know

81 Laurentin, p. 304.

83 *Origen:* Quoted in McHugh, pp. 89-90.

84 *Augustine on Joseph's adoption:* Bertrand, pp. 56-57.

84 *genealogy theories:* Brown, *Messiah*, pp. 504, 588.

85 For information on the "brothers and sisters" of Jesus, I have drawn from material in Richard Bauckham, "The Brothers and Sisters of Jesus: An Epiphanian Response," *The Catholic Biblical Quarterly* (October 1994), pp. 686-700; Bertrand, pp. 63-84; Filas, pp. 77-102; Fitzmyer, *Luke*, pp. 723-724; Hilda Graef, *Mary: A History of Doctrine and Devotion* 1 (London and New York: Sheed and Ward, 1963); *Mary in the New Testament*, eds. Raymond E. Brown, Karl P. Donfried, et al. (Philadelphia: Fortress Press; New York: Paulist Press, 1988), pp. 65-72; McHugh, pp. 200-254; John P. Meier, "The Brothers and Sisters of Jesus,"

The Catholic Biblical Quarterly 54 (1992), pp. 1-28 and "On Retrojecting Later Questions from Later Texts: A Reply to Richard Bauckham," *The Catholic Biblical Quarterly* 59 (July 1997), pp. 511-527.

86 *ecumenical task force on "Ever Virgin":* Four Catholics, four Lutherans, two Episcopalians, and two scholars from the Reformed tradition: *Mary in the New Testament,* p. 65.

86 *The Protoevangelium of James* in *New Testament Apocrypha* 1, eds. Edgar Henneke and Wilhelm Schneemelcher (London: Lutterworth, 1963), pp. 379, 383.

86 *History of Joseph the Carpenter:* Bertrand, p. 41.

87 *Origen:* Quoted in McHugh, p. 218.

87 Filas, p. 70.

87 *Jerome:* Quoted in Bertrand, p. 80.

88 Meier, "Brothers," p. 21.

89 Bauckham, pp. 694-700.

89 *Aquinas on Joseph's virginity:* Filas, p. 101.

90 Meier, "Brothers," p. 6.

90 Martin Luther, *Luther's Works* 22, ed. Jaroslav Pelikan, trans. Martin H. Bertram (St. Louis: Concordia, 1955), pp. 214-215.

90 *impossible quest?:* Meier, *Marginal,* p. 229.

Chapter 5
An Ordinary Nazorean

93 *the past as a foreign country:* L. P. Hartley, *The Go-Between* (New York: Stein and Day, 1953). Quoted in Ben Witherington III, *The Jesus Quest* (Downers Grove, Ill.: InterVarsity Press, 1997), p. 15.

94 *facts and figures:* Sean Freyne, *Galilee from Alexander the Great to Hadrian* (Wilmington, Del: Michael Glazier, Inc.; Notre Dame, Ind.: University of Notre Dame Press, 1980) and *Galilee, Jesus, and the Gospels* (Philadelphia: Fortress Press, 1988), pp. 137-163; Anne Hennessy, C.S.J., *The Galilee of Jesus* (Rome: Editrice Pontificia Università Gregoriana, 1994); Meier, *Marginal,* pp. 282-285; Witherington, pp. 14-32.

94 *changes in economy:* Witherington, p. 21.

94 *peasants:* John Riches, *The World of Jesus* (Cambridge: Cambridge University Press, 1990), pp. 25-26.

95 *family breakdown:* Bruce J. Malina, *The New Testament World* (Louisville: Westminster/John Knox Press, 1993), pp. 124-126; Witherington, pp. 27-28.

95 *cities:* Richard Batey, "Is Not This the Carpenter?" *New Testament Studies* 30, no. 20 (April 1994), pp. 249-258; Meier, *Marginal,* pp. 283-284; Riches, pp. 21-29; Rousseau and Arav, pp. 248-251; Witherington, pp. 29-31.

96 *Jerusalem, religious practice, synagogues:* Rousseau and Arav, pp. 268-272; Riches, pp. 22-24; Sanders, pp. 98-101; Witherington, pp. 22-23, 37-41.

96 *Nazareth:* Hennessy, p. 8; Elizabeth McNamer, "Jesus, the Man from Nazareth," *Scripture from Scratch* 198 (January 1998); Marianne Race and Laurie Brink, *In This Place* (Collegeville, Minn.: The Liturgical Press, 1998), pp. 47-50; Rousseau and Arav, pp. 214-216.

97 *activities:* Sanders, p. 104; John J. Pilch, "Games, Amusements, and Sports," *The Bible Today* (July 1998), pp. 250-255, and "Anyone unwilling to work should not eat," *The Bible Today* (January 1994), pp. 38-45; Malina, *Windows,* pp. 76-78.

97 *climate:* Frank S. Frick, "Palestine, Climate," in *Anchor Bible Dictionary* 5 (New York: Doubleday, 1992), pp. 119-126; John J. Pilch, "The Bible and Weather," *The Bible Today* (May 1997), pp. 171-176.

97 *dress:* Douglas R. Edwards, "Dress and Ornamentation," *Anchor Bible Dictionary* 2, pp. 236-238; John J. Pilch, "Why do you worry about clothing?" *The Bible Today* (November 1993), pp. 354-355; *Harper's Bible Dictionary,* ed. Paul J. Achtemeier (San Francisco: Harper & Row, 1985), pp. 226-229.

98 *food:* T. A. Pearson, "Biblical Foods and Eating Customs," *The Bible Today* (November 1989), pp. 372-378; John J. Pilch, "The Necessities of Life: Drinking and Eating," *The Bible Today* (July 1993), pp. 231-237; *Biblical Social Values and Their Meaning,* eds. John J. Pilch and Bruce J. Malina (Peabody, Mass.: Hendrickson Publishers, 1993), pp. 76-79; *Harper's Bible Dictionary,* pp. 141, 315-316.

98 *health:* Victor H. Matthews, *Manners and Customs in the Bible* (Peabody, Mass.: Hendrickson Publishers, 1991), pp. 236-239; John J. Pilch, "Sickness and Long Life," *The Bible Today* (March 1993), pp. 94-98; *Harper's Bible Dictionary,* p. 796.

99 *houses:* J. S. Holladay, Jr., "House, Israelite," in *Anchor Bible Dictionary* 3, pp. 308-318; "House: Syro-Palestinian Houses," *Oxford Encyclopedia of Archaeology in the Near East* 2, ed. Eric M. Myers (New York/Oxford: Oxford University Press, 1997), pp. 94-97; John J. Pilch, "House and Hearth," *The Bible Today*

(September 1993), pp. 292-299; Rousseau and Arav, pp. 128-130; Meier, *Marginal*, p. 252.

100 *languages: Harper's Bible Dictionary*, pp. 43, 361, 378; Meier, *Marginal*, pp. 255-268.

100 *money:* Matthews, pp. 247-248; *Harper's Bible Dictionary*, pp. 650-651.

100 *occupations:* John Pilch, "Anyone unwilling to work should not eat," pp. 38-45; Riches, p. 25; Witherington, pp. 28-29; Paul Hanly Furfey, S.J., "Christ as *Tekton*," *The Catholic Biblical Quarterly* 17 (1955), pp. 204-215; Meier, *Marginal*, pp. 280-285; Rousseau and Arav, pp. 339-341.

101 *travel:* John J. Pilch, "Travel in the Ancient World," *The Bible Today* (March 1994), pp. 100-107.

102 *man's world:* Archer, pp. 45, 238-250; Malina, *New Testament*, pp. 48-55; Witherington, pp. 32-34.

102 *prostitute:* Archer, p. 119.

102 *old age:* Witherington, p. 34; Malina, *Windows*, p. 35.

102 *personal space:* Malina, *Windows*, pp. 22-25; John J. Pilch, "Smells and Tastes," *The Bible Today* (July 1996), pp. 246-251.

103 *table manners:* Pearson, pp. 372-378; Dennis E. Smith, "Meal Customs," *Anchor Bible Dictionary* 4, pp. 650-653.

103 *time:* Malina, *Windows*, pp. 156-170.

103 *groups, not individuals:* Malina, *New Testament*, pp. 63-86.

104 Meier, *Marginal*, p. 252.

Chapter 6
Is That All There Is?

107 *Josephus and Tacitus:* Meier, *Marginal*, pp. 57-62, 89-91.

107 *Jerome:* Bertrand, pp. 76-80.

107 *modern scholars on the apocrypha:* Meier, *Marginal*, p. 115. See opinions cited in Brown, *Messiah*, p. 606.

108 In summarizing the apocryphal accounts related to St. Joseph, I have drawn from Filas, pp. 22-36; Tarcisio Stramare, O.S.J., *Gesù lo chiamò Padre* (Città del Vaticano: Libreria Editrice Vaticana, 1997), pp. 21-26; *The Apocryphal Jesus*, ed. J. K. Elliott (Oxford: Oxford University Press, 1996), pp. 9-50; *The Apocryphal New Testament*, ed. J. K. Elliott (Oxford: Clarendon Press, 1993); Gonzalo Aranda Perez, "Joseph the Carpenter," in *The Coptic Encyclopedia* 5, ed. Aziz S. Atiya (New York: Macmillan Publishing Co., 1991), pp. 1372-1374; *Encyclopedia of Early Christianity*, 2nd ed., ed. Everett Ferguson

(New York and London: Garland Publishing, Inc., 1998), pp. 74-77, 478, 535, 629-630, 955-956; *New Testament Apocrypha,* eds. Henneke and Schneemelcher, pp. 363-432.

108 *influence of apocrypha:* Stramare, pp. 21-22.

108 *Protoevangelium of James: Apocryphal New Testament,* pp. 57-67.

110 Fitzmyer, *Matthew's Gospel,* p. 7.

110 *Infancy Gospel of Thomas: Apocryphal New Testament,* pp. 75-83.

110 *sinister superboy:* Meier, *Marginal,* p. 115.

110 *bad mood god:* Sanders, p. 155.

111 *History of Joseph the Carpenter: Apocryphal New Testament,* pp. 114-117.

112 Filas, p. 34.

112 *Arabic Infancy Gospel: Apocryphal New Testament,* pp. 102-107.

112 *Pseudo-Matthew: New Testament Apocrypha,* pp. 410-413.

113 Filas, pp. 31-33.

113 *Church Fathers:* "The patristic age, by common agreement, ends in the West with the death of St. Isidore of Seville in the year 636 A.D., and in the East with the death of St. John Damascene in 749 A.D.": *The Faith of the Early Fathers* 1, ed. and trans. W. A. Jurgens (Collegeville, Minn.: The Liturgical Press, 1970), p. x.

114 *Bridget:* Raphael Brown, *The Life of Mary as Seen by the Mystics* (Milwaukee: Bruce Publishing Co., 1951), pp. 7-8; F. Vernet, "Brigitte de Suède," in *Dictionnaire de spiritualité* 1, eds. M. Viller et al. (Paris: Beauchesne, 1937), cols. 1943-1958.

114 *Bridget:* Quoted in Filas, pp. 514-515.

115 Mary of Agreda's *City of God,* trans. Fiscar Marison (Hammond, Ind.: W. B. Conkey Co., 1902), vol. 2, pp. 332-333; vol. 3, pp. 150-155.

115 *On Mary of Agreda:* Raphael Brown, pp. 8-17; Julio Campo, "Marie de Jesus," in *Dictionnaire* 10, cols. 508-513; Augustin Poulain, S.J., *The Graces of Interior Prayer,* trans. Leonora Yorke Smith (London: Kegan Paul, Trench, Trubner & Co., 1921), pp. 336-337; Herbert Thurston, S.J., *Surprising Mystics* (London: Burns & Oates, 1955), pp. 122-132.

115 *Mystical City of God:* Raphael Brown, p. 17; Thurston, p. 129.

115 Maria Cecilia Baij, O.S.B., *The Life of Saint Joseph,* trans. Hubert J. Mark (Asbury, N.J.: The 101 Foundation, 1996).

116 *On Maria Cecilia Baij:* J. de Guibert, "Cecile Baij," in *Dictionnaire* 1, col. 1192.

116 *On Anne Catherine Emmerich:* Raphael Brown, pp. 17-24; Winfried Humpfner, "Anne-Catherine Emmerich," in *Dictionnaire* 4, cols. 622-627; Thurston, pp. 38-99.

116 Maria Valtorta's *Poem of the Man-God,* first published as a four-volume work in 1960, positions itself as a factual account of Jesus' life, as revealed by Christ himself. Despite the author's pious motives and literary skills, the Vatican has twice condemned the work, for reasons explained in the following excerpt from a 1985 letter by Cardinal Joseph Ratzinger, as quoted in Benedict J. Groeschel, C.F.R., *A Still, Small Voice* (San Francisco: Ignatius Press, 1993), p. 58: "[*The Poem of the Man-God* has already been] examined scientifically and placed in a well known category of mental sicknesses. . . . [It] evidences being a mountain of childishness, of fantasies and of historical and exegetical falsehoods. . . . On the whole it is a heap of pseudo-religiosity."

Father Groeschel, a psychologist, adds that "it is also important to recall that Maria Valtorta is described in the preface as having spent the last decade of her life in a state similar to catatonic schizophrenia" (p. 59).

116 Thurston, pp. 79, 87.

116 Poulain, p. 329. For a helpful discussion of errors in revelations, see also Groeschel, *Voice,* pp. 23-90.

116 Groeschel, *Voice,* p. 87.

117 Groeschel, *Voice,* pp. 125-147.

Chapter 7
Communing with Saints

122 Edward D. O'Connor, C.S.C., *The Catholic Vision* (Huntington, Ind.: Our Sunday Visitor, 1992), p. 436. See also pp. 434-438 for a clear, insightful presentation of Church teaching on honoring and praying to the saints.

123 Information on the patron-client system comes from Peter Brown, *The Cult of the Saints* (Chicago: The University of Chicago Press, 1981); Roland Gauthier, "Brèves réflexions sur le patronage de saint Joseph," *Cahiers de Joséphologie* XVIII (1970), pp. 181-193; Bruce J. Malina, "Patronage," in *Biblical Social Values and Their Meaning,* pp. 133-137, and *New Testament,* pp. 101-107.

123 Malina, "Patronage," pp. 134-135.

123 Gauthier, pp. 4, 6.

124 *father:* Malina, "Patronage," pp. 133, 134, 136.

125 Peter Brown, pp. 5-6. See also pp. 50-68 on the shift from seeking invisible but nonhuman protectors (spirits, etc.) to seeking help from the saints.

126 *Bernadette:* André Doze, "Bernadette Soubirous et saint Joseph," *Cahiers de Joséphologie* XXXVII, no. 1 (1989), p. 55; René Laurentin, "Bernadette et saint Joseph," *Cahiers de Joséphologie* XX, no. 2 (1972), p. 2.

126 Malina, *New Testament,* p. 107.

126 O'Connor, p. 436.

126 *God honors saints:* O'Connor, p. 437.

127 Cardinal John Henry Newman, *Certain Difficulties Felt by Anglicans in Catholic Teaching Considered* 2 (London: Longmans, Green, and Co., 1920), pp. 26, 30-31.

127 Francis L. Filas, S.J., *St. Joseph after Vatican II* (Youngtown, Ariz.: Cogan Productions, 1981), p. 99.

128 Newman, p. 114.

129 *magical Christians:* Groeschel, *Voice,* p. 88.

129 Evelyn Underhill, *Mysticism* (New York: E. P. Dutton & Co., 1961), p. 70.

129 *devotion or magic?:* Groeschel, *Voice,* p. 90.

130 On burying St. Joseph statues see Peter Gilmour, "St. Joseph gets buried in his work," *U.S. Catholic* (March 1998), p. 7; Gary L. Smith, "St. Joseph, Realtor?" *Catholic Digest* (March 1991), pp. 65-68.

130 Filas, *Vatican II,* pp. 41-42.

132 Johannes Jörgensen, *St. Francis of Assisi,* trans. T. O'Conor Sloane (Garden City, N.Y.: Image/Doubleday, 1955), p. 262.

Chapter 8

A Father for the Church

    135 Francis L. Filas, S.J., "Barth as Seeker of God's Truth," *The Christian Century* (May 30, 1962), p. 686. The fact that Karl Barth is arguably the twentieth century's greatest Protestant theologian makes his appreciation of St. Joseph all the more striking.

    136 Gauthier, "Brèves réflexions," p. 14.

    136 Leo XIII, *Quamquam Pluries,* August 15, 1889. Quoted in Rondet, *Textes anciens,* p. 167. See also Filas, *The Man Clos-*

est to Jesus, pp. 584-596, and *The Catholic Mind* XLI (March 1943), pp. 1-6.

137 Pius IX, *Quemadmodum Deus,* December 8, 1870. Quoted in Francis L. Filas, S.J., *St. Joseph and Daily Christian Living* (New York: The Macmillan Co., 1959), p. 137.

138 John Paul II, talk given March 19, 1993. *L'Osservatore Romano,* English ed. (March 24, 1993), p. 7.

138 *Leo XIII, Quamquam:* Quoted in Rondet, pp. 168-169.

139 Joseph's mission of watching over the Body of Christ also makes him the special patron of bishops and priests, "who are entrusted with the service of spiritual and pastoral fatherhood in the ecclesial Family": John Paul II, "St. Joseph, image of God's fatherly love," *L'Osservatore Romano*, English ed. (March 24, 1999), p. 1.

139 *half the world: Time* (November 23, 1962). Quoted in Filas, *Closest*, p. 471.

140 *Pius IX:* Quoted in Filas, *Daily Christian Living*, p. 138.

140 Paul VI, talk given March 19, 1969. *L'Osservatore Romano,* English ed. (March 27, 1969), p. 1.

140 *scientists:* John J. Wynne, S.J., *The Great Encyclical Letters of Pope Leo XIII* (New York: Benziger Brothers, 1903), p. 4.

140 *Leo XIII:* Quoted in Filas, *Daily Christian Living,* pp. 141-142.

141 Benedict XV, *Actes de Benoît XV* 2 (Paris: Bonne Presse, 1924-1934), pp. 156, 155; see also Filas, *Daily Christian Living,* p. 153.

141 Pius XI, "On the Peace of Christ in the Kingdom of Christ" (*Ubi Arcano Dei*), December 23, 1922. Quoted in Anne Fremantle, *The Papal Encyclicals in Their Historical Context* (New York: Mentor-Omega/New American Library, 1963), p. 220.

141 Pius XI, "On Atheistic Communism" (*Divini Redemptoris*), March 19, 1937 (Washington, D.C.: National Catholic Welfare Conference, 1937), pp. 1, 53.

142 Nina Shea, "Terror against the Church," *Crisis* (March 1997), pp. 16-18. See also her book *In the Lion's Den* (Nashville, Tenn.: Broadman and Holman Publishers, 1997).

143 Teresa of Ávila, *The Book of Her Life*, in *The Collected Works of St. Teresa of Ávila* 1, trans. Kieran Kavanaugh, O.C.D., and Otilio Rodriguez, O.C.D. (Washington, D.C.: Institute of Carmelite Studies Publications, 1976), p. 53. On St. Teresa and St. Joseph, see also Joseph F. Chorpenning, *Just Man,*

Husband of Mary, Guardian of Christ: An Anthology of Readings from Jerónimo Gracián's "Summary of the Excellencies of St. Joseph" (Philadelphia: Saint Joseph's University Press, 1993), pp. 29-33, 239-246; Fortunato de Jesús Sacramentado, O.C.D., "Santa Teresa de Jesús y su espíritu josefino," *Estudios Josefinos* 7 (1953), pp. 9-54; Christopher C. Wilson, "St. Teresa of Ávila's Holy Patron," in *Patron Saint of the New World: Spanish American Colonial Images of Saint Joseph* (Philadelphia: Saint Joseph's University Press, 1992), pp. 5-17.

143 Teresa, *Life*, p. 54.

143 Chorpenning, *Just Man*, pp. 31, 32-33.

144 John XXIII, *Le voci*, March 19, 1961, *Cahiers de Joséphologie* IX (July-December 1961), pp. 163, 164; see also Filas, *Closest*, p. 627.

145 *John Paul II on Special Synod*: *L'Osservatore Romano*, English ed. (February 4, 1985), p. 1.

145 Cardinal John Joseph Wright, "St. Joseph and Collegiality," *Cahiers de Joséphologie* XIX (1971), pp. 10-11.

145 Ralph M. McInerny, *What Went Wrong with Vatican II?* (Manchester, N.H.: Sophia Institute Press, 1998), pp. 16-17.

145 For an explanation of the Church's teaching office, see O'Connor, *The Catholic Vision*, pp. 415-417, 419-427.

145 *Vatican II on the Church's teaching authority:* see "Dogmatic Constitution on the Church" (*Lumen Gentium*), No. 25.

146 McInerny, pp. 17-18, 158.

146 Teresa of Ávila, *Life*, p. 217.

146 Wright, pp. 10-11.

147 Quoted from Cardinal Herbert Vaughan, *The Young Priest* (London: Burns and Oates, 1904), p. 132, in Edward V. Casserly, S.S.J., "Devotion to Saint Joseph in the Josephite Society in the United States," *Cahiers de Joséphologie* (1955), p. 589.

147 Paul VI, Angelus remarks, March 19, 1970. *L'Osservatore Romano*, English ed. (March 26, 1970), p. 3.

148 On St. Joseph and New Spain see the following by Joseph F. Chorpenning: "Icon of Family and Religious Life: The Historical Development of the Holy Family Devotion," in *The Holy Family*, ed. Joseph F. Chorpenning, O.S.F.S. (Philadelphia: Saint Joseph's University Press, 1996), pp. 17-20; "The Iconography of St. Joseph in Mexican Devotional *Retablos*," in *Mexican Devotional Retablos from the Peeters Collection*, ed. Joseph F. Chorpenning, O.S.F.S. (Philadelphia: Saint Joseph's

University Press, 1994), pp. 39-92; "St. Joseph's Pilgrimage of Faith: John Paul II's Apostolic Exhortation *Guardian of the Redeemer*," *Communio* (Spring 1993), pp. 188-194. See also Christopher C. Wilson, "St. Teresa of Ávila's Holy Patron: Teresian Sources for the Image of St. Joseph in Spanish American Colonial Art," in *Patron Saint of the New World* (Philadelphia: Saint Joseph's University Press, 1992), pp. 5-15.

148 On devotion to St. Joseph in California: Larry M. Toschi, O.S.J., "St. Joseph, Father of the Birth of Christianity in Alta California," *Estudios Josefinos* 45 (1991), pp. 705-724.

148 On devotion to St. Joseph in New France see the following by Adrien Pouliot, S.J.: "L'extraordinaire dévotion de la Nouvelle-France envers saint Joseph," in *Le patronage de S. Joseph* (Montreal and Paris: Fides, 1956), pp. 361-416; "La dévotion à saint Joseph chez les Jésuites de la Nouvelle-France," *Cahiers de Joséphologie* XXIII (1975), pp. 67-99. See also Roland Gauthier, *La dévotion à la Sainte Famille en Nouvelle-France au XVIIe siècle* (Montreal: Centre de recherche et de documentation/Oratoire Saint-Joseph, 1996); Chorpenning, *Holy Family,* pp. 20-24.

148 On Our Lady of Guadalupe, see Francis Johnston, *The Wonder of Guadalupe* (Rockford, Ill.: TAN Books and Publishers, Inc., 1991), especially pp. 50-61; Ethel Cook Eliot, "Our Lady of Guadalupe in Mexico," in *A Woman Clothed with the Sun*, ed. John J. Delaney (New York: Doubleday/Image, 1990), pp. 39-60.

148 Chorpenning, *Holy Family,* p. 20.

149 Mère Saint-Joseph Barnard, O.S.U., "Un pèlerinage des Ursulines de Québec dans le domaine de saint Joseph," *Cahiers de Joséphologie* XIII (1965), pp. 19, 20.

149 Paul VI, Angelus, March 19, 1970.

150 *John Chrysostom:* Quoted in Filas, p. 385.

Chapter 9
Her Most Chaste Spouse

153 Stephen Wood, with James Burnham, *Christian Fatherhood.* (Port Charlotte, Fla.: Family Life Center Publications, 1997), p. 130.

154 Thomas Aquinas, *Summa Theologica* 3, q. 29, a. 1.

154 Leo XIII, *Quamquam Pluries, The Catholic Mind* (March 1943), p. 3.

155 *rabbinic saying:* Mordechai Akiva Friedman, *Jewish Mar-*

riage in Palestine 1 (Tel Aviv and New York: The Jewish Theological Society of America, 1980), p. 90.

155 *Augustine:* Quoted in Filas, *Closest,* p. 183.

155 Bernard A. Siegle, T.O.R., *Marriage according to the New Code of Canon Law* (New York: Alba House, 1986), p. 4.

155 Thomas Aquinas, *Summa* 3, q. 29, a. 2.

157 *patron of priests:* Edward Healy Thompson, *The Life and Glories of Saint Joseph,* p. 442.

157 *statistics:* Rutgers University's National Marriage Project findings, reported by Michael A. Fletcher, "For Better or Worse, Marriage Hits a New Low," *The Washington Post* (July 2, 1999), p. A1; Douglas J. Besharov, "Asking More From Matrimony," *The New York Times* (July 14, 1999); Michael J. McManus, online document "Overview of a Ministry," Marriage Savers, Inc., February 2, 1999.

158 Cardinal John O'Connor, *Covenant of Love* (Liguori, Mo.: Liguori Publications, 1999), pp. 102, 104.

158 Canon Jacques Leclercq, *Marriage: A Great Sacrament,* trans. the Earl of Wicklow (Dublin: Clonmore and Reynolds, Ltd., 1951), p. 53.

159 Leclercq, p. 30.

160 Roland Gauthier, S.S.C., *Saint Joseph dans l'histoire du salut* (Montreal: Oratoire Saint-Joseph, 1976), p. 11.

161 David Popenoe, *Life without Father* (New York: The Free Press, 1996), pp. 24, 5.

161 Frederic Flach, M.D. *A New Marriage, A New Life: Making Your Second Marriage a Success* (New York: Hatherleigh, 1998), p. 10.

161 David Blankenhorn, *Fatherless America* (New York: Basic Books, 1995), pp. 295, 167.

161 *learning to say goodbye:* Brenda Shoshanna, *Why Men Leave* (New York: Berkley, 1999), p. 337.

162 Leclercq, p. 67.

162 Dietrich von Hildebrand, *Marriage* (London: Longmans, Green, and Co., 1942), pp. 9-10.

163 Alice von Hildebrand, *By Love Refined* (Manchester, N.H.: Sophia Institute Press, 1989), pp. 12-13.

163 Dietrich von Hildebrand, pp. 27-28.

163 Joyce L. Vedral, *Get Rid of Him* (New York: Warner, 1993), p. xiv.

164 Leclercq, p. 62.

165 Leclercq, pp. 28, 31.

Chapter 10
Jesus Called Him Dad

167 Christella Buser, *Flowers from the Ark: True Stories from the Homes of L'Arche* (Mahwah, N.J.: Paulist Press, 1996), p. 38.

167 *daddies and mommies:* Popenoe, p. 197.

167 Paul VI, talk given May 1, 1969. *L'Osservatore Romano*, English ed. (May 8, 1969), p. 12.

167 *disengagement:* Blankenhorn, pp. 193-194.

168 *Origen:* Quoted in Filas, *Closest*, pp. 169, 170.

168 *Augustine on loyal marriage:* Quoted in Filas, *Closest*, p. 194.

168 Aquinas, *In IV Sent.*, d. 30, q. 2, a. 2, ad 4.

168 *John Chrysostom:* Quoted in Rondet, pp. 67-68; see also Filas, *Closest*, p. 178.

169 *Jean Gerson:* Quoted in Filas, p. 221.

169 Quoted in Chorpenning, *Just Man*, pp. 129, 3.

171 Witherington, p. 27.

171 Popenoe, p. 38.

171 Dana Mack, *The Assault on Parenthood* (New York: Simon & Schuster, 1997), pp. 13, 51.

171 Bronislaw Malinowski, *Sex, Culture, and Myth* (New York: Harcourt, Brace & World, 1962), p. 63.

171 *extreme form:* Popenoe, pp. 36, 52.

172 *Baius:* Quoted in Lawrence Stone, *Road to Divorce: England, 1530-1987* (New York: Oxford University Press, 1990), p. 7.

172 *rape victims:* Elisabeth Bumiller, "Kosovo Victims Must Choose to Deny Rape or Be Hated," *The New York Times*, July 22, 1999. Muslim women raped in Bosnia during the 1991-1995 conflict faced similar consequences. And in Rwanda, where Hutu soldiers also used rape as a weapon during their bloody 1994 anti-Tutsi campaign, many Tutsi women and their Hutu-fathered children are now pitiful social outcasts.

172 Popenoe, pp. 6, 175.

173 Pius IX, *Quemadmodum Deus:* quoted in Filas, *Daily Christian Living*, p. 136.

173 Leo XIII, *Quamquam Pluries:* quoted in Filas, *Daily Christian Living*, p. 146.

173 Thérèse of Lisieux, *Her Last Conversations*, trans. John Clarke, O.C.D. (Washington, D.C.: ICS Publications, 1977), p. 159.

174 Paul VI, *Discourse* (March 19, 1966), in *Insegnamenti* IV (1966), p. 110.

174 Maria von Trapp, *Yesterday, Today, and Forever* (Philadelphia: Lippincott, 1952), p. 83.

176 *subversion of parental authority:* see Mack, *The Assault on Parenthood,* especially pp. 109-229.

176 Meier, *Marginal,* p. 276.

176 de Vaux, p. 49.

177 *devout, devoted father:* Rainer Riesner, quoted in Meier, p. 277.

177 Meier, *Marginal,* p. 278.

177 *weak fathers, family dysfunction:* Blankenhorn, n. 55, p. 271.

178 Albert-Marie de Monléon, O.P., "St. Joseph Can Serve as Guide for Rediscovering Fatherhood," *L'Osservatore Romano,* English ed. (March 15, 1995), p. 7.

178 John Paul II, "St. Joseph, image," p. 1.

178 Kevin Perrotta, "Raising Children by *The* Book," *Catholic Parent* (May/June 1999), p. 35.

178 Thomas Aquinas, *Summa,* 3, q. 27, a. 4, c.

179 George T. Montague, S.M., *A Cross-Cultural Commentary on the Gospel of Matthew* (New York: Paulist Press, 1989), p. 23.

179 André Doze, *Shadow of the Father,* trans. Florestine Audett, R.J.M. (New York: Alba House, 1992), p. 17. See Teresa of Ávila, *Life,* p. 54.

179 André Doze, "Bernadette Soubirous et Saint Joseph," pp. 57-58.

180 Wood, p. 56.

180 Paul VI, talk given on March 19, 1965. *Insegnamenti* III (1965), p. 1197.

Chapter 11
Patron of What We Do All Day

183 Studs Terkel, *Working: People Talk About What They Do All Day and How They Feel About What They Do* (New York: Pantheon Books/Random House, 1972), p. 31.

183 *Benildus:* Ann Ball, *Modern Saints: Their Lives and Faces* (Rockford, Ill.: Tan Books and Publishers, Inc., 1983), p. 40.

183 Gregory F. Augustine Pierce, "A Spirituality That Makes Sense," in *Of Human Hands,* ed. Gregory F. Augustine Pierce (Minneapolis: Augsburg, and Chicago: ACTA Publications, 1991), pp. 24-25.

184 Jean-Jacques Thierry, *Opus Dei* (New York: Cortland Press, 1975), p. 152.

184 *Opus Dei patron:* Thierry, p. 13.

184 Pius XII, "Feast of St. Joseph the Workman," *The Catholic Mind* (September 1955), p. 564.

185 *goldsmith:* Timothy Sparks, O.P., and Basil Cole, O.P., *Dominicans on St. Joseph* (Rockford, Ill.: Tan Books and Publishers, 1997), p. 164.

185 Gracián, pp. 153-154.

185 Filas, *Closest,* pp. 58-59.

186 George Martin, *God's Word* (Huntington, Ind.: Our Sunday Visitor, 1998), p. 15.

186 *The Apocryphal New Testament,* pp. 60-61, 114, 78-79, 103.

186 Furfey, pp. 208-209.

187 Dorothy Sayers, *Why Work?* (London: Methuen, 1942), p. 16.

188 John Paul II, homily given May 1, 1989. *L'Osservatore Romano,* English ed. (May 22, 1989), p. 4.

188 John Paul II, talk to Olivetti workers, March 19, 1980. *L'Osservatore Romano,* English ed. (March 24, 1980), p. 12.

189 John C. Haughey, *Converting Nine to Five* (New York: Crossroad, 1989), p. 32.

190 *forbidden professions:* Arthur T. Geoghegan, *The Attitude Towards Labor in Early Christianity and Ancient Culture* (Washington, D.C.: The Catholic University of America Press, 1945), pp. 139-140.

191 *vulgar jobs:* Geoghegan, pp. 13-16.

191 *Clement of Alexandria:* Geoghegan, pp. 146-149.

191 William E. Diehl, *The Monday Connection* (San Francisco: HarperSanFrancisco, 1991), pp. 3, 11, 12.

192 Teresa of Ávila, *Life,* p. 54.

192 Meier, *Marginal,* p. 352.

192 *Joseph's earnings:* Furfey, pp. 213-214.

193 Meier, *Marginal,* pp. 284, 282.

193 Mack, p. 206.

194 Louis Uchitelle, "More Work and Less Play Make Jack Look Better Off," *The New York Times* (October 5, 1997), p. 4 wk.

194 *Canfield:* Quoted in Amy Gage, "Daddy Trap," *Pioneer Press* (July 4, 1999), p. D1, 5.

194 *child care:* Mack, p. 202.

194 *child-care directors' training session:* Amy Gage, "A New Era of Child Care," *Pioneer Press* (June 27, 1999), p. D1, 3.

194 Margaret Talbot, "Dial-a-Wife," *The New Yorker* (October 20 and 27, 1997), pp. 196-208.

195 John Paul II, talk given May 1, 1980; talk given March 19, 1981. *L'Osservatore Romano,* English ed. (March 30, 1981), p. 10.

Chapter 12
Assisted Living, Assisted Dying

197 Sarah Lyall, "Roy Porter: Making Medicine Lively (Not to Mention Intimate)," *The New York Times* (April 24, 1999), p. B11.

197 Sheryl Gay Stolberg, "Dame Cicely Saunders: Reflecting on a Lifetime of Treating the Dying," *The New York Times* (May 11, 1999), p. F7.

198 *Gracián:* Chorpenning, *Just Man,* p. 223.

198 *History of Joseph the Carpenter* in *The Apocryphal New Testament,* pp. 114-117.

198 Francis de Sales, *Treatise on the Love of God* 2, trans. John K. Ryan (Rockford, Ill.: Tan Books, 1974), p. 49; see also Joseph F. Chorpenning, O.S.F.S., "Just Man, Husband of Mary, and Guardian of Christ: St. Joseph's Life and Virtues in the Spirituality of St. Francis de Sales," in *Patron Saint of the New World,* p. 26.

198 Filas, *Daily Christian Living,* p. 125.

198 Alice von Hildebrand, *By Grief Refined* (Steubenville, Ohio: Franciscan University Press, 1994), pp. 68-69.

199 Jessica Mitford, *The American Way of Death Revisited* (New York: Alfred A. Knopf, 1998).

199 *death and funeral rites:* Raymond E. Brown, *The Death of the Messiah* 2 (New York: Doubleday, 1993), pp. 1243-1265; Archer, pp. 250-261, 278, 281-288; de Vaux, pp. 56-61.

199 de Vaux, p. 57.

200 Jean-Bernard Livio, S.J., "St. Joseph's Tomb," *Companion* (March 1999), p. 25.

200 *tombs:* Elizabeth Bloch-Smith, *Judahite Burial Practices and Beliefs about the Dead* (Sheffield, England: Sheffield Academic Press, 1992); Jack Finegan, *The Archeology of the New Testament* (Princeton: Princeton University Press, 1992), pp. 292-318.

200 Archer, pp. 255-256.

200 Zvi Greenhut, "Burial Cave of the Caiaphas Family," and

Ronny Reich, "Caiaphas' Name Inscribed on Bone Boxes," *Biblical Archaeology Review* (September/October, 1992), pp. 29-36, 38-44.

200 *Francis de Sales:* Rondet, *Textes anciens*, p. 95; see also Chorpenning, *Patron Saint of the New World*, p. 26.

201 Benedict XV, *Bonum Sane*, July 25, 1920. Quoted in Filas, *Daily Christian Living*. p. 156.

201 *St. Joseph's extended patronage:* For example, the Pious Union of St. Joseph encourages its members to "prayerfully include" caregivers, as well as "those suffering all sorts of suffering — not only those associated with the dying process, but those caused as well by the *culture of death*." Specifically mentioned are "depression, abandonment, trauma, displacement, economic disparity, racism, stress, abuse, neglect, job loss."

201 Philippe Ariès, *Western Attitudes toward Death*, trans. Patricia M. Ranum (Baltimore and London: The Johns Hopkins University Press, 1974), pp. 85, 105.

202 *Kübler-Ross search for interviewees:* Philippe Ariès, *The Hour of Our Death*, trans. Helen Weaver (New York: Alfred A. Knopf, 1981), p. 589.

202 Tom Kuntz, "Death Be Not Unpublishable: The Literature of Good Grief," *The New York Times* (November 29, 1998).

202 Bryan Appleyard, *Brave New Worlds, Staying Human in the Genetic Future* (New York: Viking Penguin, 1998), p. 11.

203 Nicholas Wade, "Longevity's New Lease on Life," *New York Times* (January 18, 1998).

203 Sherwin B. Nuland, *How We Die* (New York: Vintage Books/Random House, 1995), p. 259.

203 Vigen Guroian, *Life's Living toward Dying* (Grand Rapids, Mich.: William B. Eerdmans Publishing Co., 1996), p. 16.

203 *eighty percent:* Nuland, p. 255.

204 John J. Paris, S.J., "Active Euthanasia," *Theological Studies* 53 (1992), p. 125.

204 William L. Hamilton, "You're Not Older, Products Are Better," *The New York Times* (June 27, 1999).

204 *John Fischer:* Norman J. Muckerman, C.SS.R., *How to Face Death without Fear: Selections from the book* Preparation for Death *by St. Alphonsus Liguori* (Liguori, Mo.: Liguori Publications, 1976), p. 13.

204 Joseph Bayly, *The View from a Hearse: A Christian View of Death* (Elgin, Ill.: David C. Cook Publishing Co., 1969), p. 82.

205 *manual of piety:* John McManners, *Death and the Enlighten-ment* (Oxford: Clarendon Press; New York: Oxford University Press, 1981), p. 199.

205 Dom Hubert van Zeller, *Death in Other Words* (Springfield, Ill.: Templegate, 1963), pp. 13-14.

205 *pro-euthanasiast positions:* Patricia Weenolsen, *The Art of Dying* (New York: St. Martin's Griffin, 1996), p. 141.

206 Cardinal Joseph Bernardin, *The Gift of Peace* (Chicago: Loyola Press, 1997), p. 47.

206 Judie Brown, "Final Wish, Final Hope," *Crisis* (January 1997), p. 29.

207 *cutting death down to size:* Weenolsen, p. 247.

207 *heaven and hell:* Stephen Levine, *A Year to Live* (New York: Bell Tower, 1997), p. 54.

208 Pope John XXIII, *Journal of a Soul,* trans. Dorothy White (New York: McGraw-Hill Book Co., 1965), pp. 318, 344.

208 van Zeller, p. 24.

209 Bernardin, pp. 127-128.

Afterword
In the Family Portrait

211 Henri-Paul Bergeron, C.S.C., "La dévotion à saint Joseph chez le frère André," *Cahiers de Joséphologie* XXIII (June-July 1975), pp. 54, 47. On Brother André, see also Henri-Paul Bergeron, *Brother André, The Wonder Man of Mount Royal* (Montreal and Paris: Fides, 1958); Roland Gauthier, C.S.C., "La dévotion à S. Joseph chez le Frère André," *Cahiers de Joséphologie* XXVII, no. 2 (1979), p. 223; Bernard La-Freniere, C.S.C., *Brother André According to Witnesses* (Montreal: St. Joseph's Oratory, 1997).

211 Francis de Sales, *Treatise on the Love of God,* trans. Vincent Kerns, M.S.F.S. (Westminster, Md.: Newman Press, 1962), p. xxv.

211 John Paul II, "The Church Needs Joseph's Bold Faith for New Evangelization," *L'Osservatore Romano,* English ed. (September 22, 1993), p. 4.

212 Much of this "Holy Family" material has been inspired by: Joseph F. Chorpenning, O.S.F.S., *The Holy Family Devotion* (Montreal: Center for Research and Documentation, Oratory of St. Joseph, 1997), and "The Holy Family as icon and model of the civilization of love: John Paul II's *Letter to Families*,"

Communio (Spring 1995); Roland Gauthier, C.S.C., *La dévotion à la Sainte Famille* (Montreal: Center for Research and Documentation, Oratory of St. Joseph, 1996).

212 Chorpenning, *Holy Family Devotion*, p. 4.

212 *various writers:* Chorpenning, "The Holy Family as icon," pp. 94-95; David Herlihy, "The Making of the Medieval Family: Symmetry, Structure, and Sentiment," *Journal of American Family History* 8 (1983), p. 128.

213 *apostolic letter: Neminem Fugit.* See Chorpenning, *Holy Family Devotion*, p. 56.

214 *earthly trinity in art:* Chorpenning, "The Holy Family as icon," p. 85.

214 von Trapp, p. 47.

215 Doze, *Shadow*, p. 36.

Author's Note

In writing this book, I have come to appreciate St. Joseph's special role and presence in the Church and in my own life. I hope you have too.

I am still eagerly learning about St. Joseph and what John Paul II called his "renewed significance for the Church in our day in light of the Third Christian Millennium." This means that I continue to be very interested in other people's insights, encounters, and relationship with St. Joseph. If you have a personal story about St. Joseph and his role in your life, I would love to hear it. Please write me at the following address: Louise Perrotta, St. Joseph, Book Editorial, Our Sunday Visitor, 200 Noll Plaza, Huntington, Indiana 46750.

O Custos Jesu, esto custos noster!
(O Guardian of Jesus, be our guardian!)

(Inscribed on a statue of St. Joseph holding the child Jesus, at the Catholic University of America, Washington, D.C.)